THE
TAHIR SHAH
TRAVEL READER

TAHIR SHAH

THE
TAHIR SHAH
TRAVEL READER

TAHIR SHAH

MMXXI

Secretum Mundi Publishing Ltd
Kemp House
City Road
London
EC1V 2NX
United Kingdom

www.secretum-mundi.com
info@secretum-mundi.com

First published by Secretum Mundi Publishing Ltd, 2021
VERSION 19042021

THE TAHIR SHAH TRAVEL READER

© TAHIR SHAH

Tahir Shah asserts the right to be identified as the Author of the Work
in accordance with the Copyright, Designs and Patents Act 1988.
A CIP catalogue record for this title is available from the British Library.

Visit the author's website at:

Tahirshah.com

ISBN 978-1-912383-76-4

CONTENTS

For Paulo and Christina, with love

INTRODUCTION

Travel.

So much more than a simple word to me – it's a way of life and an obsession... a sense of magic, and of ecstatic delirium; a teacher, confidante, companion, and beloved friend.

But, most of all, travel is a way by which I make sense of the world around me. When I'm moving, my mind churns in synchronic balance.

In the way that the First Nations people of Australia walked the 'songlines' through their history, I've roamed great swathes of this planet as a direct route to finding myself.

My close friends are all aware of a secret reality... even though I appear engaging and convivial, I am at heart the most extreme form of loner you'll ever meet.

In my opinion, the truest travellers are loners lost in loneliness.

The other day, while rooting through an old box file discovered at the back of a cupboard, I chanced upon a class report from the wretched prep school I attended, aged eight to thirteen.

The form master, a cruel white Rhodesian with a seventies' handlebar moustache, had written this:

TAHIR SHAH

Tahir Shah will never amount to anything in life for a thousand reasons – the most important of which is that he is aloof, alone in both body and spirit.

For someone who got everything else about me utterly wrong, the observation – that I was 'aloof, alone in both body and spirit' – was exceptionally well observed.

While the other boys jumped to attention like little robots, doing exactly what was expected of them, I sunk down deep into the crannies of my imagination...

An imagination which could conjure the most remarkable backdrops ever dreamt up by a boy of my age.

At the time, I assumed every schoolboy was wired up just like me – that they all fantasized from one dawn to the next in blinding illusionary Technicolor, and that their every waking moment was a cornucopia of wonder, too.

But, as time passed, and as I matured from a child into a young man, I began to grasp something pivotal... something that stands prouder than proud at the helm of human civilization.

It's this:

People who shape the world are never mere passengers, but rather, they are explorers. More often than not, they're crossing a metaphorical Arctic tundra, heaving a sledge of supplies in their wake.

Forsaken by everyone else, their lot in life is to be alone, just as it is to be moving.

Like the sharks in the ocean, they cannot stop...

...because if they do, they die.

2

In the same way my close friends recognize me as a loner, they understand how I get all riled up when it comes to making an impact.

Elsewhere,[1] I've written of how my father showed me that my name was written in pencil on our family tree. It was at about the same time that the white Rhodesian was tormenting me. I suppose the result of knowing I was likely to be erased – or at least my name would be – fired me up to do something... *anything*... so as not to be eliminated.

In my yearning to appreciate how to make an impact, I clung hold of the examples of towering women and men from another age.

All were travellers. Most were Victorians.

The majority had, as children, been persecuted in classrooms just like me and, at other times, one or two had been left for dead.

I tend to be preoccupied by people who have done far more than was ever expected of them:

Writers who've published scores of books.

Walkers who've tramped across entire continents.

Linguists who've mastered a dozen languages.

Thinkers who've cracked unbreakable codes.

Even though the odds were stacked against them ever succeeding in anything, they kept going.

In my pantheon of achievers, it's the travellers I hold most dear – trailblazers like Isabella Bird and Samuel White

---

1 'Inked In', *The Reason to Write*

Baker, Gertrude Bell, Jane Digby and, of course, Richard Francis Burton.

Reading their works over and over, I hunt through thick biographies about them, seeking for lessons drawn from their lives.

More often than not, I identify how these desolate loners had an insatiable need to move… like the shark in the ocean.

Every single one of them seemed to have been well aware of it.

No surprise in that.

After all, real travellers are united in their craving for wanderlust.

If they're not planning or embarking on a journey, a real traveller is in a state of torment. Like anyone suffering from a chronic ailment, they wish they were normal – that they didn't have to roam the world in search of answers to questions yet to be asked.

They'd rather be able to sit at a fireside with a good book, reading it peacefully, without champing at the bit to be out there…

Somewhere, anywhere.

And, when the moment for rip-roaring adventure comes, they cling hold of it like a lifeline, whispering a pledge of gratitude to the universe.

Such has been my existence.

For more than thirty years I've roamed the farthest limits of land and sea – travelled to meet solitary people and indigenous tribes… to bear witness to ceremonies and feats of awe – to be free, to wonder, to worry, and to endure the unendurable.

Nothing is more delicious to me than waking from a heavy sleep, groggy and warm, and to have no sense at all of familiarity about my surroundings.

I travel to live big, to give and not to take, to appreciate my lot in life, and to grasp firmly with both hands the reins of possibility as I charge towards the next horizon.

Laid down over decades, this *Reader* contains glimpses from a wide swathe of work. Many are from adventures now long since come and gone. Others describe characters who have influenced me, experiences, and places – all of which have shaped a little of the mosaic that's me.

Although I'm a traveller, right down to the very marrow of my bones, I'm sensible to something that's never far from my thoughts:

Conjured by an ancient alchemy, it's the people and places that fate throws their way which make travellers whole.

They are what's important – not us, or our insatiable desire for movement and adventure.

The shark that cannot rest will eventually fade away, its bones and sinew melting into the brine.

When we are long forgotten, the enchanted realm, so awed with magic, will touch its wand to another generation that steps forward as we once did, wide-eyed and raw.

Tahir Shah

Damascus

SALIM THE SON of Suleiman was reclining on an ancient Damascene throne at the back of his shop.

His eyes were closed, the face around them lined with creases, its cheeks obscured by a week's growth of tattered grey beard. As he slept off a lunch of mutton kebabs, his fingertips caressed fragments of ivory inlaid on the throne's regal arm. Lost in the shadows between the front door and the chair lay a treasury of objects, a spider's web of clutter gleaned from centuries of Damascus life.

There were Crusader battle standards blackened by fire, tortoiseshell jewellery boxes, Qur'an stands carved from great slabs of teak, epaulettes and chamber pots, fountainheads fashioned in the form of gazelles, mosque lamps and astrolabes, vast gilt mirrors, and bull elephant tusks.

Before leaving home I had found a visiting card from the very same antique emporium, in a file packed with my grandfather's papers. An Afghan writer and savant, he had visited Damascus seventy-five years before me, and had written a book about the journey, entitled *Alone in Arabian Nights*. I was pleased to not only see the shop still standing, but to find it filled with such a treasure trove of wares.

At the sound of a customer's feet, Salim opened an eye. He scanned the room, jolted up, and let the kitten curled on his chest tumble to the floor.

'Can I interest you in an amulet?' he said with a grin. 'To keep you safe on Syrian roads.'

'I don't believe in all that,' I replied.

The shopkeeper's smile melted away.

'*Shhhh*!' he hissed. 'You mustn't say such things.'

'Why not?'

'Because He is listening!'

We both cocked our heads to look at the ceiling, and I changed the subject. I asked the price of a fabulous ceremonial axe that had caught my eye. Its blade was crafted from watered steel, inscribed with a spell.

Suleiman wagged a finger in my direction.

'Everything is for sale except that,' he said.

'Why is this one different?'

'I cannot tell you.'

Salim the son of Suleiman brewed a pot of tea and sat in silence, while I begged him to sell me the axe. The more I implored, the more he shook his head. After an hour of sweet tea and failed persuasion, I strolled out into the thin winter light, feeling as if I had been robbed of the opportunity of parting with my money.

Visit the old city of Damascus and it's impossible not to be struck by a sense of living antiquity, and by the gems that fill the emporia hidden within its shadows. Explore the teeming *souqs* and you descend down through layer upon layer, onion-skins of life, stretching back twenty centuries, and more.

I have never been in a place where the antiques and bric-à-brac fit so squarely against the backdrop of humanity.

Trawl through the loot on sale, and the waves of past invaders stare you in the face. The Greeks were there, and after them the Romans and Byzantine Christians. Then came the Umayyad Caliphate, its empire stretching from India to Islamic Spain and, after it, the Abbasids, the Fatimids and the Seljuq Turks. The Crusades gave way to Mameluk rule, itself followed by the conquest of Tamerlane, the Ottomans and, after them, the French.

Mark Twain was spot on when, in the 1860s, he wrote, 'To Damascus, years are only moments, decades are only flitting trifles of time. She measures time not by days, months and years, but by the empires she has seen rise and prosper and crumble to ruin.'

The American author's visit to Damascus coincided with the great Victorian preoccupation for all things Arabian. The interest was partly fuelled by the translation of *A Thousand and One Nights*, which made the Orient fashionable. European parlours were suddenly awash with exotic furniture, tiles, and silks from the Arab world. By far the best of it came from Damascus, where the remnants fill the antique shops today, and where the craftsmen still toil away making merchandise that has changed little in design in over a thousand years.

In the 1800s, intrepid adventurers like Twain visited Damascus and were awed by it, while others swapped their prim London townhouses for palaces hidden in the depths of the Old City.

The most famous of the Orientalists was Sir Richard Burton. He arrived on January 1st 1870, shortly after Mark Twain had passed through. Employed as British Consul, Burton found himself in a melting pot of ancient and modern, a rare blend of Arab life that he regarded as utter paradise. It's easy to imagine his delight, after all his consulate was housed in one of the grandest palaces of all, the fabulous Bait Quwatli. Now divided into homes and storerooms, and in a terrible state of repair, the interior harks back to a time when the Syrian capital was one of the grandest, most sophisticated cities in existence.

For me, a journey to Damascus is an amazing hunt from beginning to end, a slice through layers of history in search of treasure. Seeking out the palaces – ruined and restored – is a great way to glimpse at centuries past. Some buildings have sadly been destroyed, and others have had their beauty savaged by botched restorations, but there are riches awaiting anyone with a sense of adventure.

Look for the old palaces and, when you find them, there aren't any turnstiles or tourist lines – just a watchman, if you're lucky, to open the door. The ceilings may have fallen in, and the frescoes might be cracked, but squint a little, use your imagination, and it all comes vibrantly to life. Very soon you can hear the sound of music and staccato conversation, and smell the scent of *fleurs d'oranges* as the hostess sweeps through the room.

A Damascene mansion's reception rooms were designed to astonish visitors, aweing them with a sense of wonder. Such buildings tended to be the property of powerful political families rather than successful merchants. And so the mansions themselves were an expression of political power and aspiration. Of them all, the most extraordinary, and the easiest to visit now, is the eighteenth-century Beit Nizam, located on a narrow residential lane off Straight Street.

From the outside nothing at all is given away. It looks quite unremarkable. But ring the bell and wait for the guardian to get up from his afternoon siesta, and you enter a dream world of Arabian fantasy.

The house boasts three sprawling courtyards and many reception rooms as grand as any. There are alabaster colonnades and marble floors inset with quartz, octagonal fountains and lavish gilded doors, fabulous painted ceilings and stained glass, turquoise Iznik tiles, exquisite mosque lamps, and murals festooning the walls.

The house is silent now except for birdsong in the orange trees, the stillness bridging the century and a half since the mansion was a hub for high society. Stroll the courtyards and it's easy to picture the exiled Algerian leader, Abd al-Qadir, sitting in the shade, chatting with Burton, or their scandalous friend Lady Jane Digby revealing her latest love affair.

But the longer you spend in palaces like Beit Nizam, the more you find yourself touched by melancholy. A sense of sadness is somehow reflected in it all, as if the bandwagon rolled on.

As I traipsed around the Old City, marvelling at the shattered time-capsules of splendour, I got a sense that no one really cared – except me. The guardians were blasé to the grandeur, as were the ubiquitous families of cats perched on the rooftops; and the local Damascenes were too busy struggling with the present to give much care to the past.

The most poignant example of this sense of sorrow surrounds the home of Jane Digby. An English socialite and aristocrat, she had exiled herself to Damascus at the age of forty-five. It must have been the one place she could think of that her reputation had not yet reached.

In Europe, the drawing rooms of high society resounded with gossip of her indecent liaisons. She had been married young to an English baron, before being divorced by him after a slew of scandalous affairs, including one with her own cousin. Freed from marriage, she embarked on a catalogue of liaisons with numerous nobles, including King Ludwig I of Bavaria and, after him, with his son, King Otto of Greece.

Lady Jane spent half the year near Palmyra in goat-hair tents with her lover, a Bedouin sheikh twenty years her junior. The other six months was passed in Damascus, in a house that lies just outside the walls of the Old City.

I had heard that the building had been rediscovered by Lady Jane's biographer, Mary Lovell, a few years ago. With time to spare, I went in search of it for myself. The trouble was that no one in the Syrian capital was interested in a European woman who lived more than a century ago, and one celebrated for her promiscuity. I had inexact directions, which were of little use until, that is, I came across a little shop where electrical motors were being repaired.

Mohammed, the owner, was having lunch at a workbench strewn with wire, dismembered fans, and grease. As I entered with my makeshift map, he insisted I join him. In the Arab world, a visitor must be received with hospitality irrespective of circumstance.

Lunch was followed by tea and conversation mostly about Chinese-made fans, and a blow-by-blow account of Mohammed's youth. After that, he guided me through an album of pictures of his extended family, and served yet more tea. Three hours after my arrival, I inquired politely if he might show me the house of Lady Jane. He seemed confused, then smiled.

'Follow me,' he said.

We left the workshop and went round the corner and down an alley no wider than a man. Mohammed rang a bell high on the doorframe. After some time, an old woman poked her veiled head out and I was ushered quickly inside. The palace of Beit Nizam had impressed me for its sheer grandeur and indulgence, but rarely have I been touched as I was by the home of Lady Jane.

In the many decades since her death, the house has been divided up among as many as thirty families, but the famous octagonal parlour remains in a near-perfect state. The walls are still covered with the original handmade paper, brought from London by Lady Jane herself. Fitted cupboards stand in each corner, their doors inlaid with delicate filigree. The ceiling – alas partly concealed by a crude mezzanine floor – is octagonal, its central medallion ornamented with little mirrors.

Three generations of a family live in the two rooms now. They were clustered on vinyl couches with bouquets of plastic flowers all around, watching *Baywatch* on an old Japanese TV. Before leaving, I took a mental snapshot, and found myself wondering what the scandalous Lady Jane might have made of the scene.

Back in the covered bazaar, the traders were getting ready for the evening rush, when Damascenes take a stroll before dinner. Brisk business was being done in saffron, mothballs and in underpants, in pumice, plastic buckets and olive oil soap.

One shop was far busier than all the rest.

Its back wall was lined with jars filled with curious ingredients – sulphur, dried chameleons, oak apples and antimony. Dangling from a string near the light was a clutch of tortoise shells, eagles' wings, and a glass box filled with salamanders' tails. I watched as veiled women would wander over one by one. They would hand a scribbled list to the apothecary who, in turn, would weigh out a handful of roots, damask roses, poppy seeds or a dried starfish.

In a narrow alley a stone's throw away, a hunched old craftsman was hammering a strand of steel beside a forge. His workshop was blackened with soot, his hands as coarse as glass-paper. The swordsmith paused to greet me, and held the blade into the light for me to examine his work. Damascus was once famed for so-called 'watered steel', a technique which leaves a fluid-like grain on the metal. Blades of astonishing sharpness were fashioned until about 1700, when the technique was lost.

Nearby, in Souq al Khayyatin, the tailors' bazaar, I came across a series of chambers where red and white *kafir* headscarves were being woven on great cast iron looms, imported from France more than a century ago. The chambers were vaulted, their frescoed walls hinting at the former use of the place, as a *hammam*. The brocade spinners now populate the magnificent central steam room, its ceiling crowned by an octagonal cupola, songbirds tweeting in their cages all around.

Inspired by the ruined bathhouse, I decided to follow Arab tradition and visit a *hammam*. Bathing is extremely popular across the Islamic world, and is a way for friends to spend time together relaxing, as much as it is a means to get clean. The *hammams* of Damascus are legendary, many dating back more than a thousand years.

I had been recommended the Al Selsela, which lies close to the ancient Umayyad Mosque. Its owner, another Mohammed, was slouched on a chair near the doorway, watching an Egyptian soap opera on a portable TV.

'A clean man has a pure heart,' he whispered as I entered, quoting a favoured Syrian proverb. His family had run the establishment for generations, he said, and he knew all the customers by name. Some of them were lounging about in the central salon, chatting, smoking shisha, and drinking sweet tea.

Wrapped in a towel, I shuffled past them into the blistering steam room. The chamber was illuminated by shafts of natural light, pinpoints of radiance, like a night sky. After being scalded, then scrubbed down to the bone with a hunk of pumice, I shuffled out again squeaky clean. As I changed, I found myself pondering how the Occidental world could have lost the tradition of communal bathing – one of the pillars on which the Arab world was built.

Mohammed spat out another proverb as he took my money: 'Clean feet leave no footprints,' he said. Then he directed me to the famous Nawfara Café on the other side of the Umayyad Mosque. He said that if I heard the storyteller there, I would be the happiest man alive, a prospect too good to pass by.

Out on the street, I made my way through a river of Shi'a pilgrims, most of them women, furled from head to toe in black. There were men, too, beating their chests rhythmically as they went. They come each winter in their thousands from Iran, to pray at the shrine of the daughter of Imam Husain.

I carried on down the lane.

Even before I had turned the corner and descended the steps, I smelled the scent of apple *shisha* on the breeze.

The Nawfara Café is an institution in Damascus. You get the feeling that entire lives have been swallowed up there, a ritual of conversation, tobacco, and the bitter Arabica blend.

Inside, a waiter hurried around replenishing the *shisha* with burning coals. In the middle of the room, propped against the wall, was a kind of raised throne. Perched on it sat a grey-haired man. He was wrapped in a black robe, its lapel trimmed with gold. Nestled on his lap was a book filled with tight black handwriting. He was shouting out, waving a sword.

But no one paid any attention at all.

The reason for the lack of interest was a widescreen TV on the adjacent wall. Chelsea was playing Arsenal. Everyone in the room, except for me and the storyteller, was glued to the game.

Throughout history, Damascus has been famed for its *hakawatis*, storytellers, a tradition that was celebrated until as recently as a decade ago. But the ubiquitous satellite channels and televisions have killed the ancient Arab art of conversation. The result – a world in which storytellers are a dying breed.

And there is none in the Arab world more respected than Rachid Abu Shadi.

Silently, he finished the tale, put down the sword and the book, and slipped off his throne. The room was filled with applause, but it was not for the storyteller. No one noticed him leave, because Arsenal had just scored.

I invited Abu Shadi to join me for a cup of coffee.

'When I was young,' he said, a glint in his eye, 'my father used to bring me here and I would listen for hours on end – to the tales of Antar and Abla. You see here at Nawfara there's a tradition. Only the tales of Antar, the most famous Arab hero, are told.'

I asked about *Alf Layla wa Layla, A Thousand and One Nights*.

The *hakawati* lit a Turkish cigarette and drew the smoke through his clenched fist.

'They were told elsewhere,' he said, 'you see, each café had its own repertoire, but all that's now gone. I am the last of my kind.' He wiped his eye. 'One day the television will break,' he said darkly, 'and then they will remember me, not because of the stories, but because of the silence there will be without me, and without that vile contraption that hangs up there on the wall.'

The next day I awoke with Lady Jane on my mind.

I had dreamt of her octagonal parlour and wanted to see Palmyra for myself, where she lived half the year with her beloved sheikh. Standing two hundred kilometres to the north-east of Damascus, Palmyra once boasted a vast community, poised on the caravan routes between Persia and the Mediterranean.

Travelling there in the 1930s on camel, my Afghan grandfather was astonished by the Classical ruins. He wrote, 'To set eyes on this remote oasis is to be reminded that, however mighty an empire imagines itself to be, it is as fragile as a child's toy.'

The scale of the ruins at Palmyra are truly awe-inspiring. They stand like an ancient movie backlot, all ruined and bleak like the end of the world. But it is the silence that made the strongest impression on me. I found myself picturing both Lady Jane and my own grandfather listening to it, and to the infrequent blasts of wind ripping across the plains. It was as if the breeze were singing a warning, that civilizations crumble and fall as sure as they take seed and flourish.

Still known to the Arabs by its pre-Semitic name, Tadmor, Palmyra was once a place of decadence and wealth. Walk the ruins and you get a sense of the power of the culture that shaped it. There are vast colonnaded streets, temples and theatres, ceremonial arches and elaborate tombs, replete with exquisite funereal busts.

It's all fashioned from sumptuous honey-yellow stone, built with a confidence that must have defied anyone who questioned such a metropolis could exist in the desert. But then of course, the landscape has changed dramatically in the forty centuries or more since its founding. Palmyra's name, in its later Greek and Latin form, meaning 'the City of Palms', hints at the fertility of the oasis long gone.

Not quite so certain are the origins of this now-desolate commercial and cultural outpost of antiquity. Its name appears on stone tablets dating to the nineteenth century before the birth of Christ, and is apparently the place mentioned in the Bible's First Book of Kings as 'Tamor', a city founded by Solomon. More clear is the Roman Empire's delight at capturing the oasis, which they regarded as almost without equal. When Hadrian visited in AD 129, he renamed it Palmyra Hadriana, and proclaimed it a free city.

Sitting among the ruins in the fading light of dusk, the image of Lady Jane Digby was irresistible. I could see her quite clearly in desert robes, strolling in the long shadows thrown by towering colonnades. Like me, I am sure she was taken by the romanticism of it all, and by the desperate beauty that is so alluring as to defy accurate description.

By visiting Palmyra, I understood Damascus a little better, reminded that the circle of life stops for no man.

On arriving back in the capital, I paid Salim the son of Suleiman another visit.

As before, he was asleep, the tabby kitten curled up on his chest. In the background was the rumble of a generator, the sound drowning out the muezzin's call to prayer.

When Salim was awake, and tea had been brewed and served, I brought up the subject of the ceremonial axe. The shopkeeper smiled.

'You have earned it,' he said.

'What do you mean?'

'An object as special as that isn't for the first day,' he said, 'the fact you came back means that the axe was in your dreams. You can have it for half the price.'

From: *Travels With Myself*

Insider Information

IRRITATED BY PEBBLES, potent emetics and coal-tar soap, the delicate lining of my stomach finally began to give.

The magician's latest wheeze had played havoc with my body's finely tuned homeostatic system. Mine was a case in which the scientist had lost control of his experiment. Decreasing the temperature of 104 degrees Fahrenheit had called for drastic action. Gokul had been instructed to find a *barafwalla*, an ice seller. He ran out into the tree-lined streets of Alipore and commandeered two blocks of ice which were being lugged on the back of a cart to the nearby Zoological Gardens. Taking charge, Feroze pointed his bull's pizzle riding crop at the servant's bathtub, then at the ice and, lastly, at me. The *barafwallas* heaved their load into the bath and threw me on top.

Solace, at last.

The *barafwallas*, the Master, Rublu, and a gaggle of snorting servants gathered round to enjoy the spectacle. Each watched transfixed as I shuddered with cold and heat at the same time. First they observed the sea of soapy sweat surging like tainted spring water from my pores. Then they gawked as my steaming perspiration melted the ice – revealing an entombed frozen sewer rat.

Like an amateur mammoth hunter, Gokul chipped away at the ice with the end of a spoon to excavate the rodent.

'Good work, Gokul,' said Feroze, who was having a whale of a time at my expense. 'It's a big one, even for Kolkata. When you've extracted it, put it in the fridge... we'll do a dissection later.'

Three days passed before I could ingest any soft foods.

Even then I limited myself to a diet of soupy *daal* and mashed bananas, washed down with warm water. Ever courteous, Gokul attempted to nurse my digestive tract back to its original condition. But the damage had been done. Abdominal pain, loss of appetite and severe vomiting followed: classic symptoms of a peptic ulcer. My malady would have alarmed the most hardened of surgeons.

Fortunately, despite the grave nature of my condition, I had an incentive to recover – the prospect of revenge.

On the afternoon of the third day after the trial by temperature, Gokul stuck a hand down his *lungi* and fished something out. It was a neat bunch of *neem* sticks. He blew on them lightly, apologizing that they had become dampened by his private parts. His loins were the only place hidden from the magician's continual scrutiny. I snatched the bundle to my chest and examined it. The *neem* sticks were fastened together with three turquoise elastic bands. I hurried the contraband to my room, and hid it beneath the inner sole of my left shoe. Ready for action... All I needed now was the right moment to attack.

When I informed him of my deteriorating gastric condition, Feroze regarded the office calendar on the wall.

'It's the middle of February, fancy that…' he said dryly. 'Suppose it's about time you got out of the house… can't keep you cooped up here forever.'

'I don't know if you understand,' I said, retching. 'I think I've got a peptic ulcer. It has to be treated without delay.'

Feroze removed a doctor's notelet from a drawer in the writing bureau. Then, twisting the lid from his mandarin-coloured Parker Duofold, he scribbled a prescription.

'Go to the Swastika Chemist on Shakespeare Sarani,' he said, peering up from the paper. 'Give them this prescription and take the pills they give you… three times a day.'

As with eating, Feroze considered illness to be a waste of time. He disliked anyone associated with him to fall victim to the weaknesses of the human constitution.

'When you've got the medicine,' he went on, 'you are to go out and find your first example of insider information – the third element of your course.'

I clutched my belly like an expectant mother.

'Shouldn't I take a few days off?'

'For what?' he hissed viperously.

'Recovery,' I said. 'I once read a novel called *Broken Spirit*… the hero died an agonizing death from an ulcer much like mine.'

The Master swished his riding crop like a camel's tail.

'Sounds like a good read,' he gloated.

'What sort of "insider information" do you want me to find?'

'You'll know it when you find it,' replied Feroze. 'Now leave me… I have a rat to dissect!'

*

WITH ONE HAND on my stomach, and the other wiping the stream of sweat from my brow, I set out into Kolkata.

Through disorientation, I headed south by mistake, instead of north-east into the heart of town. Before I knew it, I was inching my way down the macadamized surface of Judge's Court Road. Famed as a haven of the sophisticated in days gone by, Judge's Court is one of Alipore's old imposing roads. Now a place of faded grandeur, it's home to a ragtag assortment of used furniture shops. Packed from floor to ceiling with roll-top desks, chandeliers, organs, and wall cabinets, bracket clocks and card tables, the shops are testament to changed taste. No longer do Kolkatans cherish the Indo-Baroque masterpieces of the past. Who wants a classical rosewood throne when they can recline in the comfort of a fluffy nylon easy chair?

As I wandered through the wide avenues of Alipore in search of a rickshaw, I considered the magician's medical prescription. How could I be taking medical advice from the person responsible for my condition?

'Bebtic ulcer very bainful,' mused the pharmacist at the Swastika Chemist.

'Yes,' I confirmed, 'it's desperately *baneful*.'

'Take six tablets every day for a week,' explained the professional.

'Shouldn't I be taking three tablets a day?'

The chemist shook his head.

'Oh, no, no, no,' he said, 'special offer... double dosage, same brice!'

I made a note of the Swastika's address. Mustn't forget about this place, I thought. This is a hypochondriac's fantasy.

'What about the pain?' I croaked. 'Will these red and white ones take away the pain?'

'Bain...?' said the pharmacist. 'Is the bain unbearable?'

'Yes, yes, yes!' I bellowed. 'That's just what it is... it's unbearable!'

The chemist screwed up his eyes like balls of paper. Then, sliding open an ankle-level drawer, he took out a brown glass bottle of lozenges.

'These relieve all possible bain,' he crowed, slapping them down squarely before me.

'How much do I owe you for them?'

'*Bain blockers,*' said the chemist grandly, tilting his head backwards, 'bain blockers, no charge... experimental.'

Sliding a wrinkled index finger to his lips, he winked.

Before choking down a bain blocker, something crossed my mind. A dangerous misunderstanding may have been about to claim a fresh victim. From the abyss of my unconscious mind a timid, lipless woman was signalling furiously. Had the chemist meant 'brain blocker', rather than 'pain blocker'? Was I about to induce a self-inflicted lobotomy? Prepared to try anything to dispel the gastric distress, I knocked a couple of the oversized chalky lozenges to the back of my throat and gulped. The experience was not unlike that of swallowing pebbles.

I counted to ten. Then to twenty. My brain still seemed to be generally intact. But, as I wandered down Shakespeare Sarani, I found myself floating like a ball of fluff in the wind. It was as if there were no gravity. The chemist's experimental painkillers obviously needed a little more work.

But as I glided towards the Maidan – Kolkata's immense central parkland – I reflected that, for the moment, the pills would be just fine.

Without faltering, I listed sloth-like and bewildered into the seething traffic of Chowringhee.

In a country where sedate driving is unknown, Kolkata's frenzied thoroughfare is the zenith of all motorway madness. Uncontrolled and maniacal, wild as a nine-headed Hydra, ferocious as ten thousand vampire bats, Kolkata's main street is more tempestuous than any act of God.

Bullock carts and Ambassador cabs, buses, their sides gashed like armour-plating peppered with anti-tank shells, herds of goats charging like migrating wildebeest, a vintage traction engine on a suicide run: fording the commotion is to play Space Invaders for one's life.

Dodge the heavy guns, and the stealthy cycle rickshaws creep up like assassins – laden high with sea trunks, and schoolchildren, *hilsa* fish and urinals, balloons and computer monitors. Miraculously, the press of wheels, spokes and tramping hooves parted, like a great sea, allowing me to cross.

In the Maidan, I drifted over to the Shaheed Minar, formerly the Ochterlony Monument – a throwback to the glory days of the British Raj.

Staggering somewhat, searching for insider information, I made my way from one performance to the next. At one, a girl of about twelve was demonstrating her ability to write with a pen held in her toes. For one rupee she would scrawl out a love poem or a secret astrological message. Opposite sat a young *swami* on crossed legs. His face was pasty, his hands tinged with orange specks. A single charred pot stood before him, positioned on a chequered handkerchief. The vessel contained crocodile fat, apparently a cure for arthritis, impotency and abdominal disorders. Beside it was a pile of 'miracle' shells from the Andaman Islands. An hour earlier, I might have solicited the luminary's advice and purchased a square of crocodile blubber. But now the pain of my peptic ulcer was nothing but a distant memory.

Further on, past a skinny boy and his tightrope-walking pye-dog, was another chap with wire-walking rats. Beyond him stood yet another lad. Like the others, he was in his early teens. But he was different. He had an engaging Charlie Chaplin smile, blinding teeth, and dimples as deep as sugar-lumps. Although tattered, his clothes were well kept. Yet it wasn't his dress which caught my attention. It was his demeanour. This boy may have been operating in Kolkata's Maiden, but he was haughty beyond belief.

His pitch was being mobbed by enthusiastic punters, all eager to get his attention. Inquisitive about the source of the commotion, I floated over. Once I had pushed my way to the front, I watched the routine.

A member of the crowd would hand the lad a hundred-rupee note, itself a tidy sum of money in India. The bill would be folded in half, and then folded in half again. Then it would be slipped into a miniature manila envelope which was placed on a brick, before a green parakeet. The bird would grip the sachet in its bill, ripping the corner. Next, the boy would throw the marked envelope into a box containing other identical, yet unmarked envelopes. He would shake the box roughly. Only then would he invite the owner of the money to search for the envelope containing his banknote.

Invariably, the marked envelope had disappeared.

Despite swaying from the bain blocker, I felt certain I could catch the boy out. What's all my training been for, I asked myself, if I can't trip up an underage hoaxer?

So when the boy challenged me, I accepted. My hundred-rupee bill was folded in half, then in half again, before being inserted into a crisp manila pouch. The parrot did its duty, and the torn envelope was thrust into the box. When the carton's lid was removed, the child – who was minting money – urged me to search for my note.

I waved the box aside. The crowd stared at me quizzically. The young magician frowned. Swaggering with all the pomposity I could muster, I ripped the stall's tablecloth away.

'This is where you hid my money!' I cried, sweeping the cloth back.

But the table was bare.

The crowd seethed with delight. Obviously expecting trouble from the foreigner, the entertainer slipped me his Charlie Chaplin smile, grabbed his parrot and props, and made off.

Back at the Alipore mansion, Feroze was pacing up and down the courtyard like a stallion before a race.

'Ah, back at last?' he puffed.

Without his captive, the magician had obviously been distraught with boredom.

'How was the rat?' I enquired, crossing the yard.

'Very interesting, actually,' replied Feroze. 'It had a tumour in its intestines. If it hadn't been frozen solid, it would have had an early death.' The Master groomed back his hair with his hands. 'That reminds me, did you get your pills?'

'Yes. Got some incredible painkillers, too. They're strong as a knockout punch.'

'Oh, can I see?'

Feroze examined the label-less bottle, then, removing the lid, he took a hesitant sniff. He raised one eyebrow, glanced at his pocket-watch, and then coughed.

'Do you mind if I take one away?' he asked.

'Help yourself. In pain, are you?'

The sorcerer chose not to answer. Instead, he enquired what example of insider information I had brought for him. When I retorted that I had come empty-handed – on account of medical reasons – he flew into a rage.

'Never...' he roared, 'never return here without completing the assignment I have set!'

Only as I apologized did I conceive the true extent of the Master's anger. By failing to bring him some nugget from my trip into town, I was in some way depriving him.

That night, in the dim light of my bedroom, I reflected on Feroze's unfounded animosity. Brooding, I tugged the inner sole from my shoe and inspected the rubber bands.

Revenge, when it came, would be sweet.

*

NEXT MORNING, FEROZE met me as I descended the antique staircase.

It was still dark outside.

'Good morning,' I said, inquisitive as to why the magician should be hovering at the foot of the stairs.

'Tahir,' he replied in an unusually sensitive tone, 'do you remember those pills you brought back yesterday?'

'Yes, of course,' I replied, 'the bain blockers.'

'I've tested the one you gave me,' Feroze explained. 'It contained mercuric chloride. Take two or three more and you'll be dead.'

'Are you sure?'

'If you don't believe me,' Feroze responded coldly, 'keep taking them and see. Don't forget, this is India – when a quack tells you a potion is "experimental", take the hint and run off!'

For a few seconds I was touched by the magician's compassionate veneer. But, as I set out in search of insider information, I remembered the past. I had endured far too much to forgive and forget.

Where does one go in a tremendous city like Kolkata to find insider information?

I recalled India's golden rule: do the opposite of what would be normal anywhere else.

The subcontinent is a fine-tuned and well-practised place. To the outsider it may appear random, or directionless. But in India, what seems haphazard is the product of five thousand years of exertion. Go with the flow, I reminded myself – never strain against the nation's natural forces… and success must soon follow.

If ordered to scour a Western metropolis for trade secrets, I would have headed straight to the heart of the city. This being India, I turned my back on central Kolkata, and strolled towards the serene banks of Tolly's Nullah canal.

I sat beneath a banyan tree to eat a packed lunch prepared by Gokul. It was five past ten, but my constitution had grown used to the Master's timetable. A group of men were gathering cress with sickles at the water's edge. Others were fishing with wiry concertina keepnets, wading up to their chests like gazelle fording a river. Behind them, a family were flipping cow dung fuel bricks in the winter sun.

Four young boys were diving into the canal in turns, clouding the water, splashing carefree, shrieking like jackals beneath a full moon.

In Europe, the last person I would turn to for help would be someone with whom I did not share a common language.

When applying the golden rule of India, such a person becomes the obvious guide.

Sidling over to a bearded man of about my age, who was flipping dung bricks like dinosaur eggs, I struck up a conversation.

'Do you know where I'd find some insider information?' I asked.

The man looked at me with blank, swollen eyes.

'In-sid-er know-ledge,' I repeated, motioning obscure gestures like a psychotic mime.

Frowning, as he strove to decipher my sign language, the brick-flipping man shook his head.

'*Haa*,' he murmured, as if he had understood my enquiry.

With a dung-clad finger he pointed at a distant building surrounded by a wall.

When I pointed to the same building, he nodded vigorously.

Excellent, I thought, I'm on to something here.

'Alipore Jail,' spluttered a boss-eyed *paan* seller, crouched outside the gate.

'Oh,' I said, sheepishly. 'That looks like a strange place to go searching for insider information, doesn't it?'

The *paan* seller clipped a pile of *sopaari*, areca nuts.
'Looking for Bhola Das?' he asked.

'Um, I'm looking for insider information,' I replied.
'Who's Bhola Das?'

The *paan* seller winked his good eye twice.

'Bhola Das... famous hangman of West Bengal!'

'Ah, yes... that's who I'm looking for. Yes, that's right. I'm
looking for the hangman!'

Who could have better trade secrets than a hangman?

'Where do I go?'

The *paan* seller motioned to a low hatch within the main
studded portal.

Pausing for a moment to get my story straight, I knocked
twice on the door. There was no reply. I knocked again.
Only then did a guard put his face to the door's grille.

'Bhola Das!' I shouted. 'I have come to see Bhola Das –
the famous hangman of West Bengal.'

The guard slid the visor back across the grille. A bunch of
keys rattled inside. The door within a door creaked inwards.

One guard ferried me to the next. To each I whispered
the cryptic password... the name of the hangman.

After a long wait I found myself sitting before the warden.

'I have come to see Bhola Das,' I explained. 'I think you
will find that he's expecting me.'

'Very good, sir,' said the warden, signing the necessary
paperwork to authorize my visit.

He pressed a button beside his desk. Before I could turn
my head, a watchman stepped from the shadows and led me
through the fabled jail of Alipore.

Up and down stairs, around corridors and along straight passageways. The soles of my shoes rasped on the flagstones as we proceeded through the maze. The liveried guard halted before a robust steel door.

'Bhola Das?' he confirmed.

'Yes, it's the hangman I've come to see.'

'Very good, sir,' squirmed the watchman, as he knocked on the door. The door opened inwards.

Inside was a square, stone-walled chamber, illuminated by natural light. A solid wood table stood in one corner. On it was a noose, crafted from coarse hemp rope. Adjacent to the table a man was sitting on a three-legged stool. His hair was snowdrop-white, his cheeks were obscured by a rough grey beard, his steely eyes hidden behind scratched lenses, and his shirt and *lungi* were old, yet neat.

'Bhola Das?' I asked.

'Yes,' said the man. 'I am Bhola Das.'

'I would like to speak with you for a few minutes.'

The hangman glanced at a clock mounted high on the wall.

'Do you have an execution to administer?'

'No,' said Das dolefully, 'I have no work today.'

Whereas other states in India elect their executioners on their own merit, West Bengal employs hangmen from a single hereditary line.

'My father and his father and his father before him were all hangmen,' exclaimed Das, stretching his spindly arms behind him like locust wings. 'My father killed more than six hundred convicts. But that was in the time of the Britishers,

34

and there were far more to execute then. My father was sent to Glasgow during the Raj. He hanged Indians at the prison there. I suppose,' said Das solemnly, 'you could say that hanging is in my blood.'

'What's it like to hang a man?'

The hangman stared at the floor, then with eyes cold as sleet, he gazed at me, taking in the features of my face.

'To kill a man,' he said softly, 'is a dreadful thing. To bring a man's life to an end is almost too much to bear. I am a hereditary executioner. This is the work of my forefathers. I do not judge the profession which they have chosen for my line. But I ensure each man I kill dies with dignity and without pain. I believe I am the finest executioner in India. I do not claim that for an idle boast. Before killing a convict I cannot sleep for three days. I cannot eat either. I spend time alone, thinking about the life which I am about to end. Then, before I place the noose in position, I ask the criminal's forgiveness. I tell him I am only doing what the government and the court has asked me to do.

'When *I* hang a man,' declared Bhola Das, pressing his thick glasses to his nose, 'the victim remains intact. Blood doesn't ooze from his nostrils, from his ears or from his mouth. That's the mark of the professional.'

'Tell me,' I intoned in a hushed voice, as the footsteps of a guard tramped past outside, 'are there any secrets of the profession which have been passed on to you by your ancestors?'

Das nodded sagaciously, staring out at a pair of pigeons which were squatting on the window ledge.

'Yes,' he replied. 'There are family secrets…'

'Could you tell me what they are?'

The hangman squinted.

'The secrets of which I speak are,' he said, 'known only to me and to the man I execute.'

'Ah,' I winced, loosening my collar, 'I understand. But isn't there some meagre tip you could give, to prove the care you take in your craft?'

Bhola Das rubbed his palms together.

'First,' he whispered, looking from right to left, 'I lubricate the noose with a bar of soap. I make sure it gets into all the creases. This reduces friction. Then I rub it a second time, with a banana. Only after that can I be certain that the knot will slide easily. But,' continued the executioner in a low voice, 'the most important thing is to weave a brass nut into the noose. While slipping the noose over the inmate's head, I position a heavy nut at the side of the neck. As soon as the trap door opens, the nut swings round to the spinal cord and snaps it cleanly.

'Half an hour later,' the hangman went on, 'when I release the rope, there's sometimes an eerie scream from the convict's mouth – it's nothing more than air escaping from the prisoner's lungs.'

'Is hanging the only method of execution in West Bengal?'

'Unfortunately, it is. Four men were recently convicted of raping a nine-year-old girl,' continued Das. 'I was told to hang them. They ought to have been thrown into a cage of lions. The noose was too good for them!'

Bhola Das removed his glasses and rubbed his eyes. He was an honourable man, maintaining the work of his forefathers.

'Do your children want to carry on the tradition?'

'Yes,' said Bhola Das. 'My elder son wants to join the business. I have taught him how to twine a rope and craft a noose. He has helped me on some occasions. But,' imparted the hangman wearily, 'he wants the position to pay more and to have better job security. Without that,' he whispered, 'he says there's no future for the profession.'

Armed with the valuable insider information, I thanked the ageing executioner and summoned the guard to escort me from the prison. Bhola Das clasped his callused hands around mine and pressed his lips to my ear.

'If you ever require my services,' he murmured darkly, as I left, 'please don't hesitate to call upon me.'

That was an honest man, I reflected, as I trekked north up Baker Road towards the magician's compound. He had inner strength, and was compassionate under testing circumstances. As for Bhola Das's offer – it was hard to say whether I would ever need to avail myself of the private services of an executioner.

But the offer, I pondered, would be good to keep in reserve... for a rainy day.

※

IT WAS WITH elation that I entered the Master's mansion.

I was eager to share my newfound insider information. But before making my report, I slipped up to my room to wash and change. Gokul's assistant was polishing the brass carpet rods on the stairs. Climbing over him, I made my way up to the first-floor corridor. My bedroom was situated at its far end. Several other rooms led off the passageway. These were usually kept locked. Feroze was obsessed that they remain so. Noticing that the second door on the right was ajar, I was suspicious. Pushing it inward, I poked my head around the door.

The casual nature of my intrusion added to the surprise.

It was a young boy's bedroom. A home-made model aeroplane was suspended from the ceiling. Below it, a clutch of toy animals were poised on the bed. A leather satchel was propped up against a chair, its buckles unfastened. A child's sketches were pinned to one wall. The low desk was strewn with the elements of childhood. A catapult, a nest of marbles, cotton reels and a decapitated doll's head. It might have been like any other boy's bedroom. But it was not. The chamber was lit by a single bare red bulb. Its shutters had been closed like an iron visor, preventing daylight from penetrating in. A ghastly scarlet light filled the place.

Rattled by the sight, I stepped back to shut the door. But as I did so, I noticed a hunched figure sitting on a low stool with his eyes closed. It was Feroze. Surprisingly, he had not heard me. I tiptoed away.

When I had changed, I went out to the kitchen to find Gokul. Surely the Master's veteran servant would explain the room's mystery.

Gokul was busy roasting a ladle of spices over a gas flame.

'Hello, *Sahib*,' he said, without turning around.

'How did you know it was me?'

'Very noisy walker,' he snorted.

'Gokul... I've just seen something rather strange.'

'What strange?'

'There's a bedroom upstairs with a red light in it. The Master is sitting there with his eyes closed.'

The manservant raised the ladle from the heat. He turned to face me.

'Long time ago,' he said tensely, 'Master's son and wife was killed.'

'How? How did it happen?'

Gokul rubbed both eyes with his left hand, and sniffed.

'They taking cycle rickshaw in Kolkata,' he said. 'Rickshaw hit by petrol tanker... Master *Sahib* has kept son bedroom same way. Today,' mumbled the servant, 'anniversary of death.'

Leaving Gokul to his spices, I returned to the main house, my head hung low. The magician may have been my tormentor, but I was willing to agree to a temporary truce. Was his venomous attitude to his pupils connected to the death of his wife and child?

An hour later, Feroze found me in the study, where I was combing a copy of *Hobson-Jobson* for magical feats. He was less vitalized than usual. His eyes were circled by heavy rings, his face was drawn and pale, and his clothes quite dishevelled.

'How did you get on?' he asked, through gritted teeth.

'Well…' I began, snapping the book closed, euphorically.

'Did you find me any insider information?'

I reflected on Alipore Jail and upon the secrets of Bhola Das – hereditary hangman of West Bengal. Should I explain first about the soap, the banana, or the brass nut which snaps the spine? I glanced at Feroze. He wasn't his usual self. How could I discuss an executioner's tips with a man whose family had themselves met such a terrible end?

'I'm so sorry,' I said, 'but my stomach has been troubling me again. I'll make sure to bring back a double dose of insider information tomorrow.'

*

NEXT DAY, WELL before Gokul had shuffled up the passageway with a pot of milky tea, I had slunk out of the house. Today, I told myself, I am going to restore my reputation.

Early morning in Kolkata is a bewitching time. Like the back lot of a Hollywood film studio, it's either teeming with people, or silent as a ghost ship. Kolkata is either off or on. It's the only city on Earth with no half-way setting.

At six a.m. – like scene shifters and extras in a film – the first people saunter on to the set. They are well rested and prepared for another day of furious activity. Some scrape out the gutters, or scrub down the cobblestones, like studio janitors making ready for the arrival of the cast. Others set out dog-eared copies of *Time* and *National Geographic* on makeshift wooden stalls.

Nearby, beggars hobble into position, bracing themselves for the crowds. Street-side astrologers prop up their hand-painted boards depicting the constellations, perfume sellers dust down their carved glass bottles, toothpick vendors arrange their stock, pickpockets step stealthily into doorways. Fruit sellers divide sour green oranges into clusters of six. Traffic policemen tighten their white steel helmets and climb up on to their rostra. Then – and only then – as if an invisible director has ordered filming to begin, Kolkata is switched on.

Within moments, the streets are choked with vehicles. The air boils with exhaust fumes. And the pavements are packed with shoals of people, jammed shoulder to shoulder like lambs in a wagon.

Nothing in Kolkata is so important as the pavement. Far more than mere conduits for pedestrians, the walkways are dormitories, typing bureaux, markets, cafés, doctors' surgeries and umbrella repair shops, rolled into an endless profusion of activity. Kolkata's pavements are wider than in most other cities, constructed by the British for a grand imperial capital. Twenty yards of Kolkata pavement has more on offer than entire countries. Plastic combs and squashy toys, shower caps in camellia pink, hard-boiled eggs in trays, reconditioned engine-blocks, Bakelite telephones, mothballs in sackcloth pouches, beetroot and jackfruit, dental floss and wooden legs, Zimmer frames and pogo sticks, turbines and theodolites.

As I recoiled from the force of the morning invasion, I noticed a man squatting outside the Writer's Building. He had no hands or feet. His stumps were well healed, their skin tight and smooth.

Dozens of unfortunates beg on Lal Bazaar Street. But this man was wearing a pair of alien antennae – popular with party-goers about twenty years before. As I bent over him, he twanged one of the springs with his stump. The bloodshot eyeball at the end jangled about, revolving wildly.

'Yes, *Sahib*...' he exclaimed eagerly, realizing that, as a customer from out of town, I was sure to buy the latest sensation. '*Panch rupia*, five rupees!'

'What would I use the apparatus for?'

'Very good quality,' he stressed, 'good price. I am crippling. No family. No money.'

I handed over the note and took the alien antennae. They might come in useful down the line, I thought. After all, this was Kolkata.

I tried on the tentacles for the first time. No one even looked round as I pushed through the crowds, the pair of demonic eyeballs jolting about above my head. Then I noticed a man waving at me from the far end of Lal Bazaar. Suspecting it to be another mendicant impatient to make an easy sale, I turned and hurried off. But a grinding of wheels indicated that the man was in pursuit. Without looking round, I slipped down a side alley, my alien eyeballs flapping about like teasels in the wind. The wheels followed.

'All right,' I snarled. 'What do you want?'

It was then I noticed that this was no cart-bound invalid, but a *rickshawalla*.

'*Jadoowalla!*' he shouted. 'Remembering? Mister Magician…?'

The man spoke gibberish.

He was sleek as a gondola, barefoot and extremely lean. His torn saffron-coloured vest revealed a scrawny back, pocked with dried sores, and with muscles as taut as a drum skin. When standing still, his body swayed back and forth. He was very drunk indeed.

'What do you want?'

The man pointed at me, then the rickshaw, and then acted out a little sketch.

He was beginning to seem familiar.

'Aren't you the *rickshawalla* who took me to Feroze's house on that first day – you were the runner in Purulia, right?'

The *rickshawalla* tilted his head from one side to the other. '*Haa, Sahib*,' he said. 'Runner. I am runner. My name is Venky.'

The *rickshawalla* cracked his knuckle joints, as if demonstrating his enduring strength.

'Where you want to go?' he asked, squinting.

'Well,' I said, 'maybe you can help me.'

He shuffled forwards in concentration.

'I am looking for a special thing,' I explained. 'I am searching for *insider information*.'

Venky the *rickshawalla* raised his eyebrows as high as he could, and swayed his head from left to right. It smelt as if he had taken a bath in *chullu*.

'Do you understand? I want to be taken to someone with insider information.'

The man patted the rickshaw's seat with his leathery palm. I climbed up and we set off. He seemed to know where he was going.

Dodging the onslaught of taxis, juggernauts, and a great caravan of marching bandsmen who were out drumming up business, the *rickshawalla* scuttled towards the Bow Bazaar. The market is famous for selling fine jewellery, produced in cramped back workrooms behind each shop. The larger emporia have resident astrologers, advising on the appropriate design of jewellery.

Without warning, Venky dug his heels into the dirt and pointed to a cow. The animal, which had a wreath of flowers around its neck, was tied to a post. Beside it was a middle-aged woman, dressed in a simple white *sari*, tied in the Bengali way.

'How can an animal have insider information?'

The *rickshawalla* hesitated.

'Do not understand,' he said.

'Then why did you bring me to this cow?'

Venky stuck out his lower lip, revealing his gums. We had only just met, but somehow it was as if I had known him all my life.

'Well, since we're here, can you ask the woman what she uses her cow for?'

Promoted from *rickshawalla* to translator, Venky struck up a conversation with the woman. She held up a bunch of rough grass stems and he slurred a number of disjointed questions.

'She says,' began Venky in his best English, 'people pay a little money to feed the cow.'

'Why do people want to pay to feed the cow?'

'Feed cow lucky,' responded the *rickshawalla*.

'Does the woman own the cow?'

Again, Venky chattered away in animated conversation.

'*Haa*,' he said after some time, 'she not own cow. Milking man own cow. She is paying milking man for cow in day.'

'You mean that the woman hires the cow each day, once the milkman's finished with it, and she lets strangers pay her money to feed it?'

Venky thought for a moment. Then he smiled.

'Yes, *Sahib*... very good!'

The genius of the arrangement bore the unrivalled hallmark of Kolkata. Where else could you find such an ingenious system? The milkman milks the cow and then, instead of looking after it all day, gives it to a woman who pays *him* for the privilege of looking after the animal. Far from being left out of pocket, the woman charges people to feed the creature a few strands of grass. In turn, the cow's devotees attain a sense of inner calm from their charity. The woman sells the dung to fuel-brick makers as a profitable sideline. This was even better than the baby rental.

'Venky!' I declared, as Mehboob's Marching Band engulfed us like a sea of crude oil. 'You're a genius!'

Buoyed by the early success of Bow Bazaar, I set my sights on the street's other professionals.

If a humble cow could reveal such hidden wonders, then what could be waiting for me further along the street?

But even before I had a chance to put away my notebook, Venky pointed at a group of men cleaning out the gutters beside his rickshaw's wheel. '*Ghamelawalla!*' he cried.

'What are you saying? What's a *ghamelawalla?*'

The rickshaw puller was perplexed that I should not understand the term.

'*Ghamelawalla,*' he repeated, 'gold sweeper!'

'Venky,' I said, 'you're obviously wrong. These men are gutter cleaners. Look – they're sweeping up all the dirt and heaving it on to a metal cart.'

The *rickshawalla* wagged a finger.

'*Ghamelawalla* is looking for gold,' he said.

With Venky translating, I resigned myself to the fact that seeking out the truth might be a slow, uphill task. His English was limited. It was like deciphering a garbled tape recording made underwater. I put his wavering linguistic ability down to the flask of opaque liquid stored in the pouch around his neck.

Bow Bazaar is a street of astounding financial wealth. Bearing this in mind, it wasn't unreasonable that people should be dredging the gutters for gold. Renewing my faith in the man who had brought me the cow keeper's secret, I licked my pencil.

Gold dealers in the West value the dirt swept from workshop floors. An elderly Hasid jeweller in Manhattan once told me he had sold the antique floorboards from his factory. Their purchaser incinerated the planks to extract the gold dust which had worked its way into the crevices over the years. But as I came to realize, the clan of the *ghamelawallas*, Kolkata's unofficial army of gold scroungers, put even the great recyclers of New York to shame.

Taking their name from their *ghamelas*, heavy iron pans, the city's *ghamelawallas* begin work in the middle of the night. Long before the bazaar's jewellers are open for business, they turn up to sweep out the workshops. Like the tiny birds which peck the teeth inside crocodile mouths, *ghamelawallas* perform a vital, if not uncelebrated, service. Every grain of dust is meticulously collected. Once the business owner is paid a few rupees, the precious dirt is taken away to be treated.

Many *ghamelawallas* make their homes on the streets of Kolkata. Nearly all are migrant workers, with wives and children who they see once a year. Most begin their careers as apprentice *ghamelawallas*, arriving to work alongside their fathers at the age of six or seven. They sleep on *charpoys*, rope beds, in alleyways, and wash at hand pumps. Wander the backstreets near the Bow Bazaar and you'll see them sitting on the pavements, toiling over the jewellers' dirt. Mixed amid the jumble of pavement life, the huddle of squatting figures could easily be dismissed without a second glance. But like so many in Kolkata, the *ghamelawallas* are masters of creating a living from almost nothing. The tattered sweepers, squatting at shin level, perform an intricate scientific procedure.

First, the scraps of paper and straw and larger pieces of rubbish are removed. These will be sold later to *ruddiwallas*, 'rag-pickers'. Then the actual dirt is washed in clean water. When it has been swilled about, a few drops of nitric acid are added. This dissolves all the metals except for the gold. The residue is then treated with a solution of barium, which amalgamates the gold particles.

After this, the remaining compound is burned in a crucible, on a *choolaah*, a little stove. As miniature hand-driven bellows blast air into the embers, a tiny nugget of gold is formed at the base of the crucible.

Some other Indian cities have *ghamelawallas* as well. But those in Kolkata dismiss their rivals as impostors. For nowhere on Earth has recycling been taken to such exalted levels as in Kolkata. Whereas *ghamelawallas* working in, say, Mumbai, treat the salvaged dirt once, their fellow gold-seekers in Kolkata are far more ingenious. When the initial burning is over, the first group of *ghamelawallas* sells the dirt from which they have extracted gold to another group of *ghamelawallas*. More impoverished than the first, the second group repeats the process, removing even more minute traces of the precious metal. These *ghamelawallas* sell the dust on to yet another team of washers, who pan it on the banks of the Hooghly. When they are finished with the dust, they peddle it to builders, who turn it into bricks.

By late morning, when the first set of *ghamelawallas* have done their round of the workshops, they turn their attentions to the gutters of the inimitable Bow Bazaar.

Armed with hard brushes, they scrub the dirt from the streets and cart it away to process. Before they leave to rest in the scorching afternoons, the *ghamelawallas* set up a complex network of miniature dams to prevent any of the valuable dirt from seeping down into the sewers. But, this being Kolkata, another regiment of *ghamelawallas* are on hand to trawl the sewers at night. If too much rubbish piles up for them to treat, they simply sub-contract the work.

Straining to translate the intricate lore of the *ghamelawallas*, Venky muttered that *ek lakh*, a hundred thousand, people work as freelance *ghamelawallas* in Kolkata. If each is making, say, twenty rupees a day – and works eleven months out of twelve – then between them, Kolkata's gold-sweepers alone must be bringing in more than thirteen million pounds a year. Not bad for making money from nothing.

As they say in Kolkata, '*Ak janar chai, annyar sona*' – 'One man's waste, another man's gold.'

From: *Sorcerer's Apprentice*

Between the Straits

THE HARVEST HAD failed again, and Nasrudin's wife screamed at him as she'd done the previous year, and the year before that. Unfazed by the run of bad fortune, the wise fool strolled down to the teahouse in high spirits.

'Can't help noticing that you're remarkably happy,' said a friend.

'Oh, yes, that I am!'

'But I thought your crops had failed for the tenth year in a row.'

'Indeed they have!' exclaimed Nasrudin with glee.

'Then, how is it you could be so happy? Anyone else would surely be suicidal by now.'

Turning to his friend, Nasrudin cracked his knuckles.

'Well, having had my crops fail for ten years in a row could mean only one thing.'

'That you're destitute?' the friend chipped in.

'No, no! Rather, that my fortune is about to change!' roared Nasrudin.

*

Three weeks ago I took Ariane and Timur to Andalucía, and watched in sheer delight as they set eyes on the Alhambra for the first time.

Both in their late teens now, they have inherited my love of travel and stories, and my insatiable need to unpick the details of the lands through which I roam.

As they've grown up, and have been shaped by experiences laid down layer upon layer, I've marvelled at the freshness with which they regard the world. Untainted by preconceptions and fears that have shaped preceding generations, they begin a new phase of their journey – a phase that I feel I have myself completed.

Bidding farewell to Granada, we drove south to the coast, and along the waterline until we reached Algeciras. An hour early for the ferry across the Straits of Gibraltar to Morocco, I begged the kids to allow me a stroll down memory lane.

As I steered the car into the backstreets, the flat winter light seemed to yellow into a summer's day thirty-two years before. My mouth dried, and I sensed my pulse hasten, as I caught snatches of the familiar.

Having parked the car, we got out and made our way along a plush residential street, the buildings drenched in fresh white paint. Timur and Ariane must have wished we'd stopped for chocolate crêpes instead. They saw the very same details as me, but my eyes caught interwoven layers from another time.

Halfway along the street I made out the facade of a dear old friend – the glorious Hostal Magnífico. Unable to help myself, my mind's eye matched its current state to how I had known it in the days of the inimitable Doña Fernández.

My conclusion: not much change at all.

So we swanned up steps I'd first climbed in borrowed shoes and luggage-less, and found ourselves in the palace of kitsch once ruled over by the empress of low-budget hostels.

As soon as we were inside, I felt the ghosts of the French musicians robbed of their instruments, and the Dutch artist in painted-on boxer shorts.

And, for a fleeting moment, I saw María, her spectral form reclining on the threadbare couch.

An eager young receptionist blustered up, looked me up and down fast, and spat:

'*Sí*, señor?'

'We're not staying.'

'Oh.'

'You see, I'm on a journey down memory lane.'

'Oh.'

'D'you know what ever happened to Doña Fernández?'

'*Doña?*'

'*Fernández*… the proprietor. I imagine she's in hostel heaven by now. She was very old even then.'

'When?'

'Oh, gosh… let me think… it was early summer 1987.'

In a well-practised movement that no doubt impressed girls, the receptionist pulled a comb from his back pocket and slid it easily back through his quiff. He didn't reply, not in words. To a spring chicken like him, the eighties were ancient history taught in school.

So, with a prayer to past glory and the ghosts, we left.

Before going back to the car, I made a second pit-stop – at the building where Señor Chen had kept me alive with the house special.

A homeless man was sitting on a bench he'd jammed into the doorway.

Timur asked what I remembered of the place.

'I remember an especially fine conversation,' I said. 'And buying Señor Chen an equally fine set of German-made pots once my money finally came in.'

'Is that all?' Ariane asked.

'No,' I countered. 'There's something else.'

'What?'

'I remember being ready to take on the world,' I said.

'And did you?'

'Did I *what*?'

'Did you take on the world?'

Considering the question before answering, I replied:

'When I was young I used to feel no one would give me a chance. They kept people like me out at all costs. With time and experience, I learned how to work the system. None of that was especially important though.'

'What *was* important, Baba?' Timur asked.

Without even thinking, an answer offered itself:

'It's this: in your life there'll be times when you're up and times when you're down. The only certainty is that when you're riding high, you will be dragged down. And, likewise, when you're down, you'll get up again, so long as you remember the ultimate secret to life.'

'Which is?'

'To keep going at any cost.'

*

FOR FIFTY YEARS, Nasrudin had hunted his nemesis, stalking him through teahouses and across deserts, along shorelines and even in and out of his own home.

Baffled at his arch-enemy's cunning, he'd made a careful study of his methods. And, tired of pursuing him, he had roamed the world in search of a quiet corner free from the wretched opponent.

Arriving in a new country, Nasrudin sat down in a modest chaikana and ordered mint tea. It wasn't long before one of the locals had engaged him in conversation, and asked the nature of his journey.

Glancing furtively from side to side, to check no one was listening, the wise fool answered:

'For half a century I've been followed by a terrible curse… a creature as cunning as any other, he always seems to know where I'll be.'

'How does he look?' the stranger asked, intrigued.

'He's always dressed in the same dark cape,' Nasrudin explained. 'Sometimes he's very short and at other times he's as tall as a house!'

'Have you ever tried to speak to him?' the man asked, sipping his tea.

'Yes, ten thousand times! I've tried to chase him, too. But when I do so he slips behind me until I run round in circles!

All I can hope is that at last I've found a kingdom where I can escape him!'

The local sighed.

'Sounds as though you've suffered,' he said.

'Oh, yes, I have!'

'Well, it seems that fortune smiles on you.'

'Really?'

'Yes! You see, in this country we all have the very same dark nemesis.'

'Noooooo!' cried Nasrudin, hands clasped to his cheeks.

'Relax, my friend,' advised the local man calmly. 'There's nothing to worry about.'

'But why not?!'

'Because, we've learnt a secret way of coping.'

'Tell me! Tell me!' gasped the wise fool.

'Very well, but you have to do exactly as I say.'

'I promise!'

'It's quite simple really,' the local said. 'All you do is ignore him.'

Nasrudin's face was masked in terror.

'If I do that he'll devour me!'

The local stretched back on the sofa.

'Don't be so sure,' he said.

*

Tangier, 2019

An hour and a half after leaving Hostal Magnífico, we were

on the ferry traversing a short stretch of water and a vast chasm of cultural divide.

Standing on the deck, I got a flash of myself tossing my wooden clogs over the handrail, my name carved into them both.

'They may get washed up in China,' my father had noted.

'So should we go there?'

'Where?'

'To China?'

'What for?'

'To wait for them,' I'd said.

The muffled wail of the muezzin's call reached us before Tangier's medieval skyline was in focus, a pall of ink-black storm clouds ominous and low.

Once we'd navigated through the ritual of Moroccan customs, we drove out of town in search of the highway to Casablanca.

'Can't wait to see Zohra,' Timur said.

'Can't wait to swim in the ocean,' Ariane said.

'Can't leave Tangier yet,' I said.

Whipping the car round in a U-turn, I steered back to the port. Parking down at the boardwalk, I thanked the kids for their understanding.

'One day you'll have memory lanes of your own,' I whispered.

We turned left, walked up the steep hill that was the narrow rue de la Plage, and stopped at a metal door.

'This is it. Villa Calpe.'

'Where your grandfather lived?' asked Ariane.

'Yes, and where he died.' I pointed to the ground under our feet. 'Just here… struck by a reversing Coca-Cola truck fifty years ago.'

As the words left my mouth, something happened. A kind of alchemical reaction felt by no one except me. Noticing my forehead beading with sweat, Timur asked if I was feeling all right.

'It's ended,' I said. 'Just now. Ended as unexpectedly as it began.'

'What's ended, Baba?'

'The quest I began thirty years ago.'

'What quest?'

'The quest for Nasrudin.'

Unbuckling my canvas bag, I pulled out my journal.

Over the span of three decades I'd had dozens of similar notebooks – filled with scribbled comments taken down as I traipsed through jungles and over deserts, across mountain ranges, and from one city to the next.

Each time I bought a new journal, I transferred something from the old to the new without a passing thought. So familiar, I only ever noticed when it wasn't there.

Opening out my journal, I flicked through pages of random notes and observations until I reached it.

The tarot card… The Fool.

'What's that?' Timur probed.

'Something precious given to me by someone who'd been instructed to do so by my grandfather.'

'Is it Nasrudin, Baba?' Ariane asked.

'Yes it is… and it's so much more. You see, it's part of a

chain of transmission that links me to you, and us to all those who came before us.'

'Who?' Timur asked.

'Admirers of wisdom and foolishness,' I said. 'The disciples of Nasrudin. But, as we stand here in this special spot where my grandfather drew his last breath, it's something else.'

'What, Baba?' Timur asked softly.

'It's the end of my journey and the beginning of yours,' I said.

Reaching out, I handed him the well-worn card...

The wise fool, Nasrudin.

From: *Travels With Nasrudin*

The Wowing

MALCOLM GLADWELL GOT a tidal wave of attention when he came up with the concept of needing ten thousand hours' experience, and quite rightly so.

But in my opinion, he could have doubled it to twenty thousand hours.

Most writers don't churn out A-grade work after such a short amount of time. Writing eight hours a day for three and a half years or so gets you to the magic figure of ten thousand hours.

Agreed, three and a half years isn't insignificant, but it's not enough to get into the maestro zone. You may say some people are naturally brilliant, and you'd be right. Even then, I'd say mastery takes longer.

What I've learned is that a real writer – who writes because if he doesn't he'll turn to stone – begins as a feeble little stream heading down a mountain. You can drop a boulder in the stream to dam the flow. It'll work, at least for a while. Then the water will well up, flow around the rock, and carry on down the mountain.

Boulders dropped into the stream are a good thing.

Good, because they force the wannabe member of the Salinger Brigade to take stock, redouble their efforts, and set off again.

Doris Lessing's letter – the one I've never re-read out of my own shamefaced sense of wretchedness – got me thinking. If I wanted to break in, I'd have to take writing seriously, and treat it like a job.

While reeling from Doris's knockout blow between the eyes, I flew down to Kenya to stay with my friend, the seasoned explorer Sir Wilfred Thesiger. He was living near Maralal, with the nomadic Samburu tribe, in a shack perched halfway up a mountainside. We'd spend the days eating over-cooked goat stew and sipping sweet tea. Between the long bouts of silence, Thesiger would recount his adventures in Africa and Arabia fifty years before.

One afternoon, we were drinking hot, sweet tea in the shade of a thorn tree as usual. It was forty-three degrees outside. Dressed in a patched tweed jacket, Thesiger was telling me about the time he attended Emperor Haile Selassie's coronation, back in 1930. I'd heard it dozens of times before – but the best stories improve with repetition, and that one certainly did.

Sir Wilfred was about to describe the Imperial procession. I knew exactly what line he would utter next, and awaited it with anticipation.

The veteran explorer gazed into the middle distance as he relived the pomp and circumstance. His lips parting, he was about to deliver the next line, when a little boy charged into the shack and yelled something loudly in Swahili.

'Be quiet Little Horror!' Thesiger yelled. 'I'm telling a story!'

Shaking his fists and stamping his feet, the boy cried the same thing over and over.

'What's he saying?'

Thesiger listened, then raised his eyebrows.

'Oh,' he said.

'What?'

'The Little Horror says there's a man in Maralal with an electric arm.'

Curious by nature, I left Thesiger to his memories, and slipped down to the Green Bar – at the time Maralal's one and only watering hole. Almost lost in the shadows was a short, stout Indian man. Around his neck were dangling three Nikon cameras and, strapped to his left shoulder, was what looked like a bionic arm.

'Nice bit of kit,' I said, pointing at the device.

'It is when it works – which is none of the time.'

'What's the trouble?'

'The heat and the dust.'

'Sorry to hear it.'

The man with the bionic arm glanced at me sideways.

'Here for the circumcision, are you?'

'Excuse me?'

'The circumcision.'

'*Circumcision?*'

'Yeah. The Samburu one. Supposed to be any day now.'

'I'm staying with Thesiger,' I said. 'Thesiger the explorer.'

'I know who he is. He usually comes to it – enjoys a circumcision, Thesiger does.'

'Does he?'

''Course he does.'

Maralal is a small town by any standards, or at least it was back then. So small that strangers get chatting in ways which might be unnatural elsewhere. In such outposts, strangers are thrust together because if they weren't, they'd go insane.

The Indian removed his arm, laid it on the table, and invited me to sit.

Without quite knowing why, I blurted out:

'Just wrote a travel book. It started with a waiter taking off his leg and using it as a pillow.'

'A writer, are you?'

'Yes.'

'What've you written?'

'A travel book. It's called *In Gondwanaland*.'

'Is it published?'

'Going to be soon,' I lied.

The man with the bionic arm stretched out a hand.

'I'm Mohamed Amin,' he said.

I believe sequences of unrelated events determine our future, and that you have to cling hold of opportunities when they come along.

Despondency at Doris's letter had led me to lie low in Samburuland with Thesiger. And, being there in the time of the circumcisions had led me to Mohamed Amin. Just as I'm a believer in key sequences of events, I've come to value the big characters life throws one's way.

Most of the time they pass you by, like fallen leaves carried down the river. They're usually moving too fast to catch, or they're obviously meant for someone else. But sometimes they head for you in a way which signals you're supposed to grab them.

Mohamed Amin was destined to influence me in an unlikely and particular way. Sitting in the cool shadows of the Green Bar, I had no idea how he would shape the course of my writing life. At the time of our first meeting, I assumed he was a nutcase with an unhealthy preoccupation with circumcisions.

A few weeks later I mentioned meeting a man with a bionic arm to Dirk, my Dutch war-junkie journalist pal in Nairobi.

Dirk rolled his eyes.

'D'you know him?'

'Sure I do. Everyone knows Mo.'

'Really?'

'He's a one-man publicity machine. I swear he had his arm blown off just for the attention.'

'How did he lose it?'

'In the fall of Mengistu.'

'Addis Ababa?'

'Yup. 'Ninety-one. An ammunition dump went up. Mo was filming right near it. God knows how he survived. A shell zipped past the soundman's head. Didn't even touch him, but the speed was enough to cave his head in. Imagine that. The same shell took off Mo's left arm.'

'Who does he work for?'

'Viznews, the BBC, anyone who pays. Mo's a gun-for-hire. He's got his own outfit in the Press Centre – Camerapix. He's still dining out on the famine.'

'Which one?'

'The big one. Korem 'eighty-four.'

'The one that kickstarted Live Aid?'

'Yup.'

'Mo was there?'

My journalist friend grinned.

'It was only because of Mo the story got out.'

'Thought it was Michael Buerk and the BBC.'

'Buerk was the face on camera, but it was Mo who got access, filmed it, and broke the story.'

'Then he's a frigging legend!'

'A legend and a shameless self-publicist.'

'I want to meet him again,' I said.

'Why?'

'To hear his stories.'

Dirk groaned.

'He's gonna gobble you up,' he said.

An hour later, I was in Mo's office at the Press Centre, the walls hung with oversized shots of him posing with celebrities and heads of state. Mo with Idi Amin, with Mother Teresa, with Mandela, Qaddafi, Clinton, George Bush Sr, and the Queen of England.

Laid along one wall were stacks of equipment – TV cameras, tripods, cables, and battered aluminium cases marked 'PRESS'. Across from them, beside a tower of coffee-table volumes, was the bionic arm sitting in its open case.

I was admiring it when Mo walked in.

'That's a fucking useless piece of shit!' he said angrily.

'How was the circumcision?'

Mo Amin scowled.

'The fucking Samburu cancelled it. Can't rely on them for anything.'

'Probably best for it to stay private,' I said.

Mo scoffed.

'They called it off because there weren't enough press.'

'You mean they want attention?!'

'Of course they do! The Samburu are sick of being outdone by the Maasai tribe.'

I sat down on the frail fold-out chair reserved for visitors, while Mo sashayed round to the far side of his voluminous desk. In his own time he lowered himself onto a plush leather throne – the kind of thing usually reserved for African dictators.

Through my own insecurity, I spewed out a random anecdote featuring a well-known actor friend. It was supposed to help me make a point about the power of the press, but it nose-dived in the most spectacular way.

Mo Amin's smile soured ferociously.

Inhaling deeply, he launched into the mother of all anecdotes that cemented his position as the most famous cameraman and news operator in the known world. It featured presidents and royalty, actors, dictators, Nobel Laureates and Live Aid, Bob Geldof, and the Rolling Stones.

When it was over, I was pinned rigid to the rickety old chair. It was as though every cell in my body had been realigned from the full force of the most impressive extravaganza in name-dropping.

'Wow,' I whispered. 'That was incredible.'

'That's nothing!' Mo growled. 'One day I'll tell you about the time I first met Idi Amin.'

Having been raised in England, a realm in which self-promotion is frowned upon, I would usually have dismissed the hype as nonsense. But there was something irresistible about it. The only other person I'd ever seen get away with laying it on so fabulously thick was when the boxer Muhammad Ali appeared on talk shows. Conceited and egotistical to the point of caricature, the legendary boxer had earned his fame through sustaining pain in the ring – just as Mo had earned it by having his left arm blown off in the fall of Addis Ababa.

For three hours I sat there as the fusillade of anecdotes was fired at me full force. In all that time I wasn't asked for my opinion once, or whether I had any stories of my own. The bombardment was the kind of thing the US military has called 'Shock and Awe', and what I came to know as 'The Wowing'.

As Mo's stock-in-trade, it was like the strutting of a peacock with his tail out for all to see, combined with the head-thrown-back howling of an Alaskan wolf. I didn't realize it, but there was a purpose to The Wowing – a purpose far more than merely making Mo feel good about himself.

I was being wowed for a reason.

That first day at the Camerapix office was a kind of interview, part of an elaborate set-up. Only later did I realize Mo had picked me out back at the Green Bar in Maralal. He'd chosen me to write for him because I possessed the one thing he regarded as supremely important – the quality that could not be bought or indeed sold:

Enthusiasm.

In the big wide world there are plenty of enthusiastic people out there – and some of them are extremely enthusiastic indeed. But I like to think my enthusiasm is in an entirely different league. That's because somehow – and I'm not sure how – I managed to maintain the enthusiasm levels of a six-year-old who's desperate to eat ice cream down at the beach.

For that reason I can 'out-enthusiasm' almost anyone I meet.

As soon as he'd experienced my enthusiasm in the fly-infested shadows of the Green Bar, Mo had wanted to fish me from the river. He knew full well that were he to catch me and wow me, I would work like a maniac… because I was running on High Octane Enthusiasm.

By the early nineties, Mo Amin was the most famous cameraman ever to have lived – thanks to the Ethiopian famine and the global Live Aid concert that followed. Long before the break onto the world stage, he'd been a news cameraman and photographer – having begun honing his craft in the sixties, in the Tanzanian capital, Dar-es-Salaam.

As a sideline to the news business, Mo had started producing guides and coffee-table books, most of them relating to Africa. By the time we crossed paths in Maralal, he had a well-developed pipeline, with glossy new titles being churned out all the time.

Mo took the pictures himself. The texts tended to be written by Brian Tetley, an affable old Fleet Street hack, who'd moved to Nairobi, lured by the prospect of cheap beer, cigarettes, and plenty of sun.

Added into the mix were a handful of submissive editorial assistants, most of them living on crumbs. Reigning over the empire that was Camerapix Publishing was Mohamed Amin: enforcer, chairman, and editor-in-chief.

The only thing lacking was an endangered species – enthusiastic young writers who'd write books under impossible conditions, and never ask questions. The problem was that writers with experience elsewhere would never work for Mo. The conditions of his employment were tantamount to slavery, and his bouts of indiscriminate rage were almost as remarkable as the intensity of The Wowing.

I can't think of any writers who stuck it out at Camerapix, except for Tetley. He was different from the keen young writers in that he'd been broken by Mo years before, like a tamed elephant toiling in the forest of the Indian hinterland. The enthusiastic new arrivals became ensnared for two or three books, before legging it.

But each of them left with the same gift as me:

The gift of belief in one's own productivity.

*

A COUPLE OF weeks after The Wowing, I was dangling from the open door of a Jordanian Air Force Super Puma above the ancient rock-hewn city of Petra.

Beside me, bionic arm strapped in place, was Mo.

I'd been conscripted to write a guidebook to Jordan, having signed the contract with no questions asked. I'd never signed a literary agreement before, and so had no reason to think the terms were odd.

On offer was:

• A luxurious two-week jaunt around Jordan
• £400 cash
• Three economy tickets on any Ethiopian Airlines flight
• A Somali passport

In return, I agreed to hammer out the full text of the guide – all 140,000 words of it – in no more than a month.

The Jordan trip had been arranged by the kingdom's royal family, and all the stops were pulled out. Having been flown in first class, I was given my own private guard and chauffeur, and permitted access to anything I liked.

During the two weeks I spent in Jordan, Mo appeared for a few days, then jetted off to pose with a line-up of African dictators at a conference somewhere far away.

Following the jaunt, I regrouped in my digs in London, trying to work out how I'd come up with a massive wordage in such a remarkably short amount of time. These were the days before the Internet, when research material had to be tracked down on foot.

That first morning, I made a list of everything which had to be covered, as well as a daily writing list. If I was to get the manuscript handed in on time I'd have to write 6,000 words a day for just over three weeks. That would give me five days to read through and correct, and a day to tie up loose ends.

Thankfully, my friend with the office let me write there again. He stretched my hours, allowing me to work there from eight pm until seven am. I later repaid him with a flight to Beijing on Ethiopian – spoils of my hard grind.

Night after night, I described the Jordanian kingdom in a way that I hoped sounded fresh and seamless. I did my level best to paper over the glaring shortcomings in my knowledge, because there'd simply been no time to do all the research. Each evening, I'd type like a maniac whose family would be put to death if he didn't complete the task.

I wrote about Jordan's history from Neolithic times right up to the current date, about the kingdom's towns and cities, the Crusader castles and the pleasure palaces of the eastern desert. I wrote about the festivals and the folklore, about the carpet-weaving, the jewellery, the minorities, and pages and pages about the royal family – who'd funded the project.

By the end of a month I was shell-shocked.

I'd forgotten how to speak, was half-blind, and my fingertips were numb. All I could think of were words and the white spaces between them. On the last night, having typed my way through the hotel listings, I'd fallen asleep at the keyboard.

My friend whose office I was using found me snoozing when he came in.

'Jesus Christ!' he yelled. 'You look like death warmed up!'

'Feel like it,' I said limply. 'But at least I'm done.'

'Hope you've learned your lesson.'

I nodded.

'I'll never work for that bastard again,' I said.

Three months later, I was back with Mo – this time in Namibia.

Having cut my teeth on the guidebook – surely the most wretched writing task in the history of wretched writing tasks – I was upgraded to produce a coffee-table book. The route from London to Windhoek, the Namibian capital, was anything but direct. Calling it 'zigzag' would have been a kindness.

It was way more indirect than that.

In addition to his book-publishing business, Mohamed Amin produced a slew of in-flight magazines as well – including for Ethiopian Airlines and Air Seychelles. In a publishing empire built on barter rather than currency, he was provided with fistfuls of tickets in return for handling the magazines.

Although there was a direct flight from London to Windhoek, I was cajoled into making the trip via Frankfurt, Addis Ababa, Mumbai, and Johannesburg.

At the time of our arrival, Namibia was the newest country in the world.

A few days before the Queen of England had come and gone, having attended a ceremony that provided a glorious chunk of Africa with full independence. Samuel Njoma had been sworn in as President – a good thing because he was Mo's closest pal. No surprise in that, of course. As Mo used to say, 'You've gotta back the winning side in Africa or else you'll never make it out alive, and your pictures won't ever see the light of day.'

As well as being skilled in identifying enthusiastic young writers to labour in his salt-mines, the veteran newsman instinctively knew who'd rise to the top – in Africa at least. For thirty years he'd befriended dictators and despots – including presidential serial killers, psychopaths, and at least two cannibals. For someone like me, who'd studied African dictatorships, his stories were irresistible. Drawn in deep, I allowed myself to be enslaved in Mo's own tyrannical regime.

With only two weeks on the ground, there wasn't a hope in hell of seeing more than a fraction of Namibia. While I was sent to the north, my friend, Tarquin Hall, who'd been drafted in to do the guidebook, was sent to the south. Mo gave strict instructions for us to meet in the middle and to tell each other about what we'd seen.

The highlight of my Namibian journey was being flown up to the Skeleton Coast, on the border with Angola, in a Cessna. The brutal Benguela current has wrecked ships there for more than a century, and has washed up whale carcasses throughout history. I was deeply affected by that secret corner of wilderness, and during the journey my love for Africa was made complete.

If the Skeleton Coast was the highlight, the lowlight was Etosha National Park.

I am by nature a lone traveller, and can't bear tourism in any shape or form. It repulses me – disgusts me in the most primeval way. The reason is that tourists don't have a reason – they're there just because they're there. So it was a terrible shock to be drafted in to an organized tour of Etosha, which bills itself as Africa's most sensational game park.

I found myself in the rear of a Mercedes tour bus packed with retired workers from a ball-bearings factory in Düsseldorf. From the moment I clambered aboard, they could smell I wasn't one of them.

As the bus traversed the desert on its way to Etosha, towering termite mounds peppering the landscape from horizon to horizon, I vowed to escape.

That's exactly what I did.

A few miles from Etosha we pulled in at a service station in the middle of nowhere. An announcement was made in German, saying we had ten minutes to use the facilities. To me, it meant I had ten minutes to come up with a plan.

The only other vehicle there was a ramshackle jalopy which looked like it had gasped its last gasp. The bonnet was open, and clouds of smoke were billowing from the engine. A pair of spindly legs were poking out from underneath, ending in worn-out boots.

I tapped one of the feet.

Shuffling and struggling, the man extricated himself, spat hard at the dirt, and greeted me with an ear-to-ear grin.

He had an ample beard – the kind Islamist suicide squads tend to sport – and big blue eyes hinting of real kindness.

'Can you take me with you?' I asked.

'Take you where?'

'Anywhere.'

'Running away from something are you?'

'How did you guess?'

'The look in your eyes. You look frightened.'

'It's the Germans,' I said, 'I'm running from the Germans. They don't like me, and I don't like them.'

The man with the jalopy held out a hand. It was callused and worn like the barnacled hull of a ship.

'I'm Hennie,' he said. 'Hennie van Wyk.'

Hennie and I spent a week together zigzagging through Namibia.

He was a scrap metal dealer on a mission, and I was a wannabe writer hiding from the Germans from Düsseldorf, and from Mohamed Amin. As Hennie explained again and again in his lyrical voice, times were bad – and in bad times you couldn't sit on your ass. That was because in the bad times you had to remind people you were their friend, so they'd be your friend when the good times finally rolled around again.

Hennie was one of the most naturally friendly people I'd ever met. His friendliness was overwhelming and bona fide – unlike Mo's friendliness, which was laid on in a frightening way as a means to an end.

When we finally rumbled into Windhoek, Hennie and I were dear friends. Hugging each other, we promised to stay in touch, and to write letters every week.

Standing on the forecourt of the hotel, I watched as Hennie's dilapidated pickup trundled away, the back brimming with twisted scrap metal, exhaust fumes streaming behind like a vapour trail.

Keeping my promise, I sent dozens of letters and postcards.

But Hennie never wrote back.

As instructed, Tarquin – who was writing the guidebook – told me about the south, and I told him about the north. Or, rather, I told him about Hennie van Wyk. I recounted every tale he'd told me – about the boom years in scrap metal, and about the dark times as well.

'Wish you could have met him,' I said with a sigh. 'Hennie was a king among men.'

'Not sure how much scrap metal talk I can squeeze into the guide,' Tarquin said.

'Pity. We should all have the gift of Hennie van Wyk. His stories have a way of opening up your mind.'

'You gonna write about him?' Tarquin asked.

'You bet I am – an entire chapter. I'll call it "Travels With Hennie". Come to think of it, I'll dedicate the book to him.'

Tarquin's face froze.

'Mo's not gonna like that,' he said.

'Why not? He's doing the pictures. The text is up to me.'

The return trip to London took me via South Africa, the Seychelles, Ethiopia, India, and Germany.

For reasons I never understood, it was necessary to fly from Addis Ababa to Mumbai twice – like a tennis ball being knocked back and forth over a net.

Mo had saved the one direct ticket to London for himself, and was waiting for me at Heathrow when I landed.

'I'll need the text in two weeks,' he snarled.

'Not sure if that's possible. I've got a week booked in the country with my family.'

'No you don't! You've got two weeks with your nose down, writing.'

'But I don't even have a computer. I have to sneak into my friend's office and work through the night.'

'Then you have two weeks of night-sneaking.'

'OK,' I said mournfully.

Mo scratched a thumbnail to his bald head as if remembering something.

'And I'll need a speech about Namibia as well. A good long one gushing with love for Namibia.'

'Where are you going to deliver it?'

'It's not for me,' Mo said. 'It's for Sam Njoma, the president.'

Falling back into my pattern of nocturnal writing, I knocked out the manuscript for *Journey Through Namibia* in under two weeks. Compared to the trial and tribulation of the guidebook, it was a cakewalk. Besides, I delighted in describing my friend, Hennie van Wyk – and wrote an effusive dedication to him at the front.

I put the typescript on a floppy disk and it was taken down to Nairobi in a diplomatic pouch. Mo Amin was all about calling in favours – and the diplomatic corps of African dictatorships was a linchpin in his favour network.

A month later, an edited, typeset version of my manuscript arrived. Eagerly, I opened it up, and turned to my florid dedication to Hennie van Wyk. It was missing – deleted, as was every mention of my dear scrap-metal-dealer chum.

Slowly, I flipped through the printout.

Almost every word had been rewritten by Tetley, the Fleet Street hack.

I sent Mo a message ordering him to remove my name from the book, saying I wanted to distance myself from him and his wretched firm.

He didn't reply, but went ahead and published under my name.

Three years passed.

Throwing myself into journalism, I felt empowered by the knowledge I could produce massive wordage with nothing to go on. From time to time I'd get an urge to reach out to Mo. Like one half of an estranged couple who'd once shared intensity, I despised him – but I missed him all the same.

One Sunday afternoon I found myself in Nairobi. I'd been up in Samburuland again – on the trail of an English woman called Cheryl, who'd married a Samburu warrior.

With a few hours to spare before my flight home, I picked up the phone and called Mo on his hotline – the one he reserved for heads of state.

Ten minutes later I was sitting on the dining chair in his office once again.

'What was all that fucking crap about scrap fucking metal?!' Mo thundered. 'Tetley had to chop it all out!'

'He rewrote every line, the bastard.'

''Course he did. That's what he gets paid to do.'

'Paid in Somali passports and zigzag flights?'

'Some people would kill for a Somali passport!' Mo growled.

'Would they?'

'Yes they would!'

'I'll bear that in mind.'

Mohamed Amin leaned back on his tin-pot dictator's chair.

'So what's next?' he asked.

'I'm going up to London to file my story.'

'Not that.'

'Then what?'

'What's next for us – for you and me?'

I let out a high-pitched giggle crossed with a scream.

'There is no *next*.'

'Got a problem with the colour of my money?'

'Your money doesn't have a colour because it's invisible.'

'Want to go to Mecca with me – full access?'

The Holy City had been at the top of my wish list ever since I'd read my father's classic travel book *Destination Mecca*.

I narrowed my eyes.

'What are you offering?'

'Flights on Ethiopian and Air Seychelles.'

'What else?'

'A diplomatic Somali passport…'

'And…?'

'And a tour of Swaziland.'

'I hate tours,' I said.

'All right,' Mo bristled, bringing out the big guns. 'I'll give you breakfast with Idi Amin.'

For me, as a former student of African dictatorships, the Holy Grail was meeting the deposed cannibalistic ruler of Uganda, and self-styled King of Scotland.

Mo's family may have been originally from the Indian subcontinent, but the fact he shared a last name with the dictator had enabled him to acquire rare and unparalleled access – access Mo exploited shamelessly.

We shook hands, and I forgave him for expunging Hennie van Wyk from literary history, and for allowing Brian Tetley to butcher my work.

The Mecca trip was scheduled for the next month, followed by breakfast with Idi Amin, who was enjoying sanctuary in Jeddah.

Returning to London, I got on with my journalism.

Three weeks later I was woken early on a Saturday morning by my sister, Saira.

Our father was dead.

It was a phone call that pressed 'pause' on my life, and an event I've never quite recovered from.

That afternoon something prompted me to turn on the TV news.

An Ethiopian Airlines flight ET961 from Addis Ababa to Nairobi had been hijacked. As fate would have it, Mohamed Amin and his sidekick Brian Tetley were on board. Mo was up front in first class, white Tetley was at the back of economy. Apparently drunk and armed with grenades, the hijackers had ordered the pilot to fly them to Australia. They'd selected the destination from the map in the in-flight magazine, *Selamta* – of which Mo was the publisher.

The hijackers had ordered the pilot to stop following the African coastline and to cross the Indian Ocean. As the plane neared the pristine beaches of the Comoro Islands, it ran out of fuel.

A wingtip brushed the water, and flight ET961 disintegrated.

Amazingly, a few passengers at the back of the aircraft survived.

Brian Tetley, the Fleet Street hack, was not one of them.

As for Mo Amin, he'd been desperately negotiating with the hijackers. Until the moment the plane hit the water, he had once again been on top of the biggest news story in the world.

On that bewitched day in late 1996, I lost my father, Mo, and all hope of ever having breakfast with Idi Amin.

From: *The Reason to Write*

The Rite of Passage

THE FIRST NIGHT we spent at the Caliph's House was a rite of passage. The guardians had pleaded with us not to stay there until the wayward jinns had been dispatched. I protested vehemently. It seemed insane to move into a hotel when we had our own home. After much wrangling, Hamza, Osman and the Bear saw that I would not be swayed. They ceded defeat, so long as we followed a few guidelines. These included all of us sleeping in the same room on a single grimy mattress, around which a circle had been etched with a lump of coal. We were instructed not to open the windows, despite the suffocating press of summer heat. Nor were we permitted to sing, laugh, or to speak in anything but a whisper. I asked why.

'Because it will anger the jinns.'

The guardians recapped the list of warnings: 'No laughing, talking, walking around, or thinking impure thoughts.'

'Is that it?' I asked.

Osman's smile vanished. 'No, no,' he said fearfully. 'There is something far, far more important to remember.'

'What?'

'Disobey, and unspeakable terror will befall you.'

My wife rolled her eyes. 'What is it now?'

The Bear swallowed hard. 'Whatever happens,' he said, stooping in dread, 'do not go anywhere near the toilet in the night.'

As I was quickly to learn, there is no place more satisfying for a mischievous jinn to lurk than just beneath the surface of water.

Rachana, who had given birth to our son, Timur, only three weeks before, choked. 'That's impossible,' she barked.

'We will do our best,' I said, meekly.

We entered the house in single file as dusk became night once again. There was no electricity and so candlelight was our guide. It threw long, spectral shadows across the walls and glistened on the backs of a thousand cockroaches, which darted in all directions at the sound of human intruders. Hamza led the way down the long corridor, across the great salon and then upstairs.

As we moved through the mansion, picking cobwebs from our faces, the thought of a hotel nearby with electric lights, television and usable toilets became all the more appealing. Once we were installed in the bedroom itself, the hotel-room fantasy beckoned again. We crouched down on the mattress, my wife holding the newborn baby to her chest and I clutching Ariane to mine. It was a miserable moment. I looked at Rachana through the flickering candlelight and whispered, 'Welcome to our new life!' We were both about to laugh, but then we remembered that laughing was forbidden, as it angered the jinns.

The square-shaped bedroom had a high ceiling, small windows and what looked like cryptic charcoal symbols strewn across the mottled walls. Some were mathematical designs, others like cave paintings of animals, sketched by primitive man.

I tucked Ariane into bed and told her a story about a brave little girl who wasn't scared, even when people tried to frighten her. There was a knock at the door, as if the tale was a cue of some kind. The three guardians were waiting. They had come, they said, to wish us luck. Osman threw a handful of salt into each of the four corners and the Bear recited a verse from the Qur'an. Before they scurried away, Hamza warned us again not to use the toilet on any account.

At first the night passed easily enough, although the chorus of donkeys from the shantytown, the mosquitoes and the stifling heat kept us awake. I was tempted to throw the windows open, but leaving them shut seemed a small price if it would keep the guardians at ease and the spirits at bay. Eventually we fell asleep, cuddled together like kittens on the vile old mattress. Then, at four a.m., came a voice from the darkness. It was hoarse and bellowing, and it was near. It became so loud that it managed to drown out the clamour of the donkeys and the savage dogs fighting in the shantytown. Rachana clutched me and Ariane began to howl with terror.

'What is it?'

'I think it's the muezzin, the call to prayer.'

I tried to get back to sleep, but was overcome by the desperate urge to pee. I held it in for an hour, until I could stand no more. The jinns would have to forgive me, I thought. Very quietly I slipped into the bathroom and began to relieve myself. The pleasure was broken when a shadowy figure with a thick moustache leapt from behind the door. It was Hamza. He flipped down the lavatory lid in mid-flow.

'Get out of here!' he whispered caustically.

'You get out of here!' I shouted.

We wrestled together for a moment or two in the blackness, I struggling to lift the lid with my free hand and he desperate to slam it shut.

'I haven't finished!'

'This is very dangerous,' he replied.

'I can't help it. It's nature's call.'

'You don't know what you're doing!' he yelled.

The baby was woken by our brawl. Then Rachana screamed for silence. I summoned all my strength and pushed the guardian out of the toilet. He disappeared into the garden, cursing.

Before I knew it, Ariane was peeling back my eyelids and looking in. Sunlight was streaming through the small windows. I could hear the melody of birds singing on the window-ledge outside, as my nostrils picked up the odour of fresh baked bread, no doubt from a stall in the shantytown. The bedroom was bathed in a blissful innocence. This is it, I thought to myself, this is our new life.

As far as the guardians were concerned, Dar Khalifa's proximity to a mosque was more than fortuitous. They regarded it as the single factor that had kept us safe during the first night. The imam's summoning of the devout to prayer was seen as a powerful purging force in itself – as if he was blessing us five times a day. To me, the raspy voice amplified through an old loudspeaker was more of an irritation than a blessing.

We had arrived in Morocco frazzled by the island culture we had left. We were paranoid, unhealthy and overworked. In the West we are driven on by an extreme form of guilt – if you are not seen to be working like a dog, you're perceived as being slothful. It was very clear that things in Morocco were quite different. A mantle of level-headed comfort enveloped life, even in Casablanca, one of the busiest of all north African cities. I found people rushed about only when they needed to, and not because they knew that others were watching them.

The first days were tranquil. We bought essentials, ate picnic meals on the overgrown lawn and set about exploring the house. Ariane liked to lead the way, tramping through the endless rooms in search of unhatched eggs in the bird nests, or chasing mice. We worked out where each corridor led, which room lay behind each door, and we trawled through the bric-à-brac left by the previous owner. The idea of renovation didn't even occur to us; it was hard enough to believe the house was ours.

Dar Khalifa is set at the far end of a long rectangular sheet of land. It looks out on the swimming pool, the gardens, stables, and an assortment of smaller buildings. The house itself has been built in stages over time. On the right side is the oldest courtyard garden, dominated by an outcrop of banana trees and towering palms. The sitting rooms, kitchens, dining room and entrance-way form the main body of the house, along with two further courtyards – one outside the kitchen, and another on the left side, which adjoins the garages. The tennis court stretches out behind, with a cluster of changing rooms, a well and servants' quarters. On the first floor there are bedrooms and an expansive roof terrace, and along the left side of the house is a later annexe of two more bedrooms with a guest suite above.

From the start the guardians were amiable, but they kept a distance. It seemed as if they were uneasy that people had moved back into the Caliph's House. They would watch us from behind a wall or a garden hedge and duck out of sight when we turned to face them. I found it amazing that in the decade the mansion had been empty the guardians had kept the stables as their hideaway. They had never opened up the house and enjoyed its space and had only ventured inside on rare occasions. I supposed it had something to do with their fear of the jinns.

We managed to get some of the lights working and cleaned the bedroom until it shone. Rachana strung up homemade curtains and I scoured ten years of algae from the toilet. Hamza found me on my hands and knees scrubbing the bowl with a toothbrush. He screwed up his face.

'There are no jinns in here, not now,' I said.

The guardian waved a finger back and forth. 'They don't like that,' he quipped. 'They like to be left alone.'

I didn't reply, but went off to buy a set of plastic garden chairs, as there was no furniture at all. Later, when I arrived home, I went for a pee. To my surprise, the toilet was filled with what looked like the leftovers from lunch. I asked Ariane if she had thrown up.

'No, Baba,' she said earnestly.

I walked out into the blazing sunshine. The guardians weren't to be seen. I called their names. No reply. So I ambled down to the stables, which are set in one corner at the end of the garden, shrouded by a mass of pink bougainvillea. I could make out the sound of feet running down a path and a door closing, but I couldn't see anyone. The stable doors were all tightly shut. I prised them open. Three were filled with broken garden tools, ladders and knots of old wire. The door of the fourth stable was ajar. I pushed it wide open.

Hamza was sitting inside on a paint can topped with a wad of grey asbestos. He was panting, as if he had been running. I asked him if he had any idea how the toilet came to be clogged with chicken stew. He stared up at me and adjusted the asbestos.

'The jinns are not happy,' he said, 'and when they are not happy they get angry.'

I was about to ask another question, but Ariane was screaming out on the lawn. I ran over to see what was going on. She was sitting under a fruit tree, hands over her eyes, bawling. Above her, on one of the low boughs of the tree, was a string. From the string there was hanging a dead tabby cat. I pulled it down and called Hamza.

'What's this doing here?'

The guardian furrowed his brow. 'It's bad,' he said.

'I know it's bad, but who did this?'

Hamza shook his head, picked up the cat and took it away.

On our third day in Casablanca, I met a French diplomat called François through a friend of a friend. He was living in a spacious apartment with his family and had a job at the French Consulate. I asked him about Morocco, expecting him to praise it – after all, he had been based in Casablanca for ten years. He looked at me across the lunch table, his sapphire eyes cool as glacial ice.

'This country's a time bomb,' he said, mimicking an explosion with his hands. 'It's a career cemetery, too. Work here and you'll never work again!'

I asked him about Moroccan people.

'Don't trust anyone,' he snapped. 'Fire the first ten people who walk into your office, and rule with an iron fist!'

'But Casablanca seems very European.'

'Hah!' cracked François. 'We're close to Europe, but don't make the mistake that I did.'

'What mistake's that?'

'Don't think for a minute people are going to be like Europeans,' he said. 'They may be wearing the latest Paris fashions, but in their minds they're Orientals.' François paused to tap a fingertip to his temple. 'In there,' he said, 'it's *Arabian Nights*.'

I told him about my experience with the toilet and the jinns.

'Of course,' said the Frenchman, 'everyone believes in that stuff... just like the tales of Aladdin, Sindbad and Ali Baba. There's no question about it. Why? Because jinns are in the Qur'an. That's why. Try to get anything done and the wall of superstition hits you face-on. Try to avoid it, pretend it's not there, and you'll trip up.'

'So what's the answer?'

François lit a Gauloise and exhaled. 'You have to learn to coexist,' he said, 'learn to appreciate the culture and to navigate through treacherous water.'

'How do I do that?'

'Shun the most obvious solution,' he said.

Back at the house, the guardians were clustered round the toilet bowl, calling prayers down to the jinns. Rachana said they had barred her way and threatened to lock the door if we continued to bother them. She was very worked up when I found her, insisting she would move into a hotel unless I sorted my workers out.

I led the guardians outside. They lined up in the long corridor, saluted, then stared at their feet.

'This can't go on,' I said. 'We need to use the bathroom. It's a matter of hygiene as much as anything else.'

The Bear squinted in the afternoon sunlight. 'The jinns want blood,' he said.

'Well, they're not going to get any. You can go and tell them.'

'A few drops would do,' said Osman.

'Absolutely not!'

'But you can prick your finger,' the Bear said. 'It wouldn't hurt. You could let the blood drip into the toilet. It would make the jinns very pleased.'

'Oh yes,' Hamza echoed, 'it would make them very pleased.'

The Bear held up a pin. He just happened to be carrying it.

I wasn't about to start feeding my blood to imaginary forces of the underworld. 'Can't one of you give them your blood?'

'No, no, no,' the Bear riposted. 'You are the new master of the house and so only your blood will do.'

We filed up to the toilet again and stared into the bowl. The thought that only my blood would suffice made me feel somehow important, indispensable – as if I was in charge. The Bear handed me the pin. I pricked my forefinger and let a large, single droplet of crimson blood splatter into the water. The guardians smiled broadly like Cheshire cats and took it in turns to shake my hand.

From then on, they seemed to regard me with a little more respect. Osman brought a pot of chicken soup for us the next night. He said his wife had made it from a recipe that had been in her family for six hundred years. One mouthful and, he claimed, we would dance like angels inside. I was touched by the thoughtfulness and rather liked the idea of dancing like an angel. The soup was flavoured with fresh coriander and saffron, and a hint of ginger. It was quite delicious and made a change from our stark diet of bread and triangles of processed cheese. The morning after that, Hamza crept into the bedroom and sprinkled us with pink rose petals while we slept. And, so as not to be outdone, the Bear presented us with talismans, fashioned from black calfskin. There was one each, of differing sizes – ranging from large to very small. We tied them round our necks dutifully and praised their craftsmanship.

The first days slipped by. Talk of jinns died down, but I knew the subject was still very much on the agenda. Hamza would roam round the house reciting verses from the Qur'an, or sketch magic squares on the whitewashed walls. He said the squares were amulets. They were formed of nine smaller squares. Add up the three numbers of any line and you got the number fifteen. When I asked what they were for, Hamza said they would help bring baraka, divine blessing, back to the Caliph's House.

The focus of his prayers was the largest courtyard, in which there lay a wonderful secret garden. It looked like the oldest part of the house. At each end there stood a long salon with a colonnaded veranda. The room at the east end had fabulous cedar doors, twenty feet high, and a pair of giant matching windows, carved with geometric designs. I planned to turn it into a library, lined with bookshelves from the floor to the ceiling.

After a week at the house, I realized that I still hadn't seen inside the room at the western end of the courtyard. I tried the handle but it was firmly locked shut. Hamza was crouching behind a squat palm tree, going over a magic square with a nugget of coal. I asked him to open the door. He saluted, then pretended not to understand. When I repeated the request, he seemed displeased and ambled off to fetch the key.

As the chief guardian, nothing was more important to him than maintaining control. He controlled Osman and the Bear, anyone who came to the house and, through skilful corralling, he managed to control us, too. The most effective method of staying in control was to lock all the doors at all times, unless one of us was in the room. Even then he quite frequently locked us inside. He kept all the keys in an old shoebox. There were hundreds of them. I would leave the kitchen for a few seconds to take a plate of food to Ariane and, when I came back, the room would be locked. The same with the bathroom – leave it for a moment and you couldn't get back in. Sometimes you would hear Hamza's worn leather-soled slippers shuffling away and the box of keys jangling.

I waited twenty-five minutes at the locked courtyard door for Hamza to return. He may have been hoping I had lost interest and had gone on to do something else.

When he did finally turn up, the shoebox under one arm, his head was stooped low. He rummaged in the box and winced in declaration: 'The key isn't here.'

'You haven't looked very hard. Let me have a look.'

The guardian covered the mouth of the box with his hands. 'I'll look, I'll look!' he said, delving a second time.

Ten minutes later he was still rummaging. 'It's not here,' he said with certainty.

'Doesn't anyone ever go in there?'

'No, they don't,' Hamza said, 'no one's been in there for years.'

The secrecy made the locked room all the more intriguing. I began to speculate what lay behind the door.

'There are other, more interesting rooms,' said the guardian. 'Don't bother with this one.'

'Have you ever been in there?'

The guardian swished the air with his hand. 'Oh, yes,' he said. 'It's very boring.'

'When did you go inside?'

Hamza thought for a moment. 'Many years ago,' he said.

'But it's an important part of the house,' I said assertively. 'Let's open it up.'

I suggested we get a hammer and break the lock. At that moment, the muezzin rang out across the shantytown.

Hamza hurried away with his shoebox of keys. 'I must go and pray,' he said, calling back.

The question of the locked room continued to grate on my mind. When I asked Osman about it, he said Hamza was the only person who had ever been inside.

'He always goes there at night,' he said.

'You mean he goes in now?'

'Of course,' said Osman. 'He goes in there every day.'

'What's inside?' I asked.

Osman grimaced, slapped his hands to his cheeks in horror and sank his teeth into his upper lip. He was wheezing.

'What's inside the locked room?' I repeated.

'I don't know,' he said. 'Really, believe me, I don't know.'

Despite the matter of the mysterious locked door, relations with the guardians continued to improve. Then, one morning as I was going into the courtyard, I spied Hamza leaving the room. The moment he saw me making a beeline for him, he slammed the door shut. I tried the handle. It was locked fast.

'Can you please open this door, right now?'

The guardian glanced away. His brow was running with sweat. 'It is locked,' he replied.

'I know that, but you just came out. You have the key.'

'I don't,' he said. 'I swear to Allah that I do not have the key.'

I was about to search Hamza, but something stopped me. For some reason I felt it better to leave him alone. I'm not sure why. It's very strange. I should have pressed him to hand over the key then and there, but I didn't, almost as if something was affecting my decision.

Although we had not started renovating the house, we did buy a few things to make life more comfortable – crockery, lamps, extra mattresses and more garden furniture. But we soon found that no taxi driver was keen to venture into the shantytown. They said its jagged track was far too rough on their precious vehicles. So I decided to hire a car.

Osman was the first to catch wind of my plan. He said it was a fine idea, that he and the other guardians would assist me as I was new to the Moroccan car-rental scene. I thought this meant they would point me in the direction of a large, well-respected rental firm. But it did not. It meant something quite different. Hamza came to our bedroom that evening and said that he and the others had arranged everything.

'What do you mean by everything?'

'No problem, Monsieur Tahir. We have found a nice car. It's very, very nice.'

He then explained that the butcher in the shantytown never drove his car because of his bad back, so it made perfect sense for me to take it on. What made less sense was the fact that the vehicle had been used for twenty years to ferry sheep carcasses from the slaughterhouse to the fly-smothered butcher's stall.

Sitting in it was like being strapped into a curious scientific experiment in which the passengers were the guinea pigs. The seats were encrusted with dead maggots and the air around them alive with flies. No matter how many you killed, there were always more.

After taking one look at the vehicle, I thanked the guardians, praised the butcher's generosity and politely refused the arrangement. 'It doesn't have enough space,' I said.

'What do you mean?' said the butcher. 'You can fit ten dead sheep in there.' He thumbed to the rear seat. 'There's plenty of room for your entire family.'

'I was hoping for a four-by-four.'

'This is far stronger than any four-by-four!' snarled the butcher.

'It has *baraka*,' said Osman. 'It will bring you good luck.'

I looked at the sordid heap of blood-splattered metal, with its cracked windscreen, smashed lights and maggot-ridden seats.

'Go on,' Osman whispered. 'Try it. For a few days only.'

'All right,' I said gruffly, 'for a few days.'

Only later did I begin to understand the game. It was a game I didn't know I was playing, a game that everyone in Morocco – not only foreigners – is forced into by their family and friends. Moroccans see it as their duty to help those they are close to. Not being of assistance at all times can bring dishonour and disgrace on the family. This wonderful tradition has evolved into a state in which everyone tries desperately to get you to do what they think is best for you. I knew the system well from years spent in Asia. Had I rented a car from Avis, Budget or Hertz, the guardians and their families would never have been able to live down the shame – the shame of not getting involved.

Like almost every other vehicle in Casablanca, the butcher's wretched Toyota was dented on every side and was falling to bits. I hated it but, at the same time, I valued it for the veil of authentic camouflage it provided. When out driving, no one would take me for a foreigner, or so I thought.

The moment I crept timidly into the ferocious stream of traffic, retching from the stench of rotting blood, I stood out like a pacifist on a battlefield. Moroccan traffic isn't like normal traffic. It's armed combat, a war of wills, in which only the very bravest have a chance to survive. Every driver, except for me, was an expert in swerving. You could veer sharply to the left or right without any warning and be quite certain that all the other cars would swerve out of the way.

On the first day on the road, I realized that I had to find someone who could help get things done and act as a bridge between us and everyone else. The constant swerving was fraying my nerves. I called François and asked him for advice on how best to choose an assistant.

'You have to show your teeth,' he said. 'It's dog-eat-dog out there. A man with no teeth is swallowed in one gulp.'

'I'll be hard,' I said, weakly. 'I'll ask tough questions. I'll bare my teeth.'

'That's not enough,' the Frenchman said frostily.

'What else can I do?'

'Tell each applicant to bring their family tree to the interview.'

'What good will that do?'

François clicked his tongue at my ignorance. 'Hire the person with the longest family tree,' he said. 'They'll have contacts. They'll be survivors.'

I thanked François, but he wasn't listening.

'Tell me,' he said, 'did you fire the first ten people who walked into your office?'

'No, not exactly, François. You see, I don't have an office and the only people I have working for me were inherited. I can't fire them. It would be unkind.'

There was silence.

'Hello. Are you there?' I stammered.

'You're going to be eaten alive,' said François.

From: *The Caliph's House*

Ali Baba's Map

So geographers, in Afric-maps,
With savage-pictures fill their gaps;
And o'er unhabitable downs
Place elephants for want of towns.

Jonathan Swift, *A Rhapsody*

AN INKY HAND-DRAWN map hung on the back wall of Ali Baba's Tourist Emporium.

Little more than a sketch, and smudged by a clumsy hand, it was mounted in a chipped gold frame and showed a river and mountains, a desert, a cave and what looked like a trail between them. At the end of the trail was an oversized 'X'.

'Is that a treasure map?'

Ali Baba looked up from the back page of the *Jerusalem Herald* and peered at me. He was an old dog of a man, whose pot belly hinted at a diet rich in fat-tailed sheep. His chin was covered with bristly grey stubble; he was bespectacled and he spoke through the corner of his mouth. Like all the other merchants in the bazaar, Ali Baba had gone to rack and ruin, but he didn't care. Lighting a filter-less Turkish cigarette, he let his chest swell with the smoke.

'That's not for sale,' he said.

'But is it a treasure map?' I asked again.

The shopkeeper grunted and returned to his paper. You couldn't accuse Ali Baba of hard salesmanship. Times had never been worse for tourism since the fighting had flared up again, and all the other traders in Jerusalem's Old City were falling over themselves to do business. But then none of them had a treasure map hanging on their walls.

'Where's the treasure supposed to be?'

'Africa.'

'Diamonds?'

'No, gold.'

'Oh,' I mouthed with mounting interest, 'pirate treasure?'

Ali Baba glanced up again from his newspaper. Then he straightened his white skull-cap, scratched a broken fingernail through his beard and replied.

'Gold mines, it is a map for the gold mines.'

'*The* gold mines?'

'The mines of Suleiman,' he growled, 'King Solomon's mines.'

The Via Dolorosa is packed with poky shops touting the latest in Virgin Mary T-shirts, playing cards bearing the head of John the Baptist, Jesus Christ bottle openers and Last Supper baseball caps.

Several merchants that morning had even offered me 'splinters' from the Cross, and one had shown me what he said were Christ's thumb bones.

The prices mentioned suggested they were fakes: they only cost two hundred dollars each. Holy Land kitsch surpasses all other forms. It seemed amazing that anyone would ever buy any of the merchandise, especially since tourists were now few and far between. Most had been scared away by the renewed Intifada.

As anyone who's ever set foot in the maze of back streets of Jerusalem's *souk* knows, everything has a price. After forty minutes of drinking dark sweet tea with Ali Baba, the map was mine. Wrapping it in his copy of the *Jerusalem Herald*, Ali Baba licked his thumb and counted my wad of notes. Then, after counting them once, he turned them over and counted them again, checking for forgeries.

'Six hundred shekels,' he said. 'Cheap at the price.'

'It may be little to you, but it's a lot to me. It's nearly a hundred pounds.'

'What do you mean?' exclaimed Ali Baba. 'This map could lead you to a treasure greater than the farthest limits of your imagination. It's been in my family for six generations. My father would slit my throat if he were alive. And my mother must be turning in her grave. I can hear my ancestors cursing me from the next world!'

'Why haven't you ever gone off to look for Solomon's mines yourself?'

'Hah!' said the merchant, recoiling. 'How do you expect me to leave my business?'

'Then why are you selling the map after so long, and why to me?'

'You seem an honourable man,' said Ali Baba, opening the door.

I thanked him for the compliment.

'You are wise too, I can see that,' he added, as I stepped into the street, 'so hang the map on your wall and leave it at that.'

All over the world unscrupulous shopkeepers have palmed me off with their most suspect merchandise.

Most tourists instinctively avoid such objects, but I can't help myself. I have an insatiable appetite for questionable souvenirs. My home is filled with useless junk from a hundred journeys. The highlights include a lucky painted sloth jawbone from the Upper Amazon, a boxed set of vintage glass eyes from Prague, and a broken boomerang purchased in a Moroccan *souq*, and supposedly once owned by Jim Morrison. I have a West African divining bowl too, made from whale bone, and a fragment of an Ainu warrior's cloak, a human hair talisman from Sarawak, and a ceremonial executioner's sword from the Sudan.

But Ali Baba's map was different.

From the moment I saw it, I knew that a great opportunity was spread out before me. No names of places or co-ordinates were marked, but it was the first fragment of a journey. Such leads are rare in life, and must be seized with both hands.

Before Ali Baba could regret the decision to sell his heirloom, I hurried out into the web of streets, past the fruit stalls and perfume-sellers, the caverns heaped with turmeric, ground cinnamon and paprika, dried figs and trays of oily baklava. The Old City was full of life, moving to an ancient rhythm which could have changed little since the time of Christ.

The Intifada might have frightened away the package tourists but, as I saw it, a visit to Jerusalem in a time of peace would strip it of a vital quality – danger. My wife has grown used to hastily planned holidays in the world's trouble-spots. As soon as there's a bomb, an earthquake, a tidal wave or a riot, I call the travel agent and book cut-price seats. I'm no fearless war correspondent, but I have come to realize that the news media has a knack of exaggerating the perils of even the worst national emergency. In any case, a little danger is a small price to pay for ridding a place of tourists. We spent our honeymoon in Alexandria, living it up in the presidential suite of a grand hotel a couple of days after a bomb had wiped out a tourist bus in the Egyptian capital. At first my wife grumbled – she had been looking forward to Venice – but over the years she's become used to holidays that come with a Foreign Office health warning. But even she wasn't prepared to accompany me to the West Bank during the worst fighting since the Six-Day War.

In more peaceful times I would have had to fight my way through the crowds to get up to the Dome of the Rock, which stands on an outcrop known to Jews as

Temple Mount, and to Muslims as Haram al-Sharif, the Noble Sanctuary. The small plateau is one of the holiest sites in Islam and is revered by Jews as well.

The Cotton Merchants' market, which was built by the Crusaders and which leads up to the sanctuary, was deserted. A pair of Israeli soldiers were standing guard at the far end of the tunnel, lit by octagonal skylights in the vaulted stone roof. Their fatigues were well pressed, but their expressions were heavy with the boredom that only conscripts know. In a synchronized movement they lifted automatic rifles to my chest and told me to turn back. Tourists were not welcome, they said. If I took another step towards the shrine, I'd be arrested and charged.

I explained that I was no tourist but a pilgrim. My father, my grandfather and his father before him had prayed at the Dome of the Rock. Now I had come to continue the tradition. Nothing would make me leave without fulfilling my duty. As I delivered my harangue, a beggar with no legs swam desperately over the flagstones, his arms flailing. He kissed my feet, rejoicing at the sight of a tourist. Until my arrival his livelihood must have been in doubt. I handed him a few small coins, for charity is one of the central pillars of Islam.

The conscripts lowered the barrels of their weapons to groin height. They were giving me a moment to persuade them of my faith.

'Tourists degrade what is holy. They are the agents of the Devil,' I exclaimed, as I spat on the ground.

The guards' eyes widened and, perhaps worried that I was a lunatic and would give them trouble, they let me through the cordon. A pair of great doors were swung open on rusting hinges, and I caught my first sight of the fabulous golden dome.

Before I had taken a single step towards the shrine, an old Arab guard hurried over and insisted that I required his services. Only he could keep me safe, he said, and besides he needed the money. His honest eyes were pale green, the colour of rock opals, his unshaven cheeks leathery and walnut brown. His front teeth were missing, causing him to whiffle when he spoke. His name was Hussein.

'My seven sons have been hungry for many weeks,' he said. 'Thank God that you have come! You were sent by God to help restore my family's fortune. I have been blessed by your arrival, and my family have been blessed! May you live for a thousand years!'

After such a welcome I had little choice but to hire the guide. He motioned to the dome and clamped his hand to my forearm, so that I might pause to savour the moment. Resting on an octagonal mosaic-tiled base, and framed in the brilliant blue afternoon sky, the great golden dome blinds all who look upon it. We shaded our eyes in the sunshine and then began to climb the steps up towards the shrine.

The floor of the main chamber is almost entirely taken up by the Rock – a broad, rolling slab of stone – which Muslims call Kubbet al-Sakhra. It is from here that the

Prophet Mohammed is said to have ascended to Heaven on his Night Journey to receive the Qur'an. Hussein pointed out the hoof-print of the Prophet's steed Buraq where he leapt into the air to carry his master heavenward. The Rock is sacred to Judaism, too, supposedly the very spot where Abraham prepared to sacrifice his son Isaac, long before the rise of Islam.

Hussein had tears in his eyes as he led me around the shrine. I was unsure whether his emotions were stirred by the thought of my custom or if, like me, he was genuinely affected by his surroundings. Perhaps it was a mixture of both, for you could stare upon the Dome of the Rock for hours and never tire of it.

As he led me down to the Well of Souls, the subterranean chamber where legend says the dead congregate to pray, Hussein wiped his eyes.

'God rewards all believers,' he said. 'Islam is the true path, of course, but we do not frown on those of the other faith. Hostility is bad for us all and it's an affront to what is sacred. Abraham is after all a prophet mentioned by the Holy Qur'an, just as Suleiman – whose great temple stood here – is honoured by Muslims.'

'Suleiman, *Solomon*... his temple was built here?'

Hussein paused to show me the niche where a strand of the Prophet's hair is kept. It is brought out only during Ramadan.

'Solomon, the wise king,' he said slowly, 'he built the most spectacular temple right here where this sanctuary now stands. How it must have looked, its walls and roofs covered in fine gold!'

'Gold... from the mines, from Solomon's mines?'

'Yes, of course,' said Hussein.

We left the Dome of the Rock and walked towards the El Aqsa mosque which stands at the southern end of the plateau. Hussein was talking, extolling the merits of Islam, but I wasn't listening. The mention of Solomon and his golden temple had distracted me.

I asked Hussein to stop for a moment. I'd stashed the map from Ali Baba's Tourist Emporium in my rucksack. We sat on the ground beside the fountain where ablutions are performed while I rummaged. Hussein was eager to tell me that Anwar Sadat had come to pray at the mosque, and to recount the day King Hussein of Jordan's grandfather, King Abdullah, was shot dead as he entered El Aqsa. With his own eyes he, Hussein, had seen the bullet enter the old king's head, his turban fall, and the dignitaries scatter like rats.

I unwrapped the gilded frame and stared at the map. Hussein glanced at the image, the bright sunlight reflecting off its glass, and fell silent.

'Solomon's mines,' he said, 'the mines in Ophir.'

I was surprised that he could recognize the map so easily, especially as there were no place names marked.

'What is Ophir?'

'The land of gold,' said the guide, 'from where the finest gold on earth was brought.'

'Where is it, this land of Ophir?'

Hussein hunched his shoulders and shook his head. 'Read the Bible for your answers.'

King David was a man of war and so was forbidden by God to construct a great temple in honour of his faith. God guided David's hand as he drew the plans, but he decreed that it would fall to his son, Solomon, to build the temple, for such a building needed a man of peace to craft it.

David paid fifty shekels in silver to a man called Araunah for a piece of land on Mount Moriah, and there, four years after David's death, Solomon began work on the temple.

First he sent word to the Phoenician king Hiram of Tyre, ordering him to fell cedar trees from his forests in Lebanon. The cedars, a symbol of strength and power in biblical times, were the most highly prized trees in the ancient world. Hiram sent timber as instructed and also skilled metalworkers, carpenters and masons. The masons knew the secret science of geometry, some of whose cryptic codes are kept alive today by the Brotherhood of Freemasons, and it was they who cut and polished the immense stone blocks. The accuracy of their work was so great that no hammers were used while the temple was being built, or so the Bible relates.

The temple was built on a conventional Phoenician design, suggesting that King Hiram's draughtsmen helped with the plans. It comprised an outer hallway, the *ulam*; a central courtyard, the *heikal*; and an inner sanctum, the *debir*, or 'Holy of Holies'. It was here, in the inner sanctum, sequestered away from the eyes of laymen, that the Ark of the Covenant was to be kept.

The stone for the temple is thought to have been quarried from beneath the city of Jerusalem. In 1854 one of the royal quarries was discovered by an American physician, Dr. Barclay, who was taking an evening stroll with his dog. The dog suddenly disappeared down a narrow shaft. Barclay enlarged the hole and found himself peering into an immense cavern. The entrance to the cave, known today as Zedekiah's Grotto, can still be seen not far from the Old City's Damascus Gate.

When the temple was finished, its decoration began, as the Second Book of Chronicles records:

'And the porch that was in the front of the house, the length of it was according to the breadth of the house, twenty cubits, and the height was a hundred and twenty: and he overlaid it within with pure gold. And the greater house he cieled with fir tree, which he overlaid with fine gold, and set thereon palm trees and chains. And he garnished the house with precious stones for beauty: and the gold was gold of Parvaim. He overlaid also the house, the beams, the posts, and the walls thereof, with gold: and graved cherubim on the walls. And he made the most holy house, the length whereof was, according to the breadth of the house, twenty cubits, and the breadth thereof twenty cubits: and he overlaid it with fine gold, amounting to six hundred talents. And the weight of the nails was fifty shekels of gold. And he overlaid the upper chambers with gold. And in the most holy house he made two cherubims of image work, and overlaid them with gold.'

The temple was completed in the seventh year of Solomon's reign and on the day of its dedication the Ark of the Covenant was carried from Mount Ophel in a grand procession, led by King Solomon himself. Priests dressed in pure white linen followed the king, blowing their trumpets, and behind them came a jubilant cavalcade. Every six paces oxen were sacrificed, drenching the road in blood. By the time the Ark was in place in the Holy of Holies, and the temple was dedicated, 22,000 oxen and 120,000 sheep had been slaughtered.

The temple served the people of Jerusalem for almost four centuries after the death of Solomon in 926 BC, but Solomon's successors lacked his wisdom and the land was misruled. The final blow came when the Babylonian king Nebuchadnezzar invaded Judah, almost annihilating its population and laying waste its cities. Jerusalem itself was besieged for a year and a half, and when the starving defenders finally capitulated, their capital was plundered. Solomon's temple was destroyed and every ounce of gold was stripped away, and carried back to Babylon.

In the Church of the Holy Sepulchre, in the Christian quarter of Jerusalem, a gaggle of nervous Russian tourists were taking in the sights and trying to remain calm.

Gunfire was ricocheting off the walls outside, but the priests said there was nothing to worry about. They'd seen much worse. One at a time the Russians stooped to kiss the Stone of Unction, where Christ's body is said to have been anointed after his death. Then they filed into 'Christ's tomb', the holiest site in Christendom.

The mood in the church was subdued, the air filled with the smell of burning beeswax and incense. The walls were filthy, especially at waist height where millions of pilgrims' hands had stroked them as they filed past. I sat on a low wooden bench and waited for the gunfire to stop, but it didn't.

I had already spent two days reading the Old Testament and staring at Ali Baba's map. The West Bank's Intifada was claiming new casualties on a daily basis and making it tricky to see the sights or even to sit in a café. To pass the time I'd bought a tattered third-hand copy of Henry Rider Haggard's *King Solomon's Mines* near the American Colony Hotel, where I was staying along with much of the world's press corps.

The book, which was released in 1885, was written by Rider Haggard when he was twenty-nine – the result of a shilling bet with his brother, who doubted he could write a bestseller. Advertised by its publisher as 'THE MOST AMAZING BOOK EVER WRITTEN', the novel was a runaway success, and more than thirty thousand copies were sold in the first year alone.

In the novel, Solomon's mines lie in what is now South Africa, but they are diamond mines, not gold mines. Rider Haggard was capitalizing on the diamond fever of the time. As a laborious introduction in my copy points out, he set the book in southern Africa because he had spent time in the Colonial Service in Natal and Transvaal, and so knew the region well. As well as an introduction my copy also contained a map. It was even sketchier than the one I'd bought from Ali Baba, marking little more than a river, a pan of bad water, 'Sheba's breasts', a kraal and a treasure cave. After going through the Old Testament for a second time, I came to the conclusion that Rider Haggard's novel, although a rattling good read, was of no use to anyone engaged in a serious search for Solomon's gold mines.

From the outset, I'd grasped that the biblical land of Ophir was the key clue to follow. The Bible can be deciphered in many ways, with an interpretation often hanging on the precise meaning of a single word. For that reason I chose to use the Septuagint version, the earliest known translation of the Old Testament. Made during the third and second centuries BC, it is still the official text of the Greek Orthodox Church. At the time it was written, the Hebrew version of the Bible still wasn't standardized.

The First Book of Kings relates that 'King Solomon made a navy of ships in Ezion-Geber, which is beside the modern city of Eliat on the shore of the Red sea, in the land of Edom. And Hiram sent in the navy his servants, shipmen that had knowledge of the sea, with the servants of Solomon. And they came to Ophir, and fetched from thence gold, four hundred and twenty talents...

'Now the weight of gold that came to Solomon in one year was six hundred threescore and six talents... And King Solomon made two hundred targets of beaten gold: six hundred shekels of gold went to one target. And he made three hundred shields of beaten gold; three pounds of gold went to one shield… Moreover the king made a great throne of ivory, and overlaid it with the best gold… And all King Solomon's drinking vessels were of gold… For the king had a navy of Tharshish with the navy of Hiram: once in three years came the navy of Tharshish, bringing gold, and silver, ivory, and apes, and peacocks.'

Stop anyone in the street today, ask them the meaning of 'Ophir', and they're likely to shake their head.

But for centuries the word was an obsession, one steeped in myth.

The Bible reveals what came from Ophir, but it does not say where it was located. Its authors took it for granted that everyone knew where it was and recorded only that those who journeyed to Ophir were away for three years. Interpreting this literally, some scholars took it to mean that the actual travelling time was three years. So they, and others, pointed to the most distant lands they knew. Ptolemy, in his maps, placed Ophir in the Malay peninsula and Christopher Columbus believed he had found Ophir in modern Haiti. Some suggested India, Madagascar, Ceylon, Arabia or even Peru, while others postulated that Ophir may merely mean 'remote'.

It was the discovery of an immense set of ruins in southern Africa – known as Great Zimbabwe – that led the Victorians to believe that they had finally discovered the Bible's Ophir. The ruins, after which Rhodesia was renamed at Independence, were found in the 1870s. To the Victorian mind, the stone workings, which lie nearly two hundred miles inland, resembled Solomon's temple. Though this was amateur archaeology at its most suspect, at the turn of the last century dozens of books appeared claiming that the riddle of Ophir had at last been solved. Rider Haggard's novel was but a fictional account of an astonishing discovery.

These days the Great Zimbabwe theory has been discredited and the location of Ophir remains a mystery.

If Ophir is the first real clue to finding the mines, then the second lies in the most famous consort of King Solomon – the Queen of Sheba.

Just as we are never told the location of Ophir, so the Bible fails to give the exact location of the Queen of Sheba's kingdom. In fact, it doesn't even tell us the queen's name, but the First Book of Kings does hint that she hailed from a land which was rich in pure gold: 'And when the queen of Sheba heard of the fame of Solomon concerning the name of the Lord, she came to prove him with hard questions. And she came to Jerusalem with a very great train, with camels that bore spices, and very much gold, and precious stones: and when she was come to Solomon, she communed with him of all that was in her heart... And she gave the king a hundred and twenty talents of gold, and of spices very great store, and precious stones... And king Solomon gave unto the queen of Sheba all her desire, whatsoever she asked, beside that which Solomon gave her of his royal bounty.'

113

As I sat in the shadows of the Church of the Holy Sepulchre that afternoon I thought of Ophir, the Queen of Sheba and King Solomon's gold.

It seemed absurd that so many generations of amateurs and experts should have searched for King Solomon's mines in such far-flung lands.

The answer, surely, must lie closer to hand.

My Michelin map of the Middle East included a large part of East Africa, stretching south as far as Lake Victoria and east to the Persian Gulf. I spread it out before me. If Solomon's ships left the port of Ezion-Geber, supposedly near modern Eliat in the Gulf of Aqaba, then his fleet would have headed south down the Red Sea in search of gold. Solomon's people had reached the Promised Land after fleeing from Egypt. They were a land-based people, not accomplished mariners, and it seemed unlikely that the king's ships would have gone further than necessary to find gold.

I knew that Ophir might have lain in southern Arabia, which may have been the Queen of Sheba's homeland, but the Sabaean kingdom probably stretched across the Bab al Mandab Straits to the African continent. The more I sat and deliberated, the stronger Africa, and in particular Ethiopia, beckoned me. I had been to a great number of African countries but had long yearned to explore Ethiopia. Like thousands of adventurers before me, I'd been bewitched by the country's history, its folklore and the strange tales of life there. Years before, I had learned that the imperial family of Ethiopia traces its descent from

114

Menelik, the son supposedly born to the Queen of Sheba and Solomon. A sacred Ethiopian text, the *Kebra Negast*, 'The Glory of the Kings', tells the story in full.

After becoming pregnant by Solomon, the Queen of Sheba returned to her native land. She left the wise king to his seven hundred wives and three hundred concubines, and departed with seven hundred and ninety-seven camels, all of them laden with gifts. The queen, who is known as Makeda in the Ethiopian texts, brought up Menelik on her own. When the boy reached adulthood, he journeyed north to Jerusalem to meet his father. The *Kebra Negast* says that as they left Jerusalem, Menelik's companions stole the hallowed Ark of the Covenant and took it back to Ethiopia. The Ark is supposedly still kept in the northern city of Axum.

I could see from the map that Ethiopia would have been easily reached from Solomon's kingdom – it was no more than a short boat trip down the Red Sea. In ancient times Ethiopia was a source of apes, ivory, frankincense and myrrh; precisely those items which the Bible says came from Ophir. And in ancient Egypt, Ethiopia was known as a land where gold could be easily mined. Even today the country has extraordinary reserves of gold and other valuable minerals and, unlike in southern Africa where you have to dig down thousands of feet to reach the ore, in Ethiopia's highlands the gold seams lie close to the surface.

I stood up, folded my map away and walked out into the afternoon sun. To the right of the main entrance to the Church of the Holy Sepulchre there is a doorway that leads to a chapel maintained by Ethiopian Christians. Once there was an Ethiopian monastery in Jerusalem, but in the seventeenth century when the monks could no longer afford the Ottoman taxes, it was forced to move here, to a series of dank rooms that lead off the roof of St. Helena's Chapel. Now a handful of monks continue to maintain a presence in Jerusalem as their forebears had done for centuries.

In one of the rooms I found a small shrine, its walls black with soot, its benches shiny and worn where thousands of robes had brushed against the wood. The walls were hung with colourful paintings showing the Queen of Sheba being greeted by King Solomon. I walked through the chapel and up a flight of stairs, out on to the roof. A bearded Ethiopian priest, dressed in a flowing black robe, a prayer book in his hands, was asleep beneath a weeping willow. As I watched him sleeping I thought about my map, and about Ophir, and about a journey.

Ethiopia was awaiting me.

On the way back to my hotel, I passed Ali Baba's Tourist Emporium once again.

I glanced in through the open door. The shopkeeper was dozing in his chair but he awoke with a start when he heard my footsteps cross the threshold. Even to the ears of such a reluctant salesman, the sound of feet meant tourists, and tourists meant trade.

When he'd wrapped the loops of his glasses around his ears and squinted in my direction, Ali Baba asked how I was enjoying the gunfire. He said that there was nothing like a little shooting to keep everyone on their toes. I told him that I'd been unable to think of anything but King Solomon's mines since buying the map, and that I had decided to look for the mines myself. I was heading for Ethiopia, I said.

Ali Baba warned me against making the journey. It would be full of dangers. He should never have sold me the map. His mother would be turning in her grave, his father would be cursing the day he was born. As he spoke I noticed something familiar hanging on the far wall of the shop. Little more than a sketch, and smudged by a clumsy hand, it was an inky hand-drawn map. I went over and compared it with my own map. Although obviously executed by the same unskilled artist, and set in identical chipped gold frames, they were different.

Furious, I demanded to know why another map was hanging in the very same spot as the one I'd purchased. Ali Baba ran a callused hand across his cheek. Times were desperate, he said woefully, and desperate times called for desperate measures.

'That's all well and good,' I said with mounting anger, 'but this is fraud. I've got a good mind to call the police.'

Sensing trouble, the old shopkeeper started to board up his emporium. He packed away the splinters from the Cross, the Virgin Mary fridge magnets, the fluorescent pink rosaries and the kitsch Nativity scenes.

'The map I sold you was the *real* one,' he said slyly. 'I'm giving you a head start in your search. You see, this other map is a fake. It'll keep the competition from your heels. Look on it as after-sales service!'

From: *In Search of King Solomon's Mines*

Rats Eating Cats

Saw a pestle hard and heavy...
With it thrashed those Giant's daughters;
Thrashed them till they bellowed loudly,
Fled and roared like Bulls of Bashan,
Fled and hid them in their wigwams.

A PAIR OF pregnant ladies sat either side of me on a bench.

They looked at each other and giggled. The one on the right made a joke in Wolof and they both rolled about in laughter.

I had come to the Clinique Troy in Castor – a suburb of Dakar – in Senegal, to get a visa for Sierra Leone. During the journey from Asia to West Africa I had tried to bury all memories of greed. The apples from Afghanistan and the mutilated bodies of the innocent had helped me to understand that treasure was more than a chest of jewels.

Wood's mention of Macumba, a magical science thought to be more comprehensive than any other, occupied my reasoning. There was one man whom I knew could assist this pursuit. His name was Max, and he lived in Freetown, the capital of the West African country of Sierra Leone. If Macumba had, as some claimed, derived from the most ancient lore in Africa, it had at least – by association – some resonance with the Gond theme.

The journey from the borderlands of Pakistan's northwest frontier, to West Africa, had been anything but simple. A travel publisher in one of Peshawar's darker backstreets had sold me a cut-price ticket. Although somehow the fare was extremely convenient, the route was not. Having diced with death by taking the 'Flying Bus' from Peshawar to Islamabad, I first flew to Damascus.

From there, I jetted on to Aden in Yemen, before taking an evening cargo flight to Moscow – then I was bustled on board puddle-hopper flight to Paris. And, it was from there – as my internal clock was spinning out of control – that I ventured on by air to Dakar.

*

WHEN I WAS told that the maternity clinic issued visas I had hardly flinched. My travels in India had made such practices seem normal. Assuring myself that the experience of Mumbai, Rajasthan and the Afghan frontier would hold me in good stead for what was to come, I was determined to press on across Gondwanaland.

My passport was examined thoroughly. A hundred irrelevant questions were asked and it was hinted darkly that maybe I just wanted to get close to expectant women, rather than to obtain a visa. I pleaded with the director – a middle-aged lady dressed in a blood-drenched surgical gown – who had just delivered twins. Finally, agreeing that a visa could be granted, she led me into the operating theatre and offered me a cigarette. The mother was recovering from the trauma of childbirth with her twin daughters.

'It will take forty-eight hours,' said the director, blowing smoke into my face.

'I was hoping to leave Dakar as soon as possible...' I said.

'All right, come back at five this afternoon.'

At five p.m. the director's assistant – who was a nurse – took my money and handed the passport back to me. I checked the visa. It filled a whole page and was striped in several colours. Just as I was leaving, I noticed that the wrong dates had been entered. Plucking up courage, I informed the assistant.

Without batting an eyelid, she ripped out the page and stamped a new visa in another part of the passport.

'Will there be anything else?' she growled.

I went back to my hotel feeling as if a piece of my anatomy had been amputated.

The Hotel Monlogie had been recommended by a burly Parisian at the airport. He had been unloading crates of gear for the Paris-to-Dakar Rally. The legendary desert race was just concluding, the first drivers having made it across the Malian hinterland to Dakar.

The tension was electrifying. People were rushing about, everyone shouting in French. It seemed that the whole of Paris was in Dakar. I had no visa for Senegal, and was very surprised to be waved through without any bureaucratic contretemps.

Hotel Monlogie was on rue Lamine Gueye. A faint line of blood could be made out about three feet up the wall: a sign, my guidebook assured, that bedbugs shared the premises.

Men in wide Mauritanian robes flapped about the dusty streets of Dakar. Their fingers were concealed, tucked into a flap of cloth around the stomach. As I stared at the fine gold embroidery, two small boys came up and started to rub my knees.

The sensation was not displeasing and I allowed them to continue for a moment, before my Western thought-patterns forced me to question the reason for their activity.

They looked rather disappointed.

Just as I was going to ask the cause of their dissatisfaction, they ran off. The smaller one tossed back a black piece of curved metal. It was the key to my hotel room.

A doddery old man staggered over to where I stood and took charge. He spoke French with a thick accent that I could barely understand. I had soon become his property and, when a younger man came up and offered to take me around the city, he protested vehemently. After a while the man, his face wrinkled with blue-black lines, gave up, and insisted I go on, even if with the other man.

The newcomer, after telling me that his name was Joseph, pulled out a lump of gold – the size of a golf-ball – and offered it to me as a gift. His legs were bulging in black denim jeans and he wore the colours of a Rastafarian. I refused the nugget, suspecting that an obligation would ensue, and asked him for a good place to eat. 'Chez Loutcha on rue Blanchot,' he said.

Joseph accompanied me there. A French woman slid a plate of spaghetti in front of me and threw a spoon at Joseph, screaming for him to leave. He shuffled his feet in the doorway, asking for a commission for bringing a customer. The woman slammed the door in his face – and turned my chair to the far wall – where a poster of the Eiffel Tower seemed to be all that was holding up the ceiling.

The next morning I went to the bus stop early and caught a coach to Barra Point. My intention was to get to Banjul, the capital of Gambia, from where the flight to Freetown would leave.

Rally cars and relay runners were bounding towards Dakar. The stripes of sponsorship and names of multinationals enveloped all. They became a blur as the vehicles pulled away, as we drove to the south of Dakar, and entered a forest of baobab trees.

Grey trunks twenty feet thick stretched from horizon to horizon. They were spread out from each other, unlike a normal forest; and somehow looked more like a herd of grazing elephants than anything else.

Baobabs are among Africa's most bizarre trees: they can live for over a thousand years. Their enormous trunks store water and in a drought they actually shrink, as the water is used up. The giant pods have seeds containing concentrated vitamin C.

Sitting next to me on the bus was a Frenchman who introduced himself as Auguste Lecomte. He fingered an immaculate copy of that very morning's *Le Monde* – Francophone Africa is splendid at distributing the papers – and read a line at a time through pince-nez. A few minutes later he looked up and spoke.

'We are nearly at the ferry point, and should get to Banjul by about six,' he said.

'Are you here on holiday?' I asked.

'My boy, my profession is to travel around the world buying excellent rare banknotes to sell to dealers. Did you know that Gambia's *dalasi* are quite sought after?'

I replied that I did not. Opening his case, he displayed perhaps a hundred currencies, each in mint condition. *Tugrik* from Mongolia, *metical* from Mozambique, Icelandic *krona*, dollars from the Solomon Islands, and many others, lay jumbled about.

I sensed a heavy breathing down my neck. Monsieur Lecomte obviously felt the draught as well. We hunched up our collars, but the cinnamon-scented breath continued. I turned around and focused on an emerald pair of eyes – which dilated with curiosity and envy. A mouth on the same face yelled:

'Hey man, how're you doing, man? I'm Oswaldo, Oswaldo Rodriguez Oswaldo.'

His vice-like hand was thrust into mine and pulled me towards the seat behind. He addressed the Frenchman:

'Hey man, d'you want any of this stuff?'

His fingers fumbled in a pouch around his waist and he fished out two handfuls of grubby Argentine banknotes. Monsieur Lecomte grimaced, appalled by the abruptness of the heavily-breathing Argentine. Declaring that the notes were worthless, he turned away to finish reading the editorial in *Le Monde*.

Oswaldo Rodriguez Oswaldo leant back, pushed a dark brown trilby onto his forehead, and sat in silence. Short, almost stunted in appearance, with well-proportioned features and an immaculate moustache, he smelt of lavender.

Outside, the baobabs stood motionless. There was no wind and the sky was free from clouds. The bus moved closer to Barra Point; it felt almost that we were driving through an oil painting.

On the ferry to Banjul a man, who claimed he was a hundred years old, changed my Senegalese *C.F.A.* currency into *dalasi*. He studied each note through thick lenses, reading the numbers aloud in Wolof.

The Argentine followed in my footsteps.

I had the feeling that I would rather be alone, but Oswaldo craved company. The money-changers, who had refused to accept his *pesos*, had asked where Argentina was. We sat on a blue iron bench and watched Gambia draw closer.

'Where are you going, man?'

'I'm on my way to Freetown, to visit a friend. What about you?' I asked.

'I'm going east.'

'How far east?'

'All the way. Came in a ship from Buenos Aires. Long long way, man!'

'Where are you from, exactly?'

'Patagonia.'

I recalled geography lessons and the teacher rolling the word *Patagonia* around his mouth with an educated satisfaction.

Oswaldo was short, no more than five foot three. He swung his stubby legs in the air and clicked a pair of decomposing cowboy boots together. He never stopped moving. Before speaking, he would rub his pencil-line moustache with his thumbnail; and would laugh loudly three times, as if to clear his throat.

A boy selling wooden pots made from the branches of the baobabs offered them around.

Oswaldo appeared to be delighted.

Grabbing the boy, he shrieked, 'That looks fantabulous, man!'

Four assorted-sized bowls were brought out and the Patagonian passed the child a bundle of Argentine *pesos*.

'Take them to the bank, OK?'

The boy shuffled away, wondering what to do with the large collection of multicoloured bills. Oswaldo opened the mouth of his voluminous rucksack. He fished out a shirt and a pair of red jeans and put the baobab bowls at the bottom. I asked why he had such a huge rucksack and only two other pieces of clothing.

'I'm stocking up on souvenirs. Love this stuff, man.'

I hoped we could get away to Banjul before the boy's father saw the *pesos*.

Having stepped off the ferry onto the shore, a child of about nine took Oswaldo by one hand and me by the other and led us to the Hotel Apollo. The wooden bowls clicked about as we took our first look at Banjul – capital city of the former British dependency.

Hotel Apollo was impressively run down. But without being discourteous, one could say that the whole of Banjul had lost any air of elegance that it might once have commanded. There were two main streets: Buckle Street and Wellington Street. Hotel Apollo had once been painted white.

The owner was named Haji, and he greeted us warmly, his long Mauritanian-type robes dragging in the dust beneath his feet. Oswaldo asked if the hotel accepted Argentine *pesos*. It did not. But, as an act of diplomacy, Haji offered to reduce our board by a third if we would pay in a European currency and stay two nights.

Having agreed, our bags were carried ceremoniously up to a terribly dilapidated room. A peculiar contraption filled one corner. The bag boy flicked the switch to turn it on.

Before it started up, I heard the sound of his bare feet pounding as fast as they could away from the room. Cogs within the machine began to grind. This was followed by the noise and vibrations, as of a pneumatic drill.

As we stood there, plugging our ears with our thumbs, water was sprayed across us and the walls. Oswaldo grappled with the apparatus, which was very like one of those machines film crews use to create wind and rain. A little plaque on the side, inscribed in Gothic script, read 'Desert Cooler'.

Oswaldo combed back his short brown hair and applied a thick layer of green brilliantine. The room now reeked of lavender.

The Patagonian pulled on his red jeans, opened his shirt to the waist and, after cackling three times, yelled, 'To the deesco man!'

He dragged me out of the hotel, hauling me up and down the two main streets, requesting that I ask for the best dance-hall in town. One man pointed left, another right, and a third looked very worried. There was a shimmering red glow coming from a bar off Buckle Street.

'Let's go there man!'

He pointed a stubby arm towards the bar and pulled his shirt front further apart, revealing a hairless white chest.

A thunderous rhythm was being beaten out on two drums. Some torn sacks had been tacked together and hung in front of the doorway, almost as if they were keeping some kind of poison gas inside. Oswaldo clicked his heels to the drum-beats, then we entered the red glare.

A room, which seemed little bigger than an aeroplane's lavatory, was packed with all kinds of life. Oswaldo ordered himself two bottles of Jewel lager, I asked for a pomegranate juice.

'Good stuff!'

Oswaldo seemed overjoyed and, in his enthusiasm for the situation, he slapped the man next to him very hard on the back. I prepared for a bar fight. But the Gambian man was too drunk to co-ordinate hostile movements. Oswaldo handed him a bottle of Jewel lager and the two men began to dance.

When the boys had stopped drumming, we each pulled up a packing crate and sat. Oswaldo's dancing partner was a Gambian named Robertson.

In his early sixties, he had a round, waxy face. Before we knew it, he'd started telling us, and anyone else who'd listen, his life story.

A career as a sailor had shown him the world. He claimed to speak twelve languages, one of which was Spanish. Oswaldo was ecstatic when he discovered his new friend had been to Argentina. He puckered his lips and kissed Robertson squarely on the forehead. The two men launched into Spanish sailing songs, acting out the sordid parts in full detail.

The manager's baby son was sucking at an empty lager bottle and making gurgling sounds from between the crates on which we sat.

Robertson patted the infant on the head affectionately as he continued with his tale. Then Oswaldo broke in, swigging from the dark green bottle in his left hand as he spoke.

Suddenly, while he was talking, the Patagonian calmly reached inside his right boot and, in one motion, pulled out a stiletto. Springing the blade open, he threw it between the fingers of the baby boy.

The drummers and the proprietor looked up.

A chicken which had been roosting in one corner flapped to the door. Robertson stopped talking and stared in horror.

Oswaldo took a sip of his lager.

Then he pulled at the knife, which was deeply embedded in the floor. A scorpion was skewered halfway up the blade.

'Big one,' he muttered, as he scraped it off with his foot onto the floor.

Robertson cheered.

The landlord, who was shaken, grasped his son in his arms. Then the drummers beat out a special rhythm to compliment Oswaldo, the unusual Patagonian. He lounged back on the crate.

The manager, who had been deeply moved by the stranger's bravado, came over. In his hands was an old biscuit tin which had lost most of its paint. He pulled open the lid. Inside was a dusty bottle of Heineken lager. Wiping a tear from his left eye, the landlord murmured gently:

'I have been keeping this for a special man and a particular night. That man and that night have now come.'

We ate breakfast the next morning at Café Express on Buckle Street. I had decided to take the evening flight to Freetown. Oswaldo said that he would like to come too, as he had never flown before. Having seen his display the previous night with a stiletto, I thought it might be to my advantage to have him along. After the meal we would go and buy tickets from the travel office.

A schoolboy arrived and climbed onto the third chair. He said nothing, just sat there motionless. His and Oswaldo's legs dangled above the ground. The Patagonian hummed what he said was the Argentine National Anthem. A single hotdog was brought over and we divided it into three. Each of us chewed at the sausage as long as was possible. The child jumped up, shouted '*Jërëjëf!* Thank you!' and ran off with his satchel swinging behind him.

A reduction was given for students on all flights to Freetown. I had no student identity card. But, in the interminable ticket queue, I managed to turn my international driving licence into student ID. The lettering was smudged but I assumed no one would be looking too closely. I showed my ID, and then Oswaldo flashed an Argentine identity card.

The clerk nodded approvingly and the tickets were written out. Oswaldo was thrilled beyond words.

'*Macanudo!*' he exclaimed.

An hour or so later I found myself on my back on the beach front of the Atlantic Hotel. Oswaldo had insisted we go to the beach as a way of celebrating.

Fleshy British package tourists waddled about, clutching towels, suntan oil, brown sauce, and plates of fish and chips all at once.

Oswaldo was fascinated by them.

I begged him not to point.

The rays burnt deep into my back and chest until I was sure that something was wrong. Gambia is near the equator and so the heat is astonishingly intense.

At three p.m. I tried to stand.

My skin had apparently shrunk, and I felt like the inside of a cooked frankfurter trying to burst out.

The Argentine appeared worried for a moment.

Then he said that we had better get to the airport.

A woman from Blackpool had given him a ballpen with a scaled-down replica of a tower trapped inside.

When he tilted the pen, the tower moved.

Delighted with his new possession he showed it to everyone he met. But I was not interested. Instead, I staggered towards the Hotel Apollo, feeling like a boiled lobster.

The Air Ghana flight was delayed three hours. The plane sat on the runway for half that time, waiting for some repairs to be done to the fuselage. Engineers with troubled expressions hurried up and down the cabin shouting, and hurling spanners like boomerangs back and forth. The lack of security checks before boarding had been rather disconcerting.

Oswaldo took the stiletto from his boot and ran it across his fingers. I told him to put it away before we were both arrested. The stewardess clambered about, handing out rock-cakes and glasses of fluorescent orange squash. An aging Ghanaian lady insisted on sharing my seat, as the plane was now full.

As we munched on our rock-cakes, the pilot suddenly hauled back the throttle and the craft swooped out of Banjul airport into the African sky. Orange juice and rock-cakes flew about as if there were no gravity. Oswaldo screamed at the top of his lungs and swung his red jeans about his head. Pulling a sick bag over my face, I pretended not to know him. The woman sharing my seat writhed about, increasing her territory.

There was an urgent tap on my shoulder.

I turned round and was handed Oswaldo's trousers which had been propelled into the row behind us.

At Freetown's immigration, our passports were taken away. They were put in a black box. Two guards patrolled back and forth for about ten minutes and then opened the box. The documents were returned, dripping with stamp-pad ink. Rumour had it that, on entry to Sierra Leone, a large amount of foreign currency had to be declared and immediately changed into *leones* at the official rate. The routine searching of luggage often resulted, a source had assured me, in the confiscation of one's belongings. Oswaldo handed me a piece of chalk.

'What's this for?'

'Cross the bags, *amigo*.'

He had noticed that all checked luggage was efficiently crossed in white chalk. But what about the currency regulations? Oswaldo leapt into the lair of officials and they forced him to hand over a wad of Argentine *pesos*. The soldiers looked as if they believed that the unknown notes might be even more valuable than dollars.

As I walked through, a very strange thing happened.

I concentrated deeply on the end of the line of salivating officials. Some were handing out forms, others brandished white chalk.

I moved straight ahead without turning. There wasn't a sound behind me. No one called back or grabbed me. For some reason I managed to get by without changing any money at the official rate. It was as if I had willed them not to see me.

Max was studying philosophy at Freetown University. He'd written in his last letter that I should to take a room at the City Hotel, as it would be more comfortable than his floor. We had not met before. When I was about twelve I had placed an advertisement to be circulated world-wide asking for interesting and unusual pen-friends. Max's letters had always been unusual. Many had been covered in blood, while others spoke of fantastic experiments and ceremonies in which he had taken part.

With one letter he had once enclosed the dried intestines of a small fly-eating lizard, together with some dogs' claws, which he said that I was to boil up into a kind of tea. He had come to West Africa to learn more of the rituals of *ju-ju* and the secret societies of Freetown.

A Frenchman from Marseilles with an aristocratic air let us share his taxi into town. He loaded four Purdey shotguns into the back of the Renault and rolled up the corners of a handlebar moustache as we jerked along.

Thick jungle undergrowth abounded on either side of the road. Monkeys swung from tree to tree and the sounds of a seething insect population hummed around us. Oswaldo began to tell the man from Marseilles all about his homeland.

Removing the stiletto from his boot, he showed it to the Frenchman, who admired the Patagonian quality.

Freetown had a dark and depressing air.

We crossed a stretch of water in a launch and walked up the slope to the City Hotel.

It was in a state poised between dilapidation and total dereliction. The crumbling facade was subsumed in moss and creepers. Yet it must once have been almost palatial. Corinthian colonnades held up the remains of the roof, and the lintel of the main doorway had been replaced with an iron bar. A symmetrical pair of flights of winding steps led to the door. The wrought-iron gates were rusted from neglect.

A European was sitting on the veranda under the light of a paraffin lamp. The proprietor, he said he could provide Oswaldo and me with a room. The Frenchman from Marseilles sniffed haughtily and carried his shotguns off into the night to find a more salubrious place to rest.

The owner was an Italian from Zurich. He'd not returned to Europe in over four decades. His skin was pallid, as if it had not been exposed to light in years. The building was bathed in an aura of decrepitude. A giant, standing at least six foot nine, moved into the lamplight and picked up our bags. The owner spoke in French, mumbling, 'This is my son, he will take you to your room.'

The creature, whose resemblance to Frankenstein's monster was more than uncanny, trod his way up three flights of stairs, whilst demonstrating his unusual talent of holding a lit candle in his teeth. The candle flickered as we progressed from one draught to the next towards the attic. The banisters, and indeed, all removable pieces of wood, so the giant said, had been incinerated to heat the house.

On the second floor, a naked man was washing a shirt in a basin. His broad smile revealed three gold teeth. The stairs creaked beneath our feet and, as we stumbled upward, Oswaldo edged closer to my side.

Two beds filled most of the attic room.

Neither had mattresses, only tattered sheets on bare springs. A swarm of mosquitos fought above the sink and flitted around the peeling pink walls. The giant strode to the sink and relieved himself in it. I asked for the room key. There was no need for a key, I was assured, as there were no locks. Instead, we were invited to come down for a drink and to get anti-mosquito incense coils. Oswaldo went down immediately, while I took a shower on the second floor.

A pleasing stream of water coursed onto my head. I washed my sunburnt body with enormous care; it could just endure the pressure of the cold water. When the drops became less frequent, I glanced upwards at the nozzle to see if it was clogged. I noticed a gap of about two inches between the boards above my head: they were the floorboards of my room.

In the candlelight, the white of a single eye rotated and blinked above me. Shrieking, I ran from the shower. The sound of footsteps pressed across the ceiling, as I made for the stairs to get to the putative privacy of the attic room.

Halfway up I met the naked man with gold teeth. We paused for a moment. I might have asked him the reason for his voyeurism, but the fact that he was naked and that my badly blistered body was protected only by a face-cloth, gagged my questions.

Oswaldo had become instantly chummy with an assortment of villainous-looking men on the veranda. They lounged about on broken chairs smoking home-made cigars. The old Swiss proprietor had passed out and was lying on a mattress on the ground, an empty bottle of whisky at his side.

A man called Olivier strode up and introduced himself. A French Senegalese priest, he said he had mastered both both yoga and karate.

An infant boy weaved between the clouds of cigar smoke and mosquitos, selling bubble gum and matches. It was easy to imagine Graham Greene lounging back on a broken wicker chair on the veranda of the City Hotel.

I tried to reach Max on an antique rotary telephone.

The dial had lost its spring and only the digit '1' worked properly. I banged the disc with my palm, but it still did not work. At that moment Oswaldo burst in and grabbed me by the shoulder.

'What's the matter?'

'Quick! Come! There's diamonds and gold!'

We charged out onto the veranda.

Oswaldo hissed that I was not to show interest, as the men suspected we were there to gain from their secret wealth.

The giant held up a flaming torch.

He, the gold-toothed man, Olivier, Oswaldo, and I climbed into the back of a jeep.

We drove out of the town into the night. I looked upwards into the night sky and saw the Big Dipper beginning to turn silently above us. The sound of bats and the chirping of crickets echoed all around as the bald tyres of the jeep spun along a muddy track. Oswaldo glanced at me nervously. Putting a fist on his left boot, he felt the stiletto, and nodded at me. We were both prepared to be robbed and left, but the opportunity to go on a midnight gold and diamond run was too great to miss.

The jeep pulled onto a side track about ten miles from Freetown. The glinting lights of the city were no longer visible; just two flares burning on the jeep. The dense undergrowth seethed with life of all types. Mosquitoes and all manner of insects buzzed around the flares and headlights. In the distance I could make out a wooden hut. The jeep pulled up at the front door and we descended. A man inside began yelling in Creole when he saw Oswaldo and me. The giant calmed him and we were all ushered into the shack.

A bottle of locally brewed alcohol was passed around. It burnt into the Patagonian's throat, making his eyes bulge as he choked aloud. Three pouches were fetched by the old inhabitant of the hut, who brought a torch closer to illuminate their contents. The pouches were upturned on a packing crate.

What looked like small pieces of ground glass sparkled in a pile. They were of irregular shapes and only some of the surfaces shone. In another heap, gold – perhaps eight to ten ounces – was admired by all. Oswaldo's and my eyes widened with avarice. The shadows of greedy men danced about the dark walls.

Pulling at Olivier's arm, Oswaldo asked where the diamonds and gold were from. The priest narrowed his eyes and whispered:

'They come from the mountains. Diamonds and gold are in the village paths and when it rains they are washed up. People come out and dig them from the ground with knives.'

A session of animated negotiating followed, lubricated with a seemingly endless supply of firewater. Some money changed hands in the untrusting candlelight and we left for Freetown with the smugglers.

As the jeep fish-tailed towards the City Hotel I thought of treasure. It was deserved far more by this sort of men. I myself no longer had a grasping fascination for such instant wealth. It was as if the appeal had been treasure for the sake of treasure: as if I had been driven by its romance, its mystique, and by its awe alone. India, Pakistan and now Africa seemed to have exorcized the lust, though not the quest.

EARLY THE NEXT morning I managed to contact Max.

He arranged to come to the City Hotel and take us to lunch. Oswaldo and I sat in the bar waiting for him.

The night had been decidedly uncomfortable.

Oswaldo had put a little beer in one of the baobab bowls, and left it on the floor. In the morning the bowl was full of cockroaches. Some survivors were crawling over the dead, their tiny antlers poking around the corpses. He gave the black insect carcasses to the boy who had been selling bubble gum the night before. The child was thrilled and plodded off to dissect the remains.

A procession of school children paraded past the hotel as we waited for Max. Dressed in neat green and yellow uniforms, some played instruments, others clapped their hands, as banners were waved from side to side.

The old owner made one of the smugglers get down from the bar where he was sleeping. There was no more beer, he informed me gravely, but appearances had to be maintained.

Max arrived.

It was odd to meet the man to whom I had been writing for so long.

Oswaldo and Max glanced at each other like different species of animal. Oswaldo, whose hair was smoothed with brilliantine, wore his brown trilby and well polished cowboy boots. Max's appearance integrated him neatly with the City Hotel. His hair was long, greasy and very black, and his face – which was dark with dirt – was peppered with infected sores. A pair of tattered sneakers were rotting about his ankles and a cluster of leather pouches hung around his neck.

We, all three, snaked our way about the silent town. Almost nothing moved. A sense of utter despondency prevailed as if Freetown was not advancing or even attempting to progress.

Max pointed out the giant cotton tree which is a landmark in the centre of town. Nearby, at the American Embassy, we were given glasses of sterilized water and allowed to see newsreels two months old. Max had adapted here as I'd done in Mumbai. Freetown had become his life, his very existence.

Outside the embassy came the sound of sirens.

Flashing red and blue lights blinked from a motorcade and five jeeps with outriding motorbikes sped past. The few people about stood still and lowered their heads. Oswaldo gasped:

'Hey man, what's that?'

'That's the president going to work!' said Max.

Like many African nations, Sierra Leone's leadership had gained power by coup d'état. Indeed, as soon as one group gets control, another is scheming secretly how they may take over. But Captain Valentine Strasser's coup was exceptional, even for Africa, for Captain Strasser was just twenty-seven, and his deputy – Solomon Musa – was a mere twenty-four years of age.

We were each presented with a bowl of boiled seaweed. It had been partially fermented and then covered in a watery meat sauce. I suspected that the meat was cow's brains. Max had ordered this delicacy for us all at his favourite restaurant. He picked up lumps of the green sludge in his nicotine-stained fingers, tossed his head back, and dropped the morsels down his throat one handful at a time. Oswaldo and I stared at each other blankly.

'Don't you like it?' huffed Max in surprise.

'Slightly too much salt for me,' I grunted.

'Lost my appetite!' squeaked Oswaldo glumly at his full plate.

Max finished the three portions. Then he sucked the ends of his fingers, which had become splayed from extensive nail-biting.

The café was behind an abattoir on the second floor, somewhere on the outskirts of the town, past the Cuban Embassy. There were no windows, but on one wall was a faded photograph of the British royal family long ago.

When Max had finished the seaweed he rubbed his hands in his hair to clean them off. Then he lit a cigarette and removed the filter. We had written about many things in our letters, such as music, our friends, and places in which we had lived. Max was an avid fan of the Grateful Dead, an American rock band. But his extreme fascination for *ju-ju* was of most interest to me.

Sinister ceremonies take place at night around the darkest corners of Freetown. A number of societies, most secret in their operations, participate in ominous rituals. Max spoke of his involvement with these groups.

He had become the pupil of a *Babalawo* – a medicine-man – one who practises *ju-ju*. Although, technically speaking, *ju-ju* refers to a fetish or image used in a magical rite, today its use is much wider.

Ju-ju can be something that causes a change in the natural and supernatural worlds. It may be a potion, an ointment, a talisman, a sign, or even a magical word or phrase.

'It wasn't easy gaining the trust of my teacher,' said Max. 'He knows that I appreciate the honour. I have immersed myself in this science: I must become one with it.'

Max paused, and I frowned, wondering exactly what he meant. Staring deeply into my eyes, he pushed up the right sleeve of his shirt. A series of dots and lines had been tattooed into his copper-coloured skin.

'What is it for?' I asked.

'This is *ju-ju* to protect. There is evil here.'

'What evil?'

'*Alé*,' said Max. 'That's *ju-ju*, or medicine, that puts harm on someone else.'

'You mean *black* magic?' I replied.

'Yes, black magic,' said Max. '*Alé* is my real interest but my teacher won't let me even think about that for years to come.'

What of the secret societies? Max had studied their history but was very unwilling to share what he knew.

'Many things are better left alone,' he said. 'These matters are taken very serious around here.'

Having read about the so-called Alligator Societies and the Leopard Societies in Sierra Leone, I asked Max if the many historical accounts could have been true.

'The Human-Alligators, as they are known,' he said, 'were at first thought to be people who were turned into reptiles by magic. They would kill someone – often eating the victim's corpse – before reappearing as humans again. Later it was found that people were just dressing up in alligator and leopard skins to kill people. That stuff has been forced deep underground following persecution by the authorities.'

'But does it really still go on?' I asked.

Max nodded slowly. 'The various societies have become more crossbred and have taken influences from new sources recently; each sect affects the practices of the next, even my Babalawo uses a Borfima,' he said.

'*Borfima,* what's that?'

'It's a symbol, a source of power, and a centre for magical activity,' replied Max.

'What *is* it?' I persisted, trying to find out more.

'I've just told you,' said Max.

'No, I mean what is it made from?'

The cook came to collect our plastic dishes. He seemed suspicious of our conversation. When he'd left, Max continued in a low voice:

'I have made Borfimas my special study,' he began. 'The most likely origin for many of the societies' cannibalistic activity seems to have started in order to feed the Borfima.'

'Feed?' I asked.

'Feed,' replied Max. 'To keep the Borfima bag as an effective medicinal tool, it must be supplied with newly killed or extracted human fat or blood. It will gain the strengths of all that is fed to it.'

I was still rather confused by what Max was saying; he saw my uncertainty and continued:

'I was just reading of a mysterious society in Angola, the Butwa sect who keep a Borfima.' He pulled a worn sheet of yellowing paper from his back pocket, and said:

'This is what the Englishman Butt-Thompson wrote of the Butwa Society's Borfima:

'*The duiker horn is said to contain human flesh, hair, nails, bone and sinew. In the larger horn are animal claws, bits of lion and leopard heart, of feet of elephants, hide of hippopotamus, shell of tortoise, bird bills, eye of osprey, eyebrow of vulture, head of the "ngweshi" snake, heart of python, head of puff-adder, nose of crocodile, brow of hyena, head of dogfish, and human and lizard gall, a tooth of a field rat, a scorpion, a burned honey bee, a baby's head, a human caul, some soldier ants, some powdered meteorites, some sand from the footprint of the founder of the Society, a head from a dead chief, a piece of tree upon which an official of the Society committed suicide.'*

When Max had finished reading, he closed his eyes and grasped one of the leather pouches which was strung around his unshaven neck.

There was a tense silence.

Oswaldo shifted nervously in his broken chair, then he gave me a tortured look as I addressed Max:

'Can we meet your teacher? I think that it's important,' I said in a wheedling tone.

'That'd be quite impossible,' he replied. 'Getting him to have anything to do with *me* was accomplishing the impossible.'

'Then Max,' I said, 'can't you make the impossible happen again?'

*

AT TWO THE next morning we crept from the City Hotel.

A cat was stalking a giant toad on the veranda next to the sleeping Swiss owner.

Enticing his master with a bottle of local whisky, Max had managed to persuade the Babalawo to meet us. As we stumbled behind him into the darkness towards the rendezvous, Max kept on repeating how difficult it had been to arrange. Understanding the gravity of the meeting, I thanked him.

Freetown seemed more alive in the hours of darkness than during the day. We left the city, walking past the abattoir and the restaurant to which Max had taken us.

A few of the shacks housed shadowy figures who could be heard talking and laughing. Insects buzzed in the undergrowth into which we walked.

Max explained that traditionally secret societies were located deep in the bush, and only the initiated had known of their whereabouts. A revival of the societies in Freetown had taken place, and men such as his Babalawo now practised very close to the city, or at times actually in it.

Initiation, Max said, was fundamental in gaining membership of a sect. The Societies native to West Africa are often formed from the people of several tribes, even of different nations.

Boys would traditionally be taken into the bush to be initiated, a process that was known to last for weeks, even months. They would be instructed in hunting, defence, and in the secret qualities of the jungle's plants. But of the greatest importance to them were their studies in the magical and occult arts.

Max explained that, as such initiates respected the force of the Babalawo's incantations, we must also do so. We agreed that we would abide by the ways of the cult.

Oswaldo was very quiet and trudged along less than enthusiastically. I sensed that he was trembling. Reluctant to have anything to do with such dark matters, he had had conventional Catholic beliefs instilled in him as a child. Max led us into the forest as if he knew each step of the path.

After half an hour of walking I smelt burning meat.

This was followed by the sound of someone whistling. Flames could be seen through the trees and, as Oswaldo and I trod softly behind Max, he also began to whistle. He led us into a clearing, illuminated by three burning torches. Between them sat a figure who poked at the embers of a dying fire.

Max greeted the man in Creole.

It was his Babalawo.

147

The mentor ignored Oswaldo and me, and continued to poke rhythmically, almost as if he were in a trance. Max told us to remove our shoes and socks, as he did the same. The ground was warm and damp underfoot, and covered in dead leaves.

I tried to make out the contours of the Babalawo's face. It was hard to tell his age, perhaps forty, perhaps sixty. His head had lost much of its hair. A striped T-shirt covered his chest: the lines of it ran from his neck to his navel. He poked away at the fire as we sat and watched. I peered up at the sky, the stars looked down and I felt a little more secure.

Max had closed his eyes and sat cross-legged in silence. The Babalawo dropped a handful of herbs onto the embers. An asphyxiating, sweet-smelling cloud ascended from the fire as the leaves ignited and were consumed in flame.

The master began to chant in Creole.

I nudged Max, hoping that we could learn of the significance of the words, but he did not translate. Instead, taking some bluish-grey dust from the fire's edge, he rubbed it across his face and over the backs of his hands.

Oswaldo and I did the same.

The ash smelt aromatic and soothing as I pressed it over the bridge of my nose and onto my cheeks. Was this the sort of ceremony that Wood had mentioned? I wondered how my mentor might have reacted if he were in my position.

Such a rite as this must have influenced the Brazilian Macumba of which Wood, my own teacher, had told me. Of that magical system, which took its roots from many lands, I longed to know more.

The Babalawo began to squeal like a tortured pig. Then, panting, he thrust his arms high above his head, shouting out what must have been the names of spirits.

Max seemed to know precisely what was going on. He stood up and made his way over to a very low-roofed hut. After a few moments he returned with something in his hands. The master took the object and, in return, passed Max some more leaves. Max motioned to us what to do.

Copying him, Oswaldo and I each pressed a broad leaf onto the roof of our mouths. My mouth was numbed by a bitter taste. And, on trying to move my tongue, I realized that it was paralyzed. I glanced in horror at the Patagonian, who winced miserably as if he, too, had fallen prey to the Babalawo's magic.

Max handed Oswaldo, and then me, an egg.

As before, we did exactly what Max did. He broke the shell and gulped down its contents. We did the same, despite the handicap of our oral anaesthetic. Then, Max put the actual shell in his mouth, crunched it up, and swallowed it. Oswaldo looked very miserable, but we both copied Max in silence. My stomach seemed to twist as it was presented with the raw egg, followed by the shell. Oswaldo's stomach also gurgled in surprise at what it had just ingested. Max looked pleased with us.

The Babalawo stood up, clasping the object that Max had brought from the shack. The size and colour of a haggis, it smelt, as it passed by me, of something which had died quite some time before. A rusty razor blade was produced by the Babalawo. He held it between his thumb and forefinger with dexterity, leading me to believe that he had handled it on many such occasions.

At that moment it became apparent that the razor was not just intended for show. It was no mere symbol, for the Babalawo wiped it, and readied it for use.

Oswaldo and I glared at Max through the orange torchlight with expressions that called for an explanation. The egg had not been pleasant, but we had swallowed it, together with shell, in the interests of magical science. But what was the blade's purpose? Max seemed a little concerned and he spoke for the first time. His words struck Oswaldo and me with horror.

He said simply:

'The Borfima is ready to be fed.'

The witchdoctor's dark shadow fell over the Patagonian, who sat cross-legged, rigid with terror, as the Borfima, blade, and Babalawo approached him.

Petrified and paralyzed, he held still as the Babalawo took his arm and prepared for the operation of drawing blood from it.

Just as the blade's edge was about to press down on Oswaldo's skin, he leapt up screaming.

The doctor fell back.

He clutched the sacred Borfima to his chest.

Unsure what to do, Max cried apologies to his master, who insisted we leave.

Oswaldo was silent as we stumbled back to Freetown, he was clearly upset and mumbled a prayer in Spanish. Max had left his Babalawo, to accompany us back through the woods. I regretted bringing the Patagonian along. But his outcry had done nothing to curb my interest in *ju-ju*. Indeed, this interest had only just begun.

Long before dawn we walked to the bus station. It was deserted. Oswaldo had made it clear that he would not spend another night, in fact another hour, in Freetown. We might have parted company then and there, but I sensed that a journey south – to Liberia – might reveal important new material.

In any case, Max was reluctant to help any more, in spite of our long postal friendship. Besides, he said that the spirit of the Babalawo would be searching for us, and if he were to find us, he would certainly feed us all to his adored Borfima.

One could never be sure when the next vehicle bound for Liberia would leave, but we stood a good chance of getting one as it was still early.

Oswaldo and I crouched in one corner of the terminal, which resembled some gigantic aircraft hangar. Still there was no light, just the sound of rats as they scuffled about. A very young girl slept against one wall; in her arms was a newborn baby. There was no sign of the mother. The two clung together to keep warm.

After about an hour, a brand new Land Rover stopped for a moment outside the terminus. Oswaldo went to ask for a ride, at least part of the way to the Liberian capital, Monrovia. We were in luck, for the driver – who was going to Kenema which was on the way – would take us there for free.

The road was excellent by African standards, and for four hours we bumped along, only stopping from time to time to get out at checkpoints. The jungle was thick and lush on both sides of the road. And, as the warm rays of dawn turned the cobalt sky pink, we could see smoke rising intermittently from a clearing, or a crook-backed woman walking to fetch water.

The Land Rover dropped us at the vegetable market of Kenema. Oswaldo bought a cucumber, cut it into slices, and squeezed the juice of a lime onto the pieces. It was a refreshing breakfast.

The market was still being set up. A selection of unusual roots and berries were displayed in round wicker baskets. Each basket was minded by a woman with a headscarf – who chattered in friendly competition about the day's business. Oswaldo led me to the bus stand as if he had been there before. He had a very good sense of direction but, when I complimented him, he just laughed his usual three times.

A yellow Peugeot 504 was filling up with passengers. In fact, it already seemed full. Ten people, a nanny goat, a large quantity of baggage, and a baby girl in the arms of her mother were already aboard. The driver assured us that his vehicle was bound for Monrovia and there was plenty of room for two more. We clambered onto the back seat. The goat was passed onto Oswaldo's lap. The baby was handed to me by its mother, who was sitting on my right.

We set off.

The communal taxi stalled four times because it was too heavy to move. The driver pumped the accelerator until the engine sounded like a dragon roaring.

Only then did the wheels begin to turn.

The driver hooted with joy and the 504 slunk its way along the craggy dust track towards Monrovia.

Oswaldo squeezed hold of the goat as the front right wheel plunged into a deep hole. Screams of panic followed, and the goat, which was bleating in terror, passed water profusely over Oswaldo's red jeans. The liquid soaked down onto the plastic seat and seeped under my thighs.

Looks of silent misery passed between us, as a dust storm filled the car.

Someone made the mistake of opening windows to release the grit. I chewed on the particles. When the animal began to choke violently, Oswaldo handed it firmly to the woman beside me. She was more willing to hold the brown goat than her own tiny infant.

The baby had begun to sweat tremendously. I pointed this out to the mother but she just shrugged her shoulders. Drawing in a monstrous breath, the infant promptly spewed the contents of its stomach over my chest and lap. It mixed with the piddle and an offensive odour penetrated the innermost reaches of the cabin. The mother caught me in an angry stare and, in the confined space, managed to turn away in disgust. All the other passengers refused to hold the child.

Four hours passed and all the initial feelings of embarking on an adventure had drained away. Arms and even toes poked about in the cab, hoping for another millimetre of space. The only breaks in routine were the strip-searches which took place at every checkpoint at least twice an hour. Twisted limbs unfurled themselves on the ground, like butterflies breaking from their cocoons.

Each passenger was led into a bamboo stall, where they removed their clothes. Anything which the soldiers thought to be contraband was confiscated. In one of the earlier searches I found a Kalashnikov AK-47 pointing at my chest.

Its owner was a boy of about sixteen.

He calmly removed my watch and put it on his own wrist. It did not seem to be a subversive item to me. So I asked politely for it back. Pushing the barrel of the AK-47 closer to my heart, the boy in fatigues replied:

'It is *my* watch now.'

Oswaldo's trilby had gone through pollution, dust and dirt, from dark brown to a shade of light tan.

He looked very miserable.

We jolted along on a track whose undulations were surely too extensive to be natural. Oswaldo suddenly gave out an unnatural, throaty laugh. Wriggling my left hand free, I manoeuvred it to pat him reassuringly on the shoulder. He was clearly beginning to crack.

At that moment the Peugeot 504 came to an abrupt stop. A soldier was waving in the road. We all trooped out. The goat and baby were passed from hand to hand and laid down on the grass.

A very stern-looking major strutted up and gave orders that all belongings were to be vigorously searched.

Parcels were unwrapped for the hundredth time and even shoes were removed. The major pointed to the car, and two young soldiers ripped out the back seats. We heard shouts as one of the lads ran to the officer with something wrapped in a cloth. All the passengers froze. The major ripped the cloth away to reveal a wad of US dollars and a large nugget of gold.

The driver was seized and put in a makeshift bamboo cell.

Another man confessed that the money and gold belonged to him. Oswaldo and I sat quietly awaiting the verdict. The officer announced that the smuggler and the driver had been arrested and the vehicle detained. Neither vehicle nor driver could be released as they had been abetting the smuggler. The major began to interrogate the two guilty men. It was then that an albino who spoke excellent English sidled up to us. He was the teacher of the local school.

Word had spread fast that two foreigners were visiting. We agreed that we were foreigners who were, in a broad manner of speaking, *visiting* the village. The albino bowed deeply and asked with ornate courtesy if we would come and talk to his pupils. Before I knew it, Oswaldo and I had jumped across a ditch and were in front of a class of maybe twenty young children.

A mouse was scuttling about in a cage in one corner of the classroom. The teacher introduced us to his students and said that we had come especially from far away to teach them. Oswaldo began a very long and serious lecture about Patagonia, the politics and tribulations of its culture and people. The children stared up blankly in silence. Oswaldo was thrilled at the opportunity of having a captive audience. It was a perfect therapy for him after the horrors of the drive.

The albino teacher told his pupils to sing the school song. They stood up and a chorus of shrill voices ran around the room.

'We have a problem here,' began the master as the children sang. 'You see we can't get the books and pens that schools in the cities can. At the moment we only have three pens for the whole class. I spend much time getting the children to learn the lessons by heart because they shall not forget them that way.'

He was a polite and apparently dedicated man.

The Patagonian dug deeply into the back pocket of his jeans. He pulled out the piece of white chalk and the ballpoint pen from Blackpool that the English woman had given him. I rummaged in my saddle-bags and found a couple of notepads.

Oswaldo handed them to the albino.

'For you, man,' he said.

The teacher looked at the ground and said that he could not take them, especially as they had come from so far away. We insisted, and Oswaldo gave him his address in Patagonia. The educator exclaimed that we would always be welcome in his school, and that he would never forget the day we came.

Oswaldo and I returned to the taxi which still had not moved.

By a great stroke of luck, it transpired that the major had once been to Banjul, where he had met Haji, the owner of the Hotel Apollo. Pleased that we shared a mutual acquaintance, he agreed to allow the driver to take us to Monrovia. Two soldiers would accompany us and afterwards would make sure that the driver returned to his bamboo cell.

One of the soldiers managed to squeeze between the mother and me. The other clambered onto the roof and banged hard when he was secure.

Just before we set off, the twenty schoolchildren appeared, led by their teacher. The eldest of the pupils tapped on the window against which Oswaldo's face was lodged. The Patagonian wound down the glass and the boy passed him a brown mouse.

'We thank you for helping us... have this,' he said. 'We will not forget you in our village.'

The wheels turned again and the students waved as the yellow Peugeot 504 left a cloud of dust in its wake.

Twenty minutes before it was due to close for the night, we arrived at the Liberian border. Two piles of forms were counted out; one for Oswaldo and one for me. We scribbled answers to what seemed like unending sides of photocopied questions.

With only five minutes left, we were less than halfway through: all the gaps had to be filled in full before we could leave Sierra Leone. It was clear that we would have to spend the night. But Oswaldo and I had no more *leones* left, and it was far too dangerous to risk exchanging foreign currency at the border on the black market. There was no official bureau-de-change.

A young Liberian man from Monrovia staggered about, clutching a bottle of whisky in one hand, and balancing a battered straw hat on his head. Oswaldo sidled up to him and began a short dissertation of the merits of Patagonian life and cuisine. Wincing, the Monrovian led us to his rented room in the middle of no-man's land.

A line of kiosks stretched the length of no-man's land. Liberia was about half a mile away. We were permitted to walk freely about the area, as all the soldiers and bureaucrats had gone to bed.

The Monrovian stumbled away into the moonless night with his bottle and straw hat, insisting that we take his bed. We explained that we had no *leones* with which to pay. But he was planning to spend the night drinking at a bar. Taking the lantern, he left us in the darkness.

Oswaldo always slept with his boots on. The left one was like a scabbard for the stiletto, which he would whip out at the first hint of trouble. We stretched out over the large bed.

A colony of insects lived in the bed. I could feel what seemed to be beetles crawling over my hands and face, searching for food, I supposed. It was almost comforting not being able to see anything in the blackness: I imagined that I was back with Osman and Prideep strolling up and down Marine Drive in Mumbai. Then Wood's form appeared and I watched him sipping vodka and feeding chapaties to a line of greedy vultures.

Oswaldo began to snore.

Just as I was falling into a deep slumber, a thudding noise hurtled across the corrugated iron roof. Instinctively, Oswaldo and I clutched each other like children terrified of a ghost. When the sound stopped we let go, both trying to conceal our fear.

Then again came the sound of feet charging at speed across the metal roof. A cat seemed to be screaming – almost a human screech – as if it were being torn limb from limb. Oswaldo and I were paralyzed with consternation.

Our imaginations ran wild.

We huddled together, all the muscles in my back and my limbs were rigid as we waited for the morning to come.

The young Monrovian was sitting outside our room, eating breakfast. A pineapple and the pelt of some small mammal lay next to where he sat. Oswaldo asked what kind of skin it was.

The youth replied:

'It's from a cat. A couple of rats killed it last night and ate it. I'm going to make a pouch from the skin.'

The Patagonian and I decided to risk entering Liberia without exit stamps from Sierra Leone: an offence said to be punishable by imprisonment. The mouse jostled about in Oswaldo's shirt pocket as we walked to Liberia. A boy on a bicycle pedalled up and said that the border guard wanted us to return to Sierra Leone. We strode on, in defiance of regulations.

At the Liberian border post we each handed five passport photographs to an officer's clerk. These were then stapled neatly into a large leather-bound tome. More forms were produced and we were led to a cell with smooth cement walls and floor.

I began to remove my clothes and empty out the contents of my saddle-bags. Squeezed from its tube, my toothpaste was inspected for diamonds. The back of my camera was prised off with a coin and the film exposed to light. All potentially subversive pictures were instantly destroyed.

Following this encounter I went to ridiculous lengths always to mail my films – and my notebooks – back to England after the last frame had been shot.

Oswaldo thought my obsession was insane.

I stood motionless, no longer caring to what lengths the conscripts went to make me angry. Then one, the youngest, picked up my stick of anti-perspirant. He removed the lid and slowly began to wind up the deodorant. Several hundred American dollars were concealed under the stick of deodorant.

The scent of sandalwood wafted about, and sweat began to drip into my eyes. The consequences of having undeclared money were very serious indeed. Unable to resist any longer, I grabbed the stick from the boy and rubbed it under my arms. The room was filled with broad smiles and laughter. Then Oswaldo and I were permitted to enter the Republic of Liberia.

Still there was no sign of the yellow Peugeot 504. We had not got round to paying for the ride, which was to be expensive. Oswaldo suggested that we could hitch with one of the trucks going to the capital, thus escaping the misery of the yellow cab. We asked around for a ride. Four lorries were going to Monrovia but still had to clear their paperwork, so we sat about waiting for the first to negotiate the red tape.

A Chevrolet station-wagon pulled up.

Clouds of exhaust fumes surrounded battered bodywork. In most other countries the vehicle would have been scrapped as a moving safety violation. I went up and asked if we could have a lift. A middle-aged man in a moth-eaten orange three-piece suit said that it would be a pleasure for him to take us. We were to be his guests. His name was Daniel, but we were to call him 'Danny'.

The Patagonian and I lounged in the back seat.

Danny's ten-year-old son and sister were also in the car. They had just come from Conakry, the capital of Guinea. The exhaust pipe of the vehicle led directly, curiously, into the car. Oswaldo and I covered our eyes and mouths with our shirt sleeves.

As soon as the windows were opened billows of black dust swept in and mixed with the carbon monoxide. For six miles the crumbling Chevy rumbled on.

Then the fan belt broke.

An assortment of worn replacements were fetched from the boot. Danny fitted one in the extreme equatorial heat. Oswaldo and I were both parched and reeling.

Another half hour passed and there was a puncture. The heat was so tremendous that it was unbearable to leave the shade of the cabin to change the wheel. A bald spare was brought out by Danny's son and we secured it with a single wheel nut. I choked as my lungs filled with dust and exhaust fumes.

Eventually we began to move.

Oswaldo's once brilliantine-soaked hair was stiff with dust and sweat, standing straight up like a sheet of cardboard. He looked at me and tried to manage a smile. Time and again he and I scrabbled under the bonnet, fumbling with the engine, scraping our knuckles as we struggled to fit yet another fraying fan belt. Neither of us had any knowledge of mechanics, but we were propelled by the desperation of survival.

Twenty miles from Monrovia, a line of metal spikes on a bar had been dragged into the road. Danny pulled over and we were made to enter an office where a man in civilian dress sat with his feet resting on the desk. He toyed with a handgun, caressing the trigger of what seemed to be a Colt .38.

Our belongings were brought and dropped on the desk. The figure shouted at me with arrogance.

'What's your purpose here?!'

'Sir, we are tourists in your country, we are travelling to Monrovia.'

'No tourists ever come here,' he exclaimed. 'You are obviously lying!' Oswaldo and I drooped silently, too weak to argue. We would have pleaded anything, said anything, just to be allowed to go on our way.

Oswaldo's shirt pocket twitched.

The man pointed to be shown what was hidden inside. A miniature nose probed for air. The Patagonian reached up and gently removed the brown mouse. The man behind the desk motioned to hold it.

The Patagonian stretched out his hand.

The official clasped the animal by the tail. Then, in one abrupt motion, he clubbed its head against the desk with the end of his revolver.

A little blood spurted from the head, before he flung the body against the far wall, dead. He snickered heartlessly. Oswaldo was close to tears. The rodent had been a symbol of the kindness of a simple people, amidst the barbarism of a totalitarian regime.

Just then, during the interrogation, came shouts from one of the soldiers outside. Danny was brought into the office, together with a box of medicines from his car. Oswaldo and I were ordered to leave. In the shade of a cement wall, Danny's son brought us each a plastic bag of water.

The liquid was cool and tasted like nectar.

An hour passed and Danny came out of the office weeping.

A conscript announced that he was to be put in prison, as he did not have the correct paperwork for his medicines. He would be taken to Monrovia under escort to face trial. My friend and I would also be arrested if we interfered. We were to leave in the next vehicle that crossed the checkpoint. I pleaded with the official in charge, but he was ready to reinforce his tyrannical orders with force. Danny was taken away.

Oswaldo went back into the office. He stooped down on the smooth cement floor and picked up the dead mouse. Then, behind the building, he dug a modest grave. The Patagonian crossed two twigs and placed them on the upturned topsoil.

As we stood in silent prayer I heard a car approaching. Oswaldo turned and pointed with the words, 'Look there on the roof!'

The Peugeot 504 taxi with the dust-covered conscript still clinging dutifully on top – brandishing a Kalashnikov – moved uneasily towards us. The car stopped and the goat leapt over the reluctant mother. I gawked at the sight of the group. All the passengers were now bedecked in gold, ivory and fine clothes. The transformation was unbelievable. It seemed incredible that the travellers could have concealed such items during the strip-searches and random checks. The driver was watched suspiciously as he went into a bush to relieve himself.

Oswaldo asked if we could have our old places back, as the Chevy's owner had been imprisoned.

It was agreed.

The soldier banged on the roof once more with the palm of his hand and we sped off towards Monrovia. Oswaldo and I were distraught at leaving Danny and his family stranded with the tyrant in civilian dress. We sat, brooding in silence, counting the minutes until we reached the war-ravaged capital.

The contents of the yellow Peugeot 504 piled out at the Disco Hotel, in a rather rough district of Monrovia. Oswaldo took the twelve-inch stiletto from his boot and stuffed it up his sleeve. He led me away from the yellow Peugeot and its soldier, sick baby, goat – which had gone into labour – and a quantity of luggage which could have sunk a ship.

Although weak and exhausted, we had been hardened by the experience of the last two days. Oswaldo's stride was longer than usual, he chewed at the inside of his cheek and scowled at all he saw in a bitter and twisted manner. I had not seen this side of the Patagonian before. No longer did he laugh or fool about. The murder of his mouse and the imprisonment of an innocent man had affected the South American deeply.

Through a series of complicated international banking transactions, Oswaldo had managed to have Western hard currency sent from his village in Patagonia to a bank in Monrovia. The financial situation in Liberia was quite bizarre.

United States dollar bills were the legal tender of the country. Instead of incinerating them, the United States sent worn-out dollar bills to Liberia. A shortage of notes prompted the Liberian government to mint its own dollar tender, with the same theoretical value as the American originals. But the black market value for the genuine American notes was much higher.

Liberia's civil war devastated the capital city and much of the countryside. The signs of combat were all around. It often happens in Africa that an unpopular president is butchered or forced to flee as his regime is toppled and replaced by another. Samuel Doe, the previous president, who had lost the battle to keep his position, had allegedly had his ears hacked off by the forces which overthrew him.

Two men were wrestling on the stairs of Maxim's Hotel. They seemed to have no intention of moving until one had fallen to the bottom. We clambered over them and found the manager holding out a key to the best room. Oswaldo snatched it as if it had been stolen from him in the first place. My clothes had been bonded to my skin with layers of black dirt.

I peeled the filthy socks from my feet.

Oswaldo leapt into the shower, and cackled so long and loudly with zest when hot water hit his back that the landlord came to see what the fuss was about. I asked him to bring a couple of towels, as none had been provided.

An hour passed.

The Patagonian had sung many a ballad, and I was getting impatient to get clean, too.

Another hour slipped by.

I hammered at the bathroom door.

Oswaldo had begun to belt out his favourite Argentine saga – 'The Life of Martin Fierro'.

Still there was no sign of the towels, so I shouted down the corridor. A faint cry radiated from some back room from which there came a distinct smell of burning.

A fist pounded at the door. I walked over and opened it, expecting to be handed two clean towels. The manager's head was servilely bent at right angles to my stomach. There was no sign of the towels. Instead, a plate was pushed at me: on it were the charred embers of something which had caught fire. The manager gasped:

'Here's your toast, sir.'

At last, I forced my Patagonian travelling companion from the bathroom and I took a long, satisfying shower. Oswaldo turned his red jeans inside out and put them on. We went out into the town to eat. Our stomachs had almost forgotten the concept of digestion. The thought of mountains of food had kept us going since Freetown. Oswaldo pulled the collar of his shirt closer to his neck and we entered an elegant Lebanese restaurant. Monrovia has been dominated economically for many years by the Lebanese community.

A menu was produced and Oswaldo waved it aside. The waiter looked displeased. I, too, was surprised.

'Sir, are you here to eat something?'

'Man…'

'Yes sir?'

'Bring one of everything!'

The mad Patagonian looked at me for approval and I nodded.

He laughed three times and I knew that everything was back to normal.

Kebabs, pizza, sirloin steaks and strawberry milkshakes were shuttled to our table by a troop of waiters. The Patagonian took alternate bites of each succulent dish. Osman would have approved.

At the next table sat a tall man with a thick black beard and Mediterranean looks, dressed in a cream gabardine suit. He was laughing at our extravagance.

Oswaldo invited him over to join us.

The figure stood up and walked over. His fingers, neck and wrists were enveloped in pieces of gold jewellery. The clasps and bracelets jingled as he sat. He spoke through a New York accent.

'I'm Jacques,' he said.

'It's nice to meet you; are you just passing through like us?' I asked.

'No, I've been living here a few years. If I can stand the place I'll stay a while longer.'

'Are you in business?' I enquired; he looked as if he was a successful man.

'Yeah, you might say that,' he murmured, 'I'm in metals.'

'Any in particular?'

'Yes,' said Jacques as he paused to sip a drink. 'Gold.'

He picked an American cigarette from a soft packet and lit it with a gold lighter which I admired:

'It's a Bic fifty-cent lighter. I made a cover in 18-carat gold. Passes the time, but I'm really getting fed up with it here.'

'Where do you get the gold from?' I asked.

'I go into the bush, three or four days' trip. Buy it there. Then I bring it back to Monrovia and melt it into ingots. Why don't you guys come around tomorrow? I'm melting in the morning.'

Placing a cream business card on the table, he sauntered off.

My stomach had surely shrunk. It felt as if food was stacked up my oesophagus, waiting to be digested. Oswaldo ploughed on. Sweat was dripping into his eyes and mixing with the tears which were pouring down his face. His greed had transcended the pain barrier. His fork was raised from the plate, his eyes spun, and he moaned, 'Just one more mouthful, man!'

Oswaldo was unable to sleep all night. His indigestion was very bad: he ran hunched to the bathroom time and again and groaned with self-pity.

Next morning we went to meet Jacques. His office was on the third floor of a modern apartment block. Security cameras moved about like eyes on stalks when I pressed the bell-push.

Jacques was berating a young African who stood in front of his desk, staring blankly. The young man left.

'What's dat problem?' Oswaldo asked.

'This city is driving me crazy!' yelled Jacques. 'I went back to the States for one week. Just one damn week, that's all. When I came back not only had my car been stolen, but my safe had knife marks in it and my partner had withdrawn a hundred thousand dollars from my account and fled. It's really beginning to get on my nerves.'

We went into a sealed-off room. Inside was a workbench and a small furnace. Jacques rotated dials and turned off the gas. What looked like a cake tin was carefully slid from the fire. When it had cooled, he tapped out a shiny brick of metal. It was solid gold. My eyes met Oswaldo's. There was no need to speak, the dilation of our pupils must have said more than words.

Jacques seemed to be the sort of man to whom one could talk at ease. He would listen and give encouragement if he thought it necessary. Oswaldo crouched over the gold ingot in the work room: he had evidently fallen in love with the substance. I sat with Jacques in his office and told him about the ceremony with Max's Babalawo. Then I began to explain to him about my interest in the Gonds and Gondwanaland.

He, too, had read about Gondwanaland and had been enthralled. He spoke of a tribe, believed to exist in Central Africa, said to be related to the Gond people of India.

'They are thought to live in Congo,' began Jacques, 'on the east side of the country... in the very heart of what was once Gondwanaland.'

'Where do they live, exactly?'

'At the summit of the Nyiragongo volcano.'

The idea of venturing to the very centre of Gondwanaland suddenly seemed important, as if the quest might provide information until now unknown.

A people related to the Gonds, could that really be true? It seemed severely implausible, especially as man had not appeared until millions of years after the continents had separated, about forty-five million years ago.

But Wood had spoken of Macumba, whose magical arts had been influenced by the peoples of Africa and India... perhaps there had been an ancient affinity – impalpable and not time-bound – between all Gondwanaland's people. Perhaps a sister tribe to the Gonds did exist; the Nyiragongo seemed a good place to look.

Wresting the block of gold from Oswaldo's clenched fingers, I began to lead him away. As we were leaving, I turned to thank Jacques. He lit a cigarette and inhaled long and hard.

'Fellas,' he said 'go to Congo, climb the Nyiragongo and breathe deeply, for you'll be standing at the core of Gondwanaland.'

Oswaldo volunteered to accompany me to Congo as long as I promised him it was to the east. Despite his love of travel, geography was apparently not his strong point, Patagonia's landscape was the extent of his knowledge. As he reminded me often, the rest of the world was to be discovered on his great adventure.

After that, he made me swear a solemn oath I'd avoid all contact with the dark arts of local magic.

Reluctantly, I gave my word.

Then I went back to the hotel to take a nap, while Oswaldo went off to tell the travel agent all about the tourist trade in his native Patagonia.

One of his cousins there had requested he drum up business wherever possible. I had suggested that there might be a lack of Liberians with the will and finances to patronize his cousin's tourist lodgings. He had looked me sternly in the eye and had cackled:

'Are you crazy?! Everyone loves Patagonia!'

As I lay on my bed dreaming of lost tribes and volcanoes, Oswaldo burst in and made an announcement:

'Hey man! We're going to Congo! The flight's at six o'clock.'

The Patagonian's first trip in an aeroplane had filled him with a new kind of excitement: one that he wanted to relive. He had developed a mysterious passion for flight, and insisted that all journeys that could be done by air, were done by air.

I rolled my eyes.

What was the point of flying?

All you got to see was sky.

From: *Beyond the Devil's Teeth*

Qualifications of a Traveller

If you have health, a great craving
for adventure, at least a moderate fortune,
and can set your heart on a definite
object, which old travellers do not think
impracticable, then travel, by all means.

The Art of Travel

MY SEARCH FOR the last refuge of the Incas had begun in the
snug surroundings of our illusionary world.

Only a man who has his health, a full stomach and wears
clean clothes would ever entertain the notion of tracking
down the greatest lost city on Earth, or venturing from such
comfort into the bitter reality of the jungle.

My obsession with the ruins had begun a decade before,
when my eyes had been drawn to the cursed name 'Paititi'
in the footnote of an obscure historical text. From the first
moment I read the word, I sensed it beckoning, daring me
to try my luck. It would have been so easy to turn the page
and move on. But, instead, I gazed coldly at the type, took a
deep breath and shut the book.

Once inside me, the corrosive allure of Paititi ran wild. For months, then years, I tried to suppress all thoughts of the Incas and their lost treasure. I undertook other projects, other journeys, but Paititi was never far from my mind. Like so many before me, my motivation was founded on greed – an overwhelming greed. Not for gold, but for glory.

Locate a lost city and your name is etched in the history books. Find Paititi, and I would be transformed overnight from a humble traveller into the world's most famous explorer.

To have a hope of discovering the lost city, I knew the key lay in the archives of the Spanish *conquistadores*. They had documented their invasion of the Americas in fine detail, but they were too busy suppressing native people to piece together the clues. For months I studied the history, reading and rereading the chronicles of Francisco de Jerez, Garcilaso de la Vega, Cristóbal de Molina, and of Felipe Guamán Poma de Ayala. The clues would be hidden, for they had eluded explorers, adventurers, archaeologists and warrior-priests for almost five hundred years. Yes, they would be concealed well, waiting to be teased out – that is, if there were any clues at all.

In the West, we are brought up to solve a puzzle with fragments of collected information, rather than by placing ourselves in the mind of the person who devised the riddle. By steeping myself in the Spanish chronicles, detailing the Incas' daily lives, folklore and beliefs, I hoped to understand how they thought. Understand that and, I hoped, I would be closer to rooting out the trail to Paititi.

When the Spanish first arrived at the coastline of Peru in the first half of the sixteenth century, they were searching for El Dorado, a land of unimaginable wealth. An Indian chief in Panama had spoken of a kingdom to the south where the only known metal was gold – where it was used for pots and pans, plates and jewellery, for hunting bows, ritualistic daggers and flutes. The *conquistadores* made a beeline southwards.

They found a vast empire that had been established only a century before, known to its people as Tahuantinsuyu, the Land of Four Quarters. Centred at the capital of Cusco, the realm stretched from Chinchaysuyu in the north to Lake Titicaca in the south, and from the Atlantic Ocean in the west to the endless cloud forest of Madre de Dios in the east.

It was a land of contrasts: stark *altiplano*, seething jungle and snow-capped mountains, populated by a people whose barbaric rituals shocked even the cruel sensibilities of the *conquistadores*. The religious figurehead of the society was the scion of the sun itself, the Inca Atahualpa.

Had it not been cut short by such an unlikely foreign invasion, the Inca Empire would surely have endured for centuries, amassing even more treasure than it did. And what of the treasure? The Spanish imprisoned Atahualpa, who feared imminent execution. He had noticed the invaders' obsession with gold and silver and, although surprised by it, he proposed what must surely be the most famous ransom in history. He scratched a line high on one wall of his cell, and pledged to fill the chamber once with gold and twice with silver in exchange for his freedom. Amazed and delighted, the Spanish readily agreed. One can only imagine their astonishment: the room measured more than twenty feet by seventeen, and the line on the wall was higher than a man: a volume of more than two thousand cubic feet.

Gold and silver were ushered forth from across the Inca Empire, a quantity that exceeded the Spaniards' wildest dreams. As one would expect, the pledge to Atahualpa was broken; the conquerors executed him, then set out to plunder his capital. But in Cusco they found relatively little gold. A rumour circulated that the bulk of the golden treasure had been hurried from the city by the Incas' supporters. It was said that they had retreated deep into the jungle, east of Cusco, where they established a magnificent city in the most inaccessible corner of the cloud forest. They called it Paititi.

I tried to put myself in the mind of the Incas, asking myself how they might have secretly passed to one another the whereabouts of their El Dorado. With the *conquistadores* all around them, they would no doubt have resorted to ciphers, unlikely to arouse the suspicions of the invading Spanish. But they had no tradition of writing, no paper or ink.

We know that they placed relatively little importance on gold. A civilization without iron, they favoured the soft yellow metal for its easy malleability, and regarded it as utilitarian rather than as a valuable commodity. The Incas placed utmost value on their fine textiles, woven in alpaca and vicuña wool. Early conquistador reports tell of the first meetings with the Incas, who came alongside the Spanish ships in flimsy craft. They presented the European visitors with exquisite woven garments, their highest honour.

Horrified at what they assumed to be an open insult, the Spanish set fire to the textiles and chased the Incas away.

The fabulous arts of weaving and embroidery had been developed by the ancient communities at Paracas and Nazca on the Peruvian coast, which flourished almost two thousand years ago. It was from them that the Incas acquired their knowledge and further developed the craft, using it to record information and ideas. These embroidered patterns, known as *quellca*, a word that is sometimes used to mean 'writing', might well have been employed to conceal the location of Paititi.

I studied hundreds of Inca textiles, hoping to decipher the meanings of the geometric patterns; and I spent a great deal of time attempting to trace the finest Inca textile ever made. It was sent to King Philip II of Spain in 1570 for the monastic walls at El Escorial, but it has disappeared without trace. One of the greatest historical treasures ever to come from the Americas, it was probably thrown away.

My studies of the *quellca* embroideries led me to consider what treasure the Incas would have taken to Paititi for safekeeping. If they did not consider gold the ultimate possession, then perhaps they would have taken their textiles instead. I knew from previous experience that the humidity of the rainforest is ruinous for cloth. If Paititi had lain in the jungle, there was little hope of any woven riches remaining intact. None the less, the draw for me was the ruins themselves, the vast stone walls like those at Machu Picchu, which would surely form the foundation of the lost city.

My obsession with Paititi, and the glory that finding it could bring, gnawed away at me. I travelled to Peru in search of the Birdmen of the Upper Amazon, a project that culminated in a book on the subject. It gave me the opportunity to do much more research, and to quiz hundreds of Peruvians on what they knew of the Incas and their last place of refuge.

I spent months combing library stacks, trawling through miles of manuscripts, many written more than four centuries ago. There were so many books, but so few clues. The only one was the recurring name Madre de Dios, the vast impenetrable jungle east of the Andes, on the southern cusp of the Amazon.

The lure of the last great lost city of the Americas had not attracted me alone: at least a dozen of the world's most seasoned explorers had just returned or were about to leave for the cloud forest. Teams from the United States and the UK, Poland, Australia and Peru itself had isolated a relatively small 'hot zone', which lay between the Piñi-Piñi and Palatoa rivers. Somewhere in there, they all claimed, lay the ruins of a tremendous civilization. Although, geographically speaking, the area is small, it's regarded as the densest stretch of jungle in the world. One adventurer told me: 'You could hide New York City in there and walk right by without knowing it.' He added that the race was reaching fever pitch. 'If Paititi exists at all,' he said firmly, 'it will be found in the next six months.'

That prediction got my blood racing. It might be the last chance I would ever get at easy fame. I had been fixated by the lure of the Inca stronghold for too long for the prize to be snatched by some other less deserving adventurer. I bought the cheapest flight to Lima I could find. It was scheduled to leave in a week's time, on Christmas Day.

Unlike most of the competition, I didn't have corporate sponsorship or a fat expense account. Nor could I boast a support team of scientists, or high-level contacts in the Peruvian government. I didn't have a headquarters either, or much in the way of specialist equipment. I owned a second-hand GPS, but hadn't a clue how it worked. It was just for show, proof of my serious intentions, as was my Gold Bug metal detector, which I had bought on my Ethiopian search for King Solomon's mines. Like a rebel fighter in a guerrilla war, I viewed my weaknesses as strengths. I was lean and mean, free from excess people and a glut of equipment. I had no one to report to, and no one except myself to please.

My wife rolled her eyes when I explained that I had to leave our poky flat in London's East End almost at once. The jungle was calling me, I said theatrically. She was very understanding, considering our little daughter's first birthday was a few days away.

I bought a copy of *Loot*, a newspaper with classified ads, and withdrew two hundred pounds from my bank account. I spread the sheets of advertisements on the sitting-room floor and searched for equipment worthy of a budget lost-city expedition. In less than an hour, I had found an old Zodiac rubber dinghy, a pair of used jungle boots, two shovels, six canvas kit bags, three tarpaulins and a pair of cheap lanterns. With the money that was left, I went to a local hardware store and bought some plastic rubble sacks, the kind used by builders to carry gravel. I splashed out on some extra batteries and a roll of bin liners too. Lastly, I went down to Safeway with my credit card and snapped up some packet soup and their entire stock of Pot Noodles. Previous experience had taught me that any expedition marches on its stomach.

It always amazes me how much money people spend on nonessential knick-knacks and mountaineering food at camping shops. A whole industry has developed touting nicely packaged rubbish to ingenuous adventurers. You're far better off buying everything second-hand, from a hardware store, supermarket or, better still, on a market stall in the country you're visiting.

These days, explorers tend to take with them from the start everything they expect to need. It's an inefficient way of operating; you get lumbered down and can hardly move. It's wiser to take only a basic core of equipment and to compensate by making anything you find you need. On rough journeys, ingenuity is the mother of success. The Victorians were masters of exploration and of solving problems, and they turned problem-solving into an art form. They could knock up just about anything from a few feet of waxed canvas, some stout cord and a cleft stick or two. For those who wanted handy tips on how to bivouac, build a camp, or cross quicksand in heavy rain, there was an invaluable guide entitled *The Art of Travel*. The book's editor was Francis Galton, a cousin of Charles Darwin and a renowned scholar and adventurer in his own right. Galton's book, which was first published by John Murray in 1855, ran to four editions, the final and most comprehensive one appearing in 1872. It was carried by explorers and soldiers, missionaries and government officials, and is an encyclopaedia of ingenuity. Much of it is regarded now as horrendously politically incorrect – especially the section on 'the management of savages' – but it contains many titbits of invaluable information. Fortunately, *The Art of Travel* had recently been reprinted. It was the last purchase I made and, without doubt, the best value.

The day after buying the equipment, I was talking to a television-producer friend, blustering on about my grand plans to find the lost city of Paititi. Like my wife, he rolled his eyes for, again like her, he had heard of my grand quests before. Just before we parted, he said that a friend of his, a Swedish filmmaker, might be interested in coming along. I barked at the thought of European company; my friend pointed out the benefit. Find Paititi, and the filmmaker could record my discovery: surely it would only add to my glory. After all, who would have cared about the lunar landings if we had not received the grainy footage of Armstrong climbing down from the NASA module onto the dusty lunar surface?

I took the Swede's number and gave him a call. We arranged to meet next day in an East End coffeehouse where the grease on the walls reflected the mud on the floor. I lurked at the back, away from the usual assortment of weirdos, a soft-covered book of Inca textiles on the table before me. As I sat there, staring at the geometric designs, two men approached. One was a good twenty years older than the other. They were both dressed in leather, the first in black suede, the younger in tan-coloured buckskin. The older was short, five foot three at the most, with dark, receding hair, swarthy complexion, pursed lips, and shoulders that were noticeably relaxed, so much so that his hands hung down at his sides like cured hams in a butcher's window. The younger had long, russet-brown hair, which covered his ears and curled down over the collar of a torn denim shirt. His face was tight and energetic, partially concealed by a straggly beard and moustaches. He looked as if he had stepped from a seventies pop-idol poster.

The pair introduced themselves as Leon and David Flamholc. They worked as a team, the father producing, the son directing. They made art-house feature films in Sweden, but they had come to London to break into the English language. Sweden was too small, too conventional, they confided darkly, and its people were too easily shocked.

I told them about my plan to venture deep into the densest jungle in the world on the trail of the fleeing Incas. 'I could do with someone to document the ruins,' I said.

I expected a barrage of questions, beginning with 'Do you really think you'll find the lost city?' But the Swedes didn't ask any questions at all. They cackled enthusiastically in their mother tongue, and noted down a few details. As they did so, I noticed a man with a large video camera standing outside the café. He was pointing the device in our direction, filming through the filthy window. 'Do you know him?' I asked.

'He follows us everywhere,' said Leon, distantly.

That afternoon I visited the hallowed halls of the Royal Geographical Society in London's South Kensington. I was in search of a map. The RGS takes the subject of exploration very seriously indeed, and tends to frown on low-budget expeditions. As far as they are concerned, the business of exploration is best left to professionals.

The secretary wrote my name in a ledger and ushered me past long, dark oils of the great explorers: Stanley, Livingstone, Burton, and some others of equal fame. Then he marched me down a corridor, striding solemnly as if we were pallbearers in a funeral cortege. A central carpet, laid over the parquet, cushioned the sound of our steps. Along the corridor ran a finely tooled display case. It housed the holy of holies, Livingstone's peaked cap and Stanley's jungle kepi, Amundsen's cooking stove and Sven Hedin's sextant. Each item bore the scars of ordeal: the ordeal of exploration.

The Map Room was lightless and cold, its walls lined with cabinets, each filled with charts and plans and miniature globes. Every inch of available space was stacked with clusters of maps, a million, billion maps. There were maps of hamlets in obscure corners of the southern African veld, city maps of Shanghai, Manila, Santiago and Trieste; maps of rivers and mountain ranges, of endless deserts and deltas, Arctic tundra and trenches on the ocean floor.

A clerk asked me to write my destination on a scrap of paper. I did so, inscribing 'MADRE DE DIOS' in small, neat capitals at the centre of the page. I slid it back across the counter. The clerk licked his thumb, scooped it up and strained through bifocals at the words. Then he scratched a rounded fingernail on his cheek.

'No, sir,' he said, in a shrill tone. 'No, sir, there is no map of Madre de Dios. There is no map at all.'

Before I knew it, I had been ushered back to the street. I felt like an outcast, as if I had sought to embarrass the Map Room by seeking out its Achilles' heel.

Much time has passed since brave Englishmen dressed in tweeds were dispatched by the RGS to fill in the blank outlines of the continents. The business of exploration has changed. There is still danger, but these days when you embark on an expedition you expect to return alive. Adventure is no longer about providing a service to humanity, but about bettering yourself, testing yourself and striving for glory.

Two days later, I had a second rendezvous with the Swedes. We met in the immense tropical greenhouse at Kew Gardens. On a hard jungle journey nothing is so important as having a team you can trust. The Swedes symbolized a lucrative source of TV funding, but there was no point in having them along if they would crack up in the climate.

As before, they arrived trussed from head to toe in leather. And, again, they were being stalked by the broad-shouldered blond man, armed with a video camera and an oversized microphone. He tracked them through the undergrowth, moving between the shrubs and fronds with impressive nimbleness.

'Who *is* that man?' I asked.

'It's Boris.'

'*Boris?*'

'He's a Bulgarian film student,' David replied.

'Oh.'

'We have a cult following in Bulgaria,' he added, by way of explanation.

Miniature beads of condensation had formed on David's costume. They grew larger and larger and ran together, then dripped silently to earth. This time his outfit was complemented by a golden medallion, hanging at the centre of his bald chest. As he moved through the festering humidity of the hothouse, it caught the light, which broke occasionally through the layers of rubbery leaves.

I warned him and his father of the certain hardship that lay ahead. The Swedes seemed unfazed by the prospect of adversity. They had been preparing, they said, grinning.

'What do you mean, *preparing?*'

'We sealed up the windows in our flat,' said Leon, 'and installed a heater from a sauna. It's a hundred per cent humidity at home, and as hot as hell.'

I was struck by their dedication, and comforted myself that Swedes knew about saunas, and could probably endure the heat better than I. The conversation moved on quickly to money. I asked what their budget was for equipment and supplies. Their confidence plunged.

'There's no money yet,' said Leon.

'But we're leaving in five days!'

'Don't worry, we have a patron.'

'Who?'

'A banker, a very rich Ukrainian banker.'

'Excellent.'

'There's a small catch,' said David, wiping his medallion with his thumb. 'We can sting him for lots of cash, but he wants to come along.'

At first I disapproved of my expedition to find the lost city becoming an upmarket package tour for middle-aged bankers, arty Swedish filmmakers and their Bulgarian groupies. But the more I thought of it, the more I came to understand that there might be strength in such an odd lineup.

Ours was not going to be a clone of the usual expeditions, oozing with sleekness. It was clear from the start that oddity was our advantage.

There are two ways to find a lost city. The first is to rely on luck alone; the second is to control all the information. My historical research had filled in some of the gaps, but it was important to hear first-hand from other Paititi-hunters. I wanted to know where they had been and what they had found. To this end, I interviewed as many as I could find, pretending that I was preparing an article about the search for Paititi. The cover story seemed to put the explorers at ease. They spoke freely about locations and methods, without fearing that I was about to steal their information. It might have been underhand, but successful explorers have always resorted to scheming, even depraved methods to ensure success.

Exploration is a dirty game. I sometimes wonder with what red herrings the great adventurers like Captain Cook and Columbus, Walter Raleigh and Drake had thrown their competition off the scent. Perhaps they were more gentlemanly then as there were more unexplored chunks of the world to go around. But now, with so few jewels in the crown of exploration still remaining, the competition is cutthroat.

I would frequently root through library stacks only to find that the relevant page of a key text had been torn out. And seasoned trailblazers would often 'shuffle' coordinates while recounting tales of their journeys. I didn't blame them. As I progressed in my search, I became as conniving as everyone else. Obsession and greed can compel a reasonable man to behave in the most appalling way.

Through a strange kind of geographic arrogance, Europeans like to think that the world was a silent, dark, unknown place until they trooped out and discovered it. They forget that when Columbus arrived in the Caribbean he came upon an orderly indigenous society, just as Pizarro did in Peru, and Captain Cook did in the Antipodes. Of course, these native peoples were regarded at the time as wild and untamed, to be taught discipline and the wisdom of the Bible.

In the same way that newly discovered landmasses had always been known about by the people who lived on them, a lost city can never really be lost at all. Tribal people know their territory inside and out. They always know where the ruins lie although, unlike us, they may have little or no interest in them. When tribal warriors stumble upon ruins overgrown in their ancestral lands, they don't waste time inspecting them. Their attention is focused on acquiring food, not antique possessions with which to spruce up their homes; indigenous people are not gripped as we are with notions of ownership, urbanism or cultural history. Just as the British developed a mania for climbing the Alps in the Victorian era, searching for a lost city is a particularly European obsession.

For this reason, I became aware early on that the best way to find Paititi was to go directly to the people who surely knew where it lay. Most expeditions don't integrate with the societies through whose lands they travel. They remain apart, superior, judgemental. As a result they are mistrusted and disliked by the locals. I had heard of the Machiguenga, a tribe whose hunting grounds stretch across much of the Madre de Dios cloud forest. They have been portrayed as a ruthless, warlike people, more eager to slay invaders than to welcome them. Thirty years ago they wiped out a French-led Paititi expedition, near the jungle village of Mantacolla.

My approach was to venture to that same village and gain the trust of the Machiguenga, the very warriors who supposedly killed the French group. We would come as equals, as friends, rather than adversaries.

Gradually, with time, I hoped to broach the subject of the lost city itself.

From: *House of the Tiger King*

Water of Paradise

FOR A WEEK after the episode with the mason and the teeth, Rachana, the children and I slept in the same bed.

I propped a chair against our bedroom door and kept an Indian dagger under my pillow. I was a coward for not dismissing Layachi right away, as he was quite obviously deranged. I didn't know how to do it and I feared he would pull out his dentures and strike again – at us.

On the eighth day I plucked up courage and found Osman raking leaves.

'I have to let your brother go,' I said diplomatically. 'He attacked the mason for no reason at all. And I just don't feel safe with him around. None of us do.'

Osman leaned his weight on the rake and wiped a hand over his chin.

'Since my brother Layachi was a small child,' he said, 'he's been crazy. He's a maniac. Everyone knows it. He should be locked up.'

'But why didn't you tell me this at the start? You brought him to me, exclaiming how trustworthy he was!'

The guardian bit his top lip.

'In our country,' he said restlessly, 'blood is thick, and where there is thick blood there is duty.'

The days were getting shorter and I could smell winter approaching from the north. In Morocco, you know the cool months are drawing near because the streets fill with carts piled high with oranges. The fruit are slightly tart at first and, each week, they become a little sweeter.

Zohra began to spend her time hounding me through Dar Khalifa, ordering me to seek help from her sorceress friend. The last thing I wanted was to follow the maid's suggestion, as doing so would have increased the power she imagined she held over me. But at the same time, I felt I had to talk to someone about the cryptic chalk symbols on the doors, as well as about my recurring magic-carpet dream.

Then Ottoman called me again. Although I knew of his past and a little of his business success, I had very little idea about his private life. I didn't even know if he was married. He was the kind of man whose personality gave off a scent, warding one away from asking certain questions.

We met at a café near his home in a fashionable suburb of Casablanca. There was the usual assortment of unshaven men in long, billowing *jelabas*. But the café was very different for two reasons. The first was that the coffee was delicious. I had grown used to slurping down the ubiquitous *café noir*, a beverage the taste buds can never quite accept. The second reason that made the café different was that there were women, plenty of them. And they were not the typical range of ruthless crones one found elsewhere, but skimpily dressed blondes, pouting mouths heavy with lipstick.

Even more unusual was that many of them were smoking.

Ottoman outlined his idea: 'We start small,' he said. 'First we'll find a storyteller and bring him to the *bidonville* where Hicham Harass lived. I will pay his wages and he will tell stories day and night, rekindling the culture that's in danger of being lost.'

I nodded, making enthusiastic sounds.

'Gradually, we will hire other storytellers,' Ottoman went on. 'Before you know it, there will be dozens of them, in cafés all over Morocco. It'll be like the old times.'

Ottoman's eyes lit up as if he was peering to make out the detail of a mirage.

'We would not need to stop there,' he said. 'We could have storytellers in railway stations, at bus stops, in markets, and even in offices!'

By this point, Ottoman, who had until then struck me as a soft-spoken man, was ranting.

'Who will pay for all the storytellers?' I asked.

'Sponsorship,' he replied. 'Companies will sponsor them. On television you have commercial breaks, so our storytellers could promote products as well.'

'So they would be travelling salesmen?'

Ottoman frowned. 'No, no, not at all,' he said. 'Not salesmen, but representatives of the big brands. Coca-Cola, Pepsi, McDonald's... imagine it!'

My problem in life is that I'm a victim. I get dragged into schemes and find myself tangled up, unable to break free. I should have shaken Ottoman firmly by the hand, thanked him for the coffee and fled. But instead I flattered his ego and his creativity.

Then I offered to help.

Six days later I saw a man sitting in Jma el Fna, the vast central square of Marrakech. He was bald, with a long tatty beard and a single silver earring reflecting the light. I knew he wasn't a Moroccan because of the look in his eye.

He looked as if he had seen a miracle.

I had headed south to begin the search for the story in my heart, and to find the first storyteller for Ottoman's grand plan. Marrakech was the obvious place to start.

The foreigner struck up a conversation. He was a German called Kaspar. He said that he had travelled for sixteen years, that almost every square inch of the world had passed beneath his feet. Sapphire eyes wide with wonder, hands out, fingers splayed, he explained that every minute until then had been preparation – the preparation for Jma el Fna, the 'Place of Execution'.

'This *is* the world,' he said in a soft Bavarian voice.

I asked him what he meant.

He smiled. 'You don't feel it?'

I didn't reply.

'You don't feel it?' he said again.

'What? Feel what?'

'The humanity,' he said.

Kaspar got to his feet and staggered away, mumbling something about a drink of cold water. Then he was gone. I stood there, gazing out at the square's stew of human life – snake handlers and fortune-tellers, healers and madmen, door-to-door dentists, witches, water-sellers, and a single blind man waiting for a coin to be pressed into his palm.

Kaspar from Bavaria was right: there is perhaps no spot on earth so alive, so utterly human, as Jma el Fna.

Like almost everyone else who has ever been there, I have tried to understand Marrakech. I have sat in Café Argana, my favourite haunt overlooking the square, and I have watched, listened and wondered. Is it Africa? Is it Morocco? Or is it a strange kind of paradise, a paradise for the senses?

The answer is that Marrakech is all of these things and it is a great deal more.

I scoured the square for Khalil the son of Khalilullah, the storyteller I had met a few weeks before. He was nowhere to be seen; nor were there any other storytellers.

When I quizzed the row of orange-juice sellers about this, they said most of them had part-time jobs because storytelling didn't pay.

'Why would you pay to listen to *them*,' said one of the juice sellers, 'when you could be at home or in a café watching television for free?'

With the light too bright for any but a Marrakchi's eyes, I slipped into the labyrinth of the medina, which spreads out behind the square in a vast cornucopia of life. Cool vaulted stone, courtyards latticed with bamboo staves, casting zebra stripes across the merchants and their stalls. Marrakech's medina is a marketplace abundant with wares – mountains of turmeric, paprika, salted almonds and dates, yellow leather slippers laid out in rows, ostrich eggs and incense, chameleons in tattered wire cages, and beef tenderloins nestled on fragrant beds of mint.

Roam the narrow passages and you are cast back in time.

Marrakech may be prosperous these days, bolstered by tourist wealth, but the medina is still intact, vibrant, raging with life. There are Chinese plastic dolls on offer these days, and second-hand TVs stacked up by the dozen, and racks of mobile phones, but Marrakech moves to an ancient rhythm. The decoration comes and goes, as do the wares, but the soul stays firm.

Of all the stalls and shops, there was one in particular I was hoping to find on my trail for a storyteller. Abdelmalik had said there was an unusual emporium to visit, called Maison de Meknès; that stepping into it would change the way my eyes saw the world. He made me memorize the directions: go to the Bab Laksour, take the third street to the left, and then fifth to the right, turn left again at the green mosque, and the second right at the butcher selling horse meat. When you see a *hammam*, turn your back to it, step two metres to the right and slip down a passage filled with a sea of rotting bread.

For three hours I traipsed up and down, lost in lanes jammed with people and merchandise. Then, quite suddenly, the directions fell into place like clues on a treasure map. I found the mosque, the butcher, the *hammam* and the rotting bread. At the far end was a low-fronted cavern, with a crude hand-painted sign. It read: *Maison de Meknès.*

There were steps going down, rounded by generations of eager feet. Inside, the ceiling was low, cobwebbed, and the shelves beneath it were cluttered with treasure. There were ancient Berber chests, silver teapots, ebony footstools, swords once used by warring tribes, cartons of postcards left by the French, Brownie box-cameras, candlesticks, silk wedding belts, and camel headdresses crafted from indigo wool.

The proprietor was a smug-faced man with tobacco-coloured eyes, and dried coffee spilled down the front of his shirt. He said his name was Omar bin Mohammed. He was perched on a stool behind a pool of light just inside the door. I didn't see him at first, not until my eyes had become accustomed to the darkness. Omar seemed greedy for business. But, as I soon found out, there was one thing he enjoyed far more than loading tourists up with loot.

He loved to tell stories.

The first thing Omar explained when I crossed the threshold was that nothing – absolutely nothing – was for sale. However much I wanted one of the ancient Berber boxes, or the rough Saharan shields, or the amber necklaces, I was out of luck, he said.

'Is it a museum, then?' I asked.

Omar bin Mohammed clawed a hand through the scrub of grey beard on his cheek.

'My shop isn't like the others in the medina,' he said bitterly. 'The others, they're frauds. They'll eat you up, sell you their mothers.'

'Is your merchandise of higher quality, then?'

Omar blew his nose into a voluminous handkerchief and rubbed his thumbs in his eyes.

'No, no,' he said. 'All this stuff I'm selling is worthless. It may look nice to you, because you don't know. The light's bad in here. I keep it like that specially. An empty tin can would look like treasure in here. Take something away and the first time you'd realize it's rubbish is when you are home.'

'I really don't understand why you're telling me this,' I said.

Omar held his right palm out in the air.

'There's a problem,' he said. 'I have put up with it since I was a child.'

I braced myself to be petitioned for charity.

'We all have problems,' I said icily.

'You are right, we all have problems,' said Omar. 'And mine is that I can't help but tell the truth.'

'That doesn't sound like a problem. Quite the opposite, in fact.'

Omar the shopkeeper blinked hard.

'You have no idea. When you're a salesman here in the Marrakech medina, lying is the first thing you learn. Generation after generation, they pass it on. It's the secret ingredient, the foundation for a salesman's success. Lie well and you make a fortune every day. Your wife purrs like a kitten and your children walk tall with pride.'

'Can't you just pretend to lie?'

'That's it,' said Omar. 'The other shopkeepers say I'm a fool, that I should simply trick the tourists like everyone else. After all, most of them will never come back. And what are tourists for but for tricking?'

'*So*?'

'So in my shop, nothing's for sale.'

'Ah,' I said.

Omar paused, flexed his neck and smiled.

'Nothing's for sale…' he repeated. 'Instead, it's all free. Absolutely free!'

I looked at the shelves. One of the ancient Berber coffers had caught my eye. The thought of getting it for nothing was suddenly very pleasing.

'Can I have that, then?'

'Of course you can,' said Omar.

'Without charge? Can I just take it?'

'I told you,' he said, 'I give the objects away.'

'I'm so glad I came inside here.'

'I'm glad you did, too,' said the shopkeeper.

I stood up and moved over to the Berber chest. Omar encouraged me to pull back the lid, revealing a faded felt-lined interior.

'Oh, there's something I should tell you,' he said gently.

'What?'

'That to every item in here there's something attached.'

Again, I didn't quite understand.

'What's that?'

'A story.'

I glanced over at the shopkeeper and narrowed my eyes.

'Huh?'

'If you want to take an item,' he said, 'then you have to buy the story attached to it.'

Omar blinked. Then I blinked. He rubbed a hand to his face again and I pondered the arrangement. In a city where competition for tourist cash had reached fever pitch, Omar bin Mohammed had come up with a ruse like none other. He grinned hard, then strained to look meek.

'What story is attached to that chest?'

The shopkeeper thought for a moment, pinching a hand to his moustache.

'It's called "The Horseman and the Snake".'

'How much does it cost to hear it?'

'Six hundred dirhams.'

'That's forty pounds,' I said. 'The chest isn't worth that.'

'I told you, the objects I'm giving away are not special at all. The chest looks nice but it's worthless.'

'Then, why should I fork out six hundred dirhams for something of such little value?'

Omar bin Mohammed wove his fingers together and bowed them towards the floor.

'For the story,' he said.

I pulled out three high-denomination bills.

'Here's the money.'

A moment later the bills had been tucked beneath layers of clothing and the Berber chest had been wrapped in sheets of crumpled newspaper.

'It's a good choice,' said Omar.

'But I thought you said you were dealing in rubbish.'

'That chest may be rubbish,' he said, 'but "The Horseman and the Snake" is worth three times the money I'm charging you for it.'

Leaning back on his stool, Omar bin Mohammed stared into the pool of light just inside his door, and he began:

'Once upon a time,' he said, 'long ago and many days' travel from where we sit, there was a kingdom called the Land of Pots and Pans. Everyone there was happy, and everyone was prosperous, made so by their thriving business of selling pots and pans to the other kingdoms all around.'

Omar the salesman paused to pass me a glass of sweet mint tea.

'Now,' he said, 'in the Land of Pots and Pans there were all sorts of animals. There were lions and tigers and crocodiles and even kangaroos. There was every imaginable kind of animal, everything except for snakes. No one had ever seen a snake and no one had ever imagined such a creature.

'One day a woodcutter was asleep in the forest, when a long green serpent slithered up to him and slid into his open mouth and down his throat. The woodcutter woke up as the snake suffocated him. Panicking, he managed to stand up and flap his arms about, moaning as loudly as he could.

'As luck would have it, a horseman was riding by at that precise moment. He saw the woodcutter waving his arms in distress. Having come from the neighbouring land where snakes were plentiful, he realized immediately what had happened. Pulling out his whip, he leapt from his steed and began to lash the poor woodcutter's stomach with all his strength.

'The woodcutter tried to protest, but half-suffocated by the serpent and wounded from the horseman's seemingly unprovoked attack he could do nothing except fall to his knees. Displeased at the discomfort of its hiding place, the snake reversed up out of the woodcutter's throat and slithered away. When he saw that the woodcutter was out of danger, the horseman jumped back on to his mount and rode off without a word. Hailing from a land where such attacks were frequent, he didn't give the matter a second thought.

'As he caught his breath, the woodcutter began to understand what had happened, and that the horseman had attacked him in silence because time was of the essence, before the reptile had injected venom into his bloodstream.'

Omar bin Mohammed held up the Berber chest wrapped in newspaper and grinned.

'Don't forget the story,' he said. 'You may appreciate it all the more because you have paid to hear it. Allow it to move around your head; the more it does so, the more its real value will reveal itself to you.'

An hour later, I was sitting in the barber's across the street from Maison de Meknès along with my Berber chest, waiting for a storyteller to arrive. The rendezvous had been brokered by Omar bin Mohammed, before he rushed out to splurge the prized income generated by 'The Horseman and the Snake'.

Omar had exclaimed that the storyteller, called Murad, was no ordinary raconteur, but a man whose ancestors had been telling tales for twelve centuries. His pedigree was so established, Omar had said, that the man's biology had been affected in some strange and unlikely way. I had asked him to elucidate. The shopkeeper had risen up to his full height of five foot five and punched his arms out above him like pistons, baring his wrists to God.

'His body doesn't have blood like you or I have,' he boomed, 'but its veins flow instead with words!'

In true Moroccan style, the *coiffeur* thought nothing of my sitting on his threadbare couch, waiting for someone to arrive. While I was waiting, I asked if he had heard of a storyteller by the name of Murad. No sooner had he heard the name than his face lit up.

'The sound of his voice is like the singing of a thousand angels,' he said. 'Murad will hypnotize you with the stories that stream from his lips, in a waterfall of words.'

'Is he well known?' I asked.

The barber brushed one palm over the other.

'To every man, woman and child in Marrakech,' he said, gasping. 'People cry his name from the balconies of their houses and tear their hair out when he leaves their sight!'

The build-up was almost too much for me to take. I sat there, squirming in the barber's rotting couch, eager to meet the great Murad. Forty minutes passed. The barber opened a drawer below the mirror, fished about for an old CD, lathered it with shaving cream, rinsed it off. Then he blow-dried it with care and loaded it into the stereo he kept in a box under the sink. The sound of Bob Dylan's 'Tambourine Man' rang out through the streets of old Marrakech.

It was at that moment that Murad the storyteller swept in.

When I was eight years old, my father arrived home from a journey to the East with a pair of tanned leather suitcases packed full of gifts, and a stout lisping red-headed figure following behind. My childhood was full of people coming and going. Most of the time I never quite knew who any of them were. As far as I could understand, they were a human stew, a jumble of all people, who came because my father was there.

The red-headed man with the lisp moved into an attic room, from where he would appear from time to time and tell stories. I don't remember his name now, or quite where he came from. I used to like to think my father had found him in some distant land and coaxed him to return to our home near Tunbridge Wells.

Over the months he stayed, the red-head revealed to us some of the great characters of Arabian folklore. He lisped his way through dozens of tales from *A Thousand and One Nights*, then moved on to stories from other collections lesser known in the West – such as *Antar wa Abla* and the *Assemblies of Al Hariri*. A child's mind pieces things together in a way that makes perfect sense, creating a kind of story from fragments overheard. We assumed that the portly red-headed figure was there to entertain us. And he was. But as the years have passed, I have come to understand that the man had been brought as a sort of tutor as well.

Each one of his stories was chosen for the inner properties contained within it. Like the peach, the story was the delicious meat, which allows the nugget in the middle to be passed on and eventually be sowed. Every day, the red-headed man would sit in our playroom at the top of the house, with my sisters and me. Sometimes our friends would be there, too, clustered round. When we were all listening, the lisping voice would begin.

Of all the stories he told, the one that took root the deepest was 'The Water of Paradise'.

Long ago, a Bedouin shepherd was crossing the vast expanse of the Southern Desert, when he noticed one of his sheep licking at the sand. The shepherd staggered over and, to his great surprise, he found a spring. He bent down and tasted its water. No sooner had his tongue touched one drop than he realized that this was no ordinary water. It was the most delicious liquid imaginable, even more perfect than any refreshment experienced in his dreams.

The shepherd drank a little more, before coming to understand the grave duty before him. As a humble subject of the great Harun ar-Rachid, it fell to him to take a gift of the water to the caliph himself.

Having filled his most reliable water skin with the Water of Paradise, the shepherd entrusted his flock to his brother and set off across the dunes towards Baghdad. After many days of struggle and thirst, he arrived at the gates of the palace. The royal guards pushed him away at first, threatening to hack off his head for wasting their time. But he pleaded, held up the water bottle and shouted, 'I have a gift for the caliph. It is the Water of Paradise.'

The great gate of the palace opened a crack and the Bedouin shepherd was pulled in. Before he knew it, he was crouching in the throne room at the feet of Harun ar-Rachid himself. While minions scurried about attending to their duties, the caliph demanded to know why the shepherd had come.

Holding out the putrid water bottle, the Bedouin said, 'Your Majesty, I am a simple man from the inner expanse of the Southern Desert. I have never known luxury, not until now. While herding my sheep, I came to understand that we had happened upon the most delicious liquid on the earth. Our fathers and forefathers have spoken of it, but none has ever tasted it. Not until now. Your Majesty, Your Magnificence, I present you this, the Water of Paradise.'

Harun ar-Rachid clicked his fingers and a solid gold cup was borne forth on a jewel-encrusted tray. He gave a nod towards the water skin and a finely dressed servant snatched the skin and poured a few drops into the royal cup. A bodyguard tasted the liquid first and, when he did not fall to the ground, the goblet was passed to the caliph.

Harun pressed its rim to his lips, sniffed and then tasted the Water of Paradise. The shepherd and all the courtiers leaned forward in anxious anticipation. Harun ar-Rachid, the Commander of Day and Night, said nothing. After several minutes of silence, the grand vizier bowed until his mouth was a fraction of an inch from the caliph's ear.

'Shall we chop off his head, Your Magnificence?'

Harun stroked a hand over his chin.

He thanked the shepherd for the gift and whispered a secret instruction to his vizier.

'Have him taken back to his flock under the cover of darkness,' he said, 'and on the way neither let him see the mighty Tigris River, nor taste the sweet water that we find so ordinary. Then present him with a thousand pieces of gold, and tell him that he and his progeny are appointed guardians of the Water of Paradise.'

From: *In Arabian Nights*

Balkh

ONE NIGHT WHEN Nasrudin was coming home from the teahouse he spotted something at the side of the road – a huge strongbox. Excited, he opened it up and found a fabulous treasure.

Bursting into laughter, he slapped his thigh, then walked on.

'When will Providence stop trying to test me in such an obvious way?' he mumbled to himself.

*

Until the aftermath of 9/11, the name 'Afghanistan' was rarely spoken in the West.

Overnight, everything changed.

Newspapers and TV networks were plastered with maps of the war-torn country, along with descriptions of its geography and culture. I remember hearing that the United States was going after Bin Laden in the Tora Bora cave complex with 'bunker-busting' bombs, and reflecting on what my father and grandfather would have made of it all.

For three-quarters of a century, our family had droned on about Afghanistan. In 1927, my grandfather published his first book on the country – *Afghanistan of the Afghans* –

in which he did his level best to package a description of the kingdom for the Occidental world. Throughout his life, he published books and articles about his homeland. Having eloped to the Hindu Kush with him, my Scottish-born grandmother followed suit – writing dozens of articles about Afghan culture and folklore, as well as penning two travel books, *My Khyber Marriage* and *Valley of the Giant Buddhas*.

My father continued the mission, writing masses on Afghanistan, as though his life depended on it – doubling and redoubling his efforts when the Russians surged across the border on Christmas Eve 1979. Delving deep into centuries of ancestral folklore and knowhow, he churned out a best-selling novel, *Kara Kush*.

Stretching to twelve hundred pages in manuscript form, the book was a veritable instruction manual on Afghanistan. One morning when I asked him how the book was going, he wagged a finger at me.

'I'm not writing a book,' he said.

'But you're typing away day and night.'

'Yes, but it's not a book that I'm creating.'

'What is it, then?'

'A horse.'

'Huh?'

'A Trojan Horse!'

The way my father saw it, the West had to be informed about the war in Afghanistan, but educated through Oriental thinking. Only then, he would tell us, would people fully understand what was going on.

So, fashioning a Trojan Horse from paragraphs and lines, he packed it with information that would be ingested along with the story.

'When you want to tell a child something,' he said, 'the best way to do it is not by telling it to them straight out. Most of the time they'll listen and then forget, or not listen at all. If you want it to get through, rooted in their subconscious, there's only one way to do it.'

'How, Baba?'

'By giving them a story.'

The story my father spun from the threads of Afghan folklore told of a massive treasure, hidden somewhere in the mountains:

The lost treasure of Ahmed Shah Durrani.

When *Kara Kush* was launched in 1986, it was a runaway success.

My father was pleased – not because he'd turned himself into a best-selling novelist, but because he had succeeded in creating the ultimate Trojan Horse.

Three years later – nine years since its invasion – the Russian military machine withdrew back across the border, having been routed, just as my father maintained it would be right from the start.

By the time US forces began storming Tora Bora with their bunker-busting bombs, my family had single-handedly written more books on Afghanistan than any other in the Western world. My grandfather, grandmother, father, and aunt were responsible for showing the country to the outside world in a way it would understand. Shortly before the 9/11 atrocities, my sister, Saira, made her award-winning documentary, *Beneath the Veil*.

A full five years after the first bunker-busting bombs were dropped at Tora Bora, I arrived in Kabul with my Swedish film crew from Caravan Film.

I had arrived there for a thousand reasons.

At the top of the list was to continue the tradition of showing Afghanistan from the inside out. At the same time, I longed to find Nasrudin in the land of my forefathers, and to observe the country through the lens of the wise fool.

We set ourselves what seemed to be an obvious task: to locate the massive lost treasure of Ahmed Shah – valued at $520 billion.

Landing at Kabul Airport early in 2006, we were enthusiastic, although a little less than usual, having been locked up for sixteen days in a torture jail while doing pre-production in Pakistan.

Medieval to the core, Afghanistan doesn't run along the lines to which most other countries ultimately conform. An enchanted realm of preposterously back-to-front behaviour, it's like nowhere else. On my search for the lost treasure of Ahmed Shah, I was constantly exposed to Nasrudin.

He was everywhere – in caravanserais and teahouses, on buses and in bazaars, walking over mountains and along streams.

Spend time in Afghanistan and you find yourself wishing everywhere else could be like it, at least some of the time. Because in the Land of Nasrudin anything is possible, except of course the probable.

Crisscrossing the country, I took with me a caged hoopoe. A storyteller in Kabul had informed me that only a man carrying one – the favourite bird of King Solomon – had a hope of finding the treasure of Ahmed Shah. When the hoard was near, he revealed, the hoopoe would sing.

Over weeks, I followed all kinds of clues, working with leads laid down by my father and grandfather – searching frantically for a hollowed-out mountain, where they both hinted the treasure lay.

From the moment I reached Kabul, it dawned on me that mounting a quest for the lost treasure of Ahmed Shah was possibly an act of foolishness worthy of Nasrudin.

At a time at which the Americans and their allies were dropping bunker-busting bombs with reckless abandon, I was roaming the country, caged hoopoe in hand, hunting for a cave system in which the treasure might be hidden.

One of the first destinations on a journey of spectacular danger was Balkh, in northern Afghanistan. It was there that Alexander the Great built his capital, while planning an advance into India… an advance that never came.

By the time I arrived at Balkh, it was a backwater in the shadow of nearby Mazar-i-Sharif. Although gracious, the locals were uneasy at finding a film crew searching for a lost treasure – as though fearing our mission might somehow end in an airstrike.

On our first night, the owner of the *chaikhana* in which we were staying came over with a scrap of paper as I got ready for bed.

'I do not know about the treasure,' he said, 'but my

brother-in-law does. When I told him what you are looking for, he wrote down these instructions. If you leave Balkh early, you may reach the place by dusk.'

Taking hold of the scrap, I gave thanks, and heard a voice in my head pronounce a favourite Afghan expression, 'Send the fool another mile!'

Being the fool, I gave the order for the film crew to rise early, so we might leave at dawn.

By dusk the next day, we were far from Balkh.

Despite the distance, I could hear the owner of the teahouse and his extended family hooting with joy at ridding themselves of their perilous guests.

Being so far off the beaten track, I was on edge, and suggested we spend the night at a little village reached by crossing fields on foot.

No people on earth welcome travellers as Afghans do. A throwback to an ancient time, the hospitality extended is part of a code of honour binding man to man.

The village was far too small and too remote to have a teahouse. So, seeing us approach over the fields, a farmer took us in. His head was crowned in a voluminous turban, his long broad form wrapped up in a sheepskin coat.

Before we knew it, his family were fussing over us. They moved out of their wattle and daub home, insisting we stay there as long as we wished.

That evening, the villagers came together. Slaughtering

a sheep, they brought out a carpet usually reserved for weddings, and burned precious paraffin in their lamps.

We presented gifts, then feasted under a full moon and a bewitching canopy of stars. A truly enormous pilau was served, with great chunks of mutton buried in it. As we gorged ourselves, I pondered how best to bring up the quest of the lost treasure.

Every time I framed a sentence enquiring about it in my mind, the farmer would coax me to eat more.

After the meal, the villagers filed away into the darkness, against the strains of a donkey braying as though the end of the world had come.

Ascending a rickety wooden ladder at the side of the adobe building, I climbed up onto the roof. Tilting my head back, I viewed the heavens, the full moon at their heart.

Little by little, my view ranged downwards, taking in a chain of hills lost in shadow. Nestled among them was a small lake, the moon reflecting over its surface in a sheet of silver light.

In the morning, I climbed up onto the roof again and peered down at the lake. Sapphire blue, it was supremely secretive and mysterious.

When the farmer joined me on the roof, I remarked how fortunate the villagers were to have such a fine lake so close.

'It must be wonderful for fishing,' I said.

To my surprise, the farmer replied that it was not.

'We don't drink its water, or fish in it,' he said.

'Really? Well, I'm sure you swim in it in the summer at least.'

'No, we don't.'

'Is it poisoned, or contaminated with a dangerous substance?'

'No.'

'But then, if it's not causing offence to ask, why do you not take advantage of such a fine-looking water source?'

The farmer pressed his hands together.

'There's a reason,' he said, 'a reason which explains what you're asking. It sometimes sounds strange to those who have not heard it before.'

'I'm intrigued,' I replied.

The farmer invited me back down to ground level, where breakfast was waiting along with a handful of villagers. I got the feeling he hoped I would forget about the lake.

'Would you tell me the reason?' I prompted.

The farmer conferred with the others.

'You will not believe us if we tell you,' he said.

'I promise to believe you, even if I do not,' I replied, in a curiously stupid sentence.

Again, the villagers conferred.

'Very well,' the farmer said, his expression grave. 'We will tell you why we do not use the lake.'

I listened intently, and this is what the farmer said:

'When people go into the water, they become the other person who goes in with them. They look the same in every way, but their minds are switched over.'

'Oh,' I said. 'I wouldn't have guessed that.'

The villagers seemed pleased the situation had been explained.

'Now you understand,' the farmer's brother said.

'Yes I do, and then again, no I don't. You see, if someone who goes in the water becomes the person in there with them, why don't you just go in one at a time?'

The farmer nodded.

'The water simply remembers who was in it last. So the person who goes in will become the last person who went in.'

'A delayed reaction?'

'Yes.'

'It doesn't just affect swimming,' a villager called out. 'It even happens when you go fishing, wash there, or fill a bucket with water.'

'How does the water taste?' I asked.

The villagers shook their heads.

'We don't know. None of us have ever drunk it because we will become one another.'

'But how do you know all this?'

The farmer conferred with his brother, and then all the villagers talked together.

'No one told us,' one of them said. 'We've always known it, just as our parents and grandparents did.'

'One last question...' I said. 'What happened to the very first person who went in the water? If they were the first person, surely they weren't swapped with someone else.'

Again, the villagers conferred.

'Even though he's long dead, he must be in a kind of limbo.'

I motioned something to one of our team and he gave a thumbs up.

'Would you mind if we do an experiment?' I asked.

'What kind of experiment?'

'Would you allow me to go down to the lake with my colleague who is sitting over there, and both touch it at the same time?'

The farmer whispered to his brother, and his brother whispered to the others.

'You are welcome, but we warn you of the danger.'

'I will take the risk in the name of science,' I replied.

As the sun rose over the valley, the film crew and I, followed by the villagers, streamed down to the lake.

The body of water was even more striking by day than by night, so much so I was at a loss for words. On the way down to it, we passed children running back and forth to gather water from a far-off stream.

The villagers held back from getting too close, fearful of being splashed. The director of our film crew and I wended our way down to the edge of the lake. Even before we were close we could see the fish darting through the clear water.

The farmer held up a hand.

'You are our honoured guests,' he said. 'Please don't continue, as you will become one another!'

'It's a risk we are prepared to take,' I replied. 'In any case, there's something I haven't told you. We may be brave but even we are not going to dare touch the water without protection.'

Fumbling in my shirt pocket, I pulled out a loop of green nylon parachute cord. The crew's director did the same.

In time with one another, we put them around our necks.

'These cords are amulets which will protect us,' I explained.

'Are you sure?' someone called out.

'Yes, we are absolutely certain.'

With the villagers watching us in trepidation, we took off our shoes and socks, and stepped into the lake.

'Have you become each other?' one of them cried out.

We shook our heads.

'It takes time to happen,' the farmer mumbled knowingly.

'We will wait,' I said.

So we waited and waited, until our feet were wrinkly, and our bodies were frozen to the bone.

After two hours of waiting, the villagers asked again.

'We are still ourselves,' we both said.

'The amulets are strong,' the farmer's brother muttered. 'Where did you get them?'

'From an astrologer in Kabul,' I replied.

On hearing the news the villagers seemed sorrowful. Kabul was too far, and even if any of them went there, none had money with which to buy amulets.

'How many of you live in the village?' I asked, as I dried my feet.

The farmer counted on his fingers.

'There are sixty-three of us, including the children.'

I thanked God.

'That's exactly the number of amulets we have.'

The farmer's brother broke into a grin.

'But do they all have the same power over the lake?' one of the villagers called out.

'Oh, yes, yes… they're all exactly like the one I'm wearing.'

Once back in the village, I raced over the fields, made sixty-three loops as quickly as I could, and was soon back at the farmer's house.

Giving thanks for the hospitality, I turned to the farmer, as the villagers clustered around.

'By the same power that gave our amulets their strength,' I said, 'the astrologer in Kabul foresaw us coming here to your village. He knew there were sixty-three of you, and so he sent that number of amulets.'

I passed over the loops.

'There's a chance that they'll wear out,' I went on, 'or that you will need more when children are born. If that happens, there's a solution. Before we left the astrologer in Kabul, he turned a very long piece of the same material into an amulet.'

I pulled a two-hundred-foot roll of green parachute cord out from my daypack. 'Whenever you need one of the amulets, all you have to do is to make a loop and give it to whoever you like.'

The villagers appeared overcome with joy.

'The astrologer has strong magic,' stated the farmer's brother.

'Yes he does,' I replied. 'So strong in fact, that he added another spell to the amulets. If they're used by everyone in the village they have an extra power.'

'What is it?' asked someone at the back.

'Well, if you all wear the amulets, and go down to the lake every day, and use it for drinking water, fishing and swimming, you'll break the spell of the jinn that guards the lake. If you do so, by the next full moon none of you will need to ever wear amulets again.'

From: *Travels With Nasrudin*

Inca Trail Warriors

IT WAS WELL below freezing as I stumbled out of my tent into the blackness, a torch in one hand, a soggy roll of loo paper in the other.

With the night to cloak me, I went in search of a patch of field in which to purge my faltering digestive tract. Within a week I'd ripened from headstrong adventurer with a quest, to incontinent wreck.

I had arrived in Lima with the intention of picking up the trail to the elusive Birdmen, whoever they might be. I had no idea where the path might lead, or the hazards which might line its route. My *modus operandi* was to forge ahead, quizzing anyone and everyone for scraps of information. Looking back, I can only marvel that I embarked on such a long journey with so little in the way of concrete data. But, in hindsight, this lack of research may have been my greatest asset.

Weighted down instead with equipment, I made a beeline to the ancient city of Cusco. From there I signed up for the Inca Trail, the trek across the mountains to Machu Picchu. The Incas' most sacred city seemed the obvious place to pick up the trail in search for the Birdmen of Peru.

The four-day hike was described by my guidebook as 'ten times harsher than Everest'. Waving it off as no more than a piffling stroll, I had thrust my trekking pole into the dirt. A man with as much gear as me, I mused, was surely unstoppable.

Since my rendezvous with Deiches, I'd read what little I could find regarding flight in antiquarian times. The line between myth and fact was clouded in uncertainty. Cold hard facts were few and far between. I scrutinized the more reputable ancient texts, hunting for clues.

I read of a man named Ki Kung Shi who supposedly built a chariot with wings in the reign of Chinese Emperor Ch'eng T'ang, eighteen centuries before the birth of Christ. The chariot looked rather like a paddle steamer. Another source recorded that two thousand years ago, in the Chinese kingdom of Ki-Kuang (its people, supposedly, had one arm and three eyes each), flying machines were common. And, in Ancient Greece, Archytas of Tarentum, a friend of Plato, had constructed a wooden dove. When it flew it became one of the wonders of the ancient world.

Dig deep in folklore and you start unearthing examples of primitive flight. Most test the boundaries of belief. Danish legends tell of flying sun chariots over Trundholm two millennia ago; the Indian epics Ramayana and Mahabharata contain references to flight – the most famous being the Zeppelin-like *Vimana* aircraft. Zimbabwe had 'towers of the flight'; the Maoris had a tradition of flying-men, as did the English, beginning with King Bladud.

For some reason the notion of Incan flight shone more brightly for me than all the rest. Perhaps because the empire of the Incas rose at a time when a few scientists and free-thinkers in Europe were working on the idea of flight. Roger Bacon, Leonardo Da Vinci and others gave serious thought to the problem of sustaining a man's weight in air. But they were lampooned for using hammers and nails rather than magic, alchemy, and other accepted tools of the time.

*

ON THE THIRD night on the Inca Trail, after a suspect bowl of stewed *cuy*, which we know as guinea pig, I asked the guide, Patricia, if she had heard whether the Incas flew. A sensitive woman with deep-set eyes and an infectious smile, she'd laughed at my question. Only when I declared that I wasn't joking did she become more serious. Like many Peruvians I quizzed, she was capable of extraordinary perception in esoteric matters. And, as with many others, she had a nugget of information to pass on.

'When my grandfather was a young man in Urubamba,' she said, stirring her guinea pig goulash to cool it, 'he was walking in the woods near his home. At the foot of a tall tree he came across a young condor. Its wing had been broken. Taking pity on it, my grandfather gave the bird a little meat. He took it home, where he cared for it through the winter. After many weeks, when it had recovered, he let it go free.'

Patricia slurped her stew and stared into the camp fire.

'From that day on he had wild, vivid dreams,' she said. 'He dreamt he was an Inca flying, gliding through the empty sky... he dreamt he was part-condor, part-man, a man from ancient times.'

*

By the time I had struggled back to my tent from the lavatory field, Patricia was ready to leave. It was just before three a.m. She supervised the porters, two of whom had been assigned to haul my luggage across the passes to Machu Picchu.

Laden down with non-essential knick-knacks, I limped forward on bleeding feet. I cursed myself for giving in to the salesman's tempting merchandise – and I damned Deiches. If it hadn't been for him, I would have been tucked up at home dreaming of adventure. The porters scuttled ahead under the weight of survival gear, their sandals biting into the granite-paved path. All around us the jungle slept.

Patricia told me to keep a look out for *Cuscomys ashaninka*, a new genus of mammal, the size of a domestic cat, which had been discovered in the hills for the first time a few days before. But I was in no mood for nature. I inched forward through the darkness, my hand on Patricia's shoulder, like a gas victim from a forgotten war.

Four hours later, the undergrowth appeared to know that dawn was near. The food chain had woken and was hungry. In what was a consummate ceremony of breakfasting, one creature would become an early meal for another with wider jaws.

A thousand birds nudged about in the foliage, restless to take flight. Each nest sheltered a clutch of mouths waiting to be fed. Darkness lifted by gradual degrees, although there was still no real light. At last the first shades of cypress and olive green came to life.

The track had levelled out, and was now clearly visible. I responded by moving faster, bounding across the neatly fitting flagstones. A thermometer, distress whistle, and signalling mirror clattered from my jacket, like tools hanging from an astronaut's suit.

Turning a sharp bend, I was struck dumb by the view. Stretching out ahead was a valley. At its centre lay the ruins of a city. The valley was like no other I have ever witnessed, just as the city itself has no equal. The colours, the shadows and the sense of secrecy were bewitching.

I rested there at Intipunku, the Gate of the Sun, before starting the short walk down into the ruins. The air, which had shed its nocturnal blanket, smelled of fennel, although I could not see that aromatic herb growing among the smooth-edged granite stones. As I descended, the first fragment of dawn rose out over the dark peaks, giving them colour. No more than a glow of light at first but, as the moments passed, the glow transformed into a bolt of gold. I watched transfixed and, as I did so, it struck the ancient ruins of Machu Picchu.

The Spanish ravaged the Incan kingdom, stripping away its riches. But they missed this, the greatest jewel of all. Before walking the Inca Trail I had wondered how the sacred city could have eluded the Conquistadors. Far too steep for their horses, the trail – supposedly the original route of pilgrimage – appears to lead nowhere. Only after four days of hiking across mountain passes do you reach the city itself. The elusive path had kept the Incas' secret safe.

Current thinking says that Machu Picchu was probably deserted before the Conquistadors arrived. Some experts say it was abandoned after a plague; others that the religious centre may have moved elsewhere.

The American scholar Hiram Bingham is credited with rediscovering Machu Picchu. Leading a Yale University team to the site in July 1911, he claimed to have found the Incan stronghold of Vilcabamba. A historian rather than an archaeologist, Bingham knew how to put together an expedition and his team was remarkably well equipped. When I read his book *Inca Land*, I wondered if he'd visited the same mountaineering shop as me. The inventory of his equipment suggested that superior salesmen had been at work.

Bingham's gear included: a mummery tent with pegs and poles, a hypsometer, a mountain-mercurial barometer, two Watkins aneroid barometers, a pair of Zeiss glasses, two 3A Kodak cameras, six films, a sling psychrometer, a prismatic compass and clinometer, a Stanley pocket level, an eighty-foot red-strand mountain rope, three ice axes, a seven-foot flagpole with an American flag and a Yale University flag, four Silver's self-heating cans of Irish Stew, a cake of chocolate, eight hardtack biscuits, as well as raisins, sugar cubes and mock-turtle soup.

Gazing down across the valley, it was hard to imagine that until Bingham's arrival Machu Picchu was lost in jungle. The canopy of trees which had hidden and protected the sacred city for centuries has long since been hacked down. Modern times have brought mod cons in abundance, paving the way for the tourist bandwagon. The most notable additions were an exclusive hotel and the railway, which runs from the nearby town of Aguas Calientes down to Cusco. Each year brings newer and more costly comforts. The latest idea is to build a cable car which will ferry even more tourists up to the sacred city from the valley floor.

But for two hours each morning, Machu Picchu belongs to the weary, stomach-clutching legion of Inca Trail warriors. The ruins are deserted and lie silent. For those who have staggered over the passes, the reward is like slipping into Disneyland before the gates open. You have a chance to breathe deeply, to soak up the textures, and to absorb the lack of human sound. But then, on the dot of nine, as if some invisible gong has been struck, the first of a thousand tourist coaches winds its way up the hairpin bends to Machu Picchu. Within moments, the turnstiles are spinning, the flush toilets are churning, and soft drinks fizzing, as the seething mass of Banana Republic explorers descends.

Tour groups, speaking every language in the world, crisscross the place like spiders weaving a giant web. Stubbing out their duty-free cigarettes underfoot, rubbing sun cream into their wrinkles, troop after troop of khaki-clothed tourists hustles forward, desperate to get their money's worth in this, the greatest archaeological theme park on earth.

*

ON THE WESTERN edge of Machu Picchu, we came across a group of seven Eastern Europeans, clustered around a curiously shaped granite block. The tourists, dressed in matching lilac robes, were barefoot, except for one woman who was wearing purple moonboots. They were chanting some kind of invocation. Patricia frowned, then shook her head woefully.

'They are always doing this,' she said.

'Who?'

'Those purple people. They come from Poland and think they are Incas. They come to take power from the Intihuatana, the Sacred Stone.'

We watched as the Poles, their palms pressed against the granite surface and their eyes tightly closed, sapped the rock's energy.

'What's so sacred about that stone?'

'The Incas used to tie the sun to it,' said Patricia. 'It proved their power over nature. When the Spanish found those special stones, they broke them up. I wish this one could be broken,' she said, her voice rasping with anger, 'then maybe the Polish people would go away.'

Soon after, Patricia's wish was granted. The sacred stone was crushed to bits during the filming of a beer commercial.

Without wasting time Patricia led me from the holy rock, down through the terraced ruins, pointing out the principal buildings along the way.

Since Bingham, every generation has dreamed up new theories to explain the ruined city. Experts have claimed it was a fortress, a private *hacienda*, a nunnery, centre of learning or religion, even an observatory.

'Look at this place,' Patricia said, sweeping her arm in an arc over a bluff of rocks, 'this is called the Temple of the Condor.'

I entered the shrine.

'To me it does look like a temple dedicated to birds,' said Patricia. 'See here, how the wings of the condor are represented by the rock. And here, how the image of a condor has been carved from a piece of granite.'

The guide wiped her neck with her hand. 'But has it got anything to do with birds at all?'

'What do you mean?'

'Bingham thought it was the prison, where convicts were chained up or killed,' she said. 'Others have said it's a princess's tomb, a kitchen, or a place where maize was stored.'

I stepped out of the way as a river of retired Israelis flooded in. Before we knew it they were upon us. We held our ground. The Israeli leader, waving a pink flag – embroidered with the legend *Moses Basket Tours* – was a force to be reckoned with. He spewed out a couple of lines about the temple, clapped his hands signalling for photography to begin, clapped again, and led the way to the Temple of the Rainbow.

Every three minutes another wave of white-skinned, blue-rinsed retirees splashed in, and swirled around us. Between the waves, I made a hurried inspection of the sanctuary. The form of the condor was blatantly obvious, lying outstretched on the floor, its wings writhing behind, and its beak lurching ahead. This was no prison block or princess's tomb, but quite obviously a shrine dedicated to flight.

Patricia pointed out the groove in the bird's ruff, where sacrificial llama blood might once have run. A rush of energy gripped me as the next swell of Israelis surged into the cove. Surely this, the Temple of the Condor, was connected to the Birdmen?

Patricia noticed my particular interest in this shrine.

'Why are you so interested in birds?' she asked, scrunching her cheeks into a smile.

'I have heard that the Incas glided over the jungles,' I said.

'They may have done so,' Patricia said. 'But you don't understand.'

'Understand, what?'

'You are thinking of the flight itself, which is meaningless,' she said. 'And, you're missing the real question.'

I paused, as another wave of tourists hurled themselves into the temple. A moment later they were gone.

'What is the *real* meaning, the *real* question?'

Patricia ran her fingers across the stylized stone wing of the condor.

'Whether the Incas flew or not is irrelevant,' she said. 'Instead, you must ask why they wanted to fly.'

Reflecting on Patricia's words, I recalled that, on a trip to Mexico, I had once come across a *fiesta* in the small Yucatan town of Ticul. The highlight of the festival was a ceremony, called Volador. It's said to have been started by the Aztecs. Three men, guised as birds, with papier-mâché beaks and feathered robes, leapt off a miniature platform at the top of a towering pole. Each had a cord tied to his ankles, which had been wound around the pole. As the men vaulted from the platform, they swung round and round, unwinding as they flew.

A Mexican friend told me that Volador represented freedom, and the devotion of man to God. For years I had puzzled over this. But it helped me to understand why the Incas might have wanted to fly. It wasn't about getting from A to B. It was about something far more fundamental, far more spectacular.

The Incas could have had no need to use flight as a means of transport. Such a thing would surely have trivialized what they considered to be a sacred medium. Yet they must have had good reason for yearning to glide, to soar free in the air. Perhaps, like the condor, the Incan Birdmen were messengers to the Gods.

Two hours later I was perched up on the summit of Huayna Picchu, the sugar-loaf peak which overlooks the ancient city. The climb is strenuous, especially when you have a bout of the runs. Crawling on my hands and knees up the sheer faces of stone, I began to wish that I'd stayed with Patricia. I had left her in the café down below, with a plate of roasted guinea pig.

Staring out across the valley, down to the Urubamba River, was invigorating beyond words. The light was now a syrupy yellow, bright yet not harsh. A chill wind ripped through my hair, whistling between the crags. I yelled at the top of my voice. But no one heard me. Then, like a cat stuck in a tree, I peeped down at the ruins. The lack of safety devices was unnerving, but at the same time exhilarating. One slip of the heel and Huayna Picchu would have embraced another victim.

The rush of the wind was telling me to thrust away from the rock and jump.

'You will fly! You will fly!' it called.

'But I have no wings. It'll be suicide.'

'Make a canopy,' urged the wind. 'With a sail streaming above you, you'll glide down to earth.'

I closed my eyes and sensed the current of air on my face. Then I breathed in deeply.

'Trust me, and I will protect you… I will hold you as you fly.'

I opened my eyes a crack, and began to understand the significance of Machu Picchu. Stretching out in symmetrical flanks, on east and west, the ruins were arranged as wings. Once I saw them, I couldn't get them out of my mind. They gleamed up at me, glinting in the yellow light.

Machu Picchu was laid out in the shape of a condor.

I would have slithered my way back down to the café much sooner, but a refined-looking Peruvian man was watching me.

'It's a condor!' I shouted. 'Machu Picchu's a gigantic condor!'

The man was dressed in a sheepskin jacket, with the flaps of a woollen hat pulled down snugly over his ears. His nose was streaming, and his cheeks were scarlet. In his hands was a tin, and in it were coca leaves.

'The condor is the messenger,' he said in English, offering me some of the leaves.

'Whose messenger?'

Resting the tin on his knee, the man washed his hands over his face.

'The condor links us to heaven,' he said. 'Just as it did the Incas. It is the bridge, the bridge between man and God.'

'Could the Incas glide like condors?'

The man twisted the corners of his mouth into a smile.

'We can all fly,' he said.

'*All* of us?'

The man nodded.

'*Sí*, all of us.'

He paused, to regard me sideways on.

'*Todos tenemos alas*, we all have wings,' he said, 'but we have forgotten how to use them.'

From: *Trail of Feathers*

In a Shrunken World

PEOPLE OFTEN SAY the world has become very small.

By that, I always assume they're referring to travel and communication. After all, venturing to the most obscure places on the planet – or communicating with them – has been made ridiculously easy.

A century ago no one would have been heard moaning that it had taken an hour longer than expected to fly from London to Tokyo. Or that you'd been stuck for a few minutes in a tunnel under the English Channel.

Back then, few could have dreamt of a day when racing from London to Berlin for lunch would not only be conceivable, but affordable, too.

Until relatively recently, most societies had little or no interaction with others far away. Indeed, until a couple of centuries ago, almost no one ever ventured beyond the borders of the territories in which they lived.

A few intrepid explorers did reach far-flung lands, of course, and lived to tell the tale to a wide-eyed audience. Bringing with them strange new fabrics, fruit, or exotic spices, they would have wowed those around them.

In our time, in which just about anything and everything is freely available, it's challenging to conceive how things must have been in our great-grandparents' time.

Imagine, for instance, that in Georgian England, pineapples were so rare that the well-to-do would rent one for the evening – not to eat, but to show off to their friends.

A century ago, the vile onslaught of the Great War led to the opening up of cultures on a monumental scale – far more than had ever taken place throughout human history. European nations and the United States, began influencing not only the lands bordering them, but others on the far side of the globe – on a mass scale.

As regions such as the Indian subcontinent, the Middle East, and Africa increased their exposure to the world outside their own borders, there was a direct influence on their societies, and on their ancient cultural systems as well. Newly introduced products and ideas had an irreversible effect – from Buenos Aires to Bangkok.

A profound knock-on effect took place, as the prevailing winds of change tore through great cities, towns, villages, and hamlets. All of a sudden, it was possible to buy a Savile Row suit in Mexico City, Swiss clocks in Vladivostok, or indeed a pineapple in Bradford.

Within Britain's Victorian age, all areas of life witnessed monumental change and upheaval. With a plethora of goods and services to supply, its mighty empire sought to recalibrate the world. As it did so, it ended up being transformed as well – influenced by immigrants and their unfamiliar ways of life.

Change ripped across each continent in turn, forcing fragile societies that had been isolated for thousands of years to adapt or be relegated to extinction – as so many inevitably were.

They say history is written by the victors.

More fundamentally, it's written by those whose cultures endure, rather than be annihilated.

Through the readings in this book, we'll see how certain civilizations have boomed, while others have had their ancient cultural heritage diluted, and destroyed.

The Gond tribe of Central India, for instance, the indigenous Ainu of Japan, and the so-called 'Kafirs' of Afghanistan: each was compelled to abandon traditions and beliefs that had evolved through centuries.

The enduring mantra of the time was very much one of 'adapt or die'.

In the northern Japanese island of Hokkaido, the few pure Ainu that remain were forced to abandon antique ways of life – tailored to their individual circumstances. As has taken place with ubiquitous regularity, the new realm decreed that one size and shape of culture fits all.

Similarly, the Gonds of Central India were driven from their lands, destined to become inferior, eking out a living at the margins of society. And, as in the case of some ancient Kafir tribes, they were dispossessed, left with little choice but to sell traditional carvings to tourists.

Parallels can be drawn between such people as the Gonds, the Ainu, and the Kafirs. We will see how each culture was once autonomous, self-reliant, and calibrated to the place where they resided.

Such societies had no need for the world beyond the frontier, or the trappings of its commercialization. But, as secluded communities fell under the jurisdiction of others, and as bureaucracy developed, they were stripped of their own systems of regulation and control.

The increased interaction between people of different nations leads to complexities on all fronts. With conflict the name of the game, it became necessary to establish legislative systems to preside over cases with foreign elements.

At the same time, enslaved people shipped to the New World in their millions did their best to cling on to indigenous beliefs. These convictions, reflected through faiths, were influenced by fresh environments. The philosophies of First Nations melded with the principles of certain West African secret societies, to create extraordinary new hybrids, such as 'Macumba'.

Dance, music, and other key cultural constituents travelled westwards with the human cargo, forcibly transported to the New World. Having reached their destination, they continued to develop.

Spurred on substantially by the rise in technology, the last century has brought riches to a select few, just as it's robbed many more of their culture, work, and land. Many countries, such as some in the Arab world, benefited – at least on the surface. All of a sudden there was a value in the unseen wealth lying beneath the sands they'd roamed for an eternity.

At its height, an Arab caliphate stretched the width of Africa, and across much of Asia, lasting for centuries.

In that time, it produced some of the most magnificent architecture, literature, and art of any civilization.

But even the greatest empire eventually comes to an end.

Within Europe, the great Islamic dominion of the so-called 'Golden Age' eventually broke up. The Moors, who had ruled the Iberian Peninsula for more than seven centuries, were defeated. Those not expelled were driven into subservience. Converting on pain of death, these *Moriscos* ('Little Moors') endured. Against extraordinary odds, some even managed to continue their Islamic beliefs in secret, and even produced a considerable body of literature.

Now that communication has become faster and easier, we are informed about cultures from every corner of the earth. But, rather than merely observing them – in books, documentaries, and online – we must learn about them in a deep-down way. By studying their ancient methods, we have a hope of solving the problems we ourselves face.

Our society is riddled with trials and tribulations of all kinds – predicaments and problems that are endemic in all the lands we have influenced and changed.

The papers in *Cultural Research* illustrate a sense and sensibility that we've lost but can and *must* re-learn. Through reading of the experiences of others, we can understand our own society and seek answers, not only to our own problems, but to those of the wider world.

From: *Cultural Research*

India Considered

I LIKE TO think of a travelling life as a mosaic pattern, the kind that adorns the fountains in the rambling Moroccan labyrinth that has been my home through the last dozen years and more.

Observed from a distance, it is a study in gentle and serene elegance.

Different colours, interwoven shapes and varying motifs, conjuring an expression of beauty that tantalizes one's sight, as the sound of trickling water soothes the soul.

But draw in closer, and the effect changes.

As one nears, inch by inch, a secret world is revealed.

A world formed from detail.

The tiniest fragments of mosaic, shaped with absolute skill, form patterns and sub-patterns, like the strokes made by an artist's brush.

I am enchanted by the mastery of the mosaic makers. I love to observe how each individual fragment has been cleaved into the perfect outline, so that it lies snug with the others around it.

In the way that I perceive the world, the mosaics themselves are the journeys I have made. They are the countries my feet have traversed. The experiences that have in their own way fashioned me deep-down, from the inside out.

But, stare at the mosaic fountain long enough, and you begin to distinguish another layer... a dimension that was previously concealed.

Most artists cling to what is obvious, drawing delight in the onion's outer-most layers. While doing so, they fail to understand that there is not one, two, or even three layers, but many hundreds – lying beneath the surface, waiting to be discovered.

Although enchanted by the mosaics themselves, I have come to appreciate that they are neither the thing of greatest beauty, nor of real significance. They are the delicious flesh of the peach, but not the stone.

Look beyond the mosaics, focus on the slender lines that hold them in place, and you observe the thing of true value.

And so it is with travel.

To almost anyone who set eyes on a mosaic fountain, the grouting is invisible.

As with travel, we mesmerize those around us with tales of grand experience, adventure, and even bravery. We recount exploits tinged with intrigue, our stories framed in superlatives.

Yet, as we do so, we fail to pass on the kind of details which make the path of a lone traveller into an experience that shapes one from the inside out.

For me, it's the onion's deepest layers that hold the greatest riches.

Layers that are rarely the easiest to uncover or understand.

But, tease them out, decipher them, and a world comes into sharp focus that is more fantastical than anything untrammelled vision could ever discern.

Through my own journeys, detail has been both my currency and my matrix of discovery: the way I have sought to take inspiration from the lands that have passed beneath my feet.

As I sit here, pondering the subject, a memory is nudging me:

A long while ago I was studying magic in Kolkata. It was the kind of thing that so-called 'godmen' pass off as *real* magic, a realm pioneered by Harry Houdini a century ago. My magician master, a sadist called Hakim Feroze, insisted that I search for detail. Without it, he said, I could never hope to understand the rich textures of his illusionary world.

One afternoon, I came to be sitting at a Kolkata café. It wasn't much more than a cluster of tables and benches in the sidewalk's shade. I'd been sitting there for hours, having decided not to leave until I glimpsed something that wasn't obvious.

Anyone who's been to India will know that there's never any shortage of fodder to amaze and entertain. But what I was looking for wasn't the wild rumpus of life so overwhelming to the newly arrived.

I was searching for a whole other level.

So for the thousandth time I glanced out at the street, and found myself looking at an old woman and a cow. It's something you see across the subcontinent and isn't very unusual at all.

People paid a rupee or so to the woman, who sold them a handful of succulent green grass, which they fed to the cow.

I stared and I stared, and I stared and I stared.

And, as I stared, I took notice of the details:

The bright orange colour of the woman's *sari*.

The mottled pattern of the cow's hide.

And the way the grass had been heaped up.

The more I looked at it, the more I began to think it was ordinary. I'd been looking at it for so long that I wasn't doing more than scratching the surface.

But suddenly, it was as though something shifted inside me – as if a gear lever had been moved.

At that moment, I worked out what was really going on:

The woman didn't own the cow – the milkman did. But, after milking the animal in the early morning, he wanted to go around selling the milk. So, he rented the cow to the old woman. Each morning she'd pluck some grass in a field, and would lead the creature to the city.

As I had seen, people would pay her a rupee or two for some grass, and feed it to the cow.

By deciphering the system, I witnessed a genius – a genius that served everyone:

The milkman was happy because he was paid for having his cow looked after and fed all day.

The woman was happy because she had a livelihood.

The passers-by were happy because they received divine blessings for feeding a sacred animal.

But, best of all, the cow was thrilled because she was getting fed and loved by everyone all day long.

As with the memory of that street scene in Kolkata, or the pattern of the mosaic fountain, I like to delve down deep.

To search for the story behind the story, and question what the senses feed us.

After all, the most intoxicating value of life is surely to discover that which has been earned – by challenging what we hold to be true.

From: *The Clockmaker's Box*

The Place of Gold

The Desert of the Danakil is a part of the world
that the Creator must have fashioned when he
was in a bad mood.

Ladislas Faragó, *Abyssinia Stop Press*

IT TOOK ALL evening to dismember the dead she-camel.

The men worked together, cutting the flesh from the
carcass, draining the hump of its liquid, removing the
entrails and cooking the bones for their marrow. For once
Kefla stood back and let the others do the work. The dead
camel was his favourite. He had bought her as a calf and
they must have travelled the route together hundreds of
times. The rest of the party were sensitive to their leader's
loss. One of them put out a mat for him to sleep. He
crouched on it but refused to lie down.

The air was heavy with the smell of his beloved camel
roasting.

The last time I'd eaten camel was in the Jordanian
desert where it was made into *mensaf*, cooked in milk and
served in a rich *pilau*. The Bedu had prepared the dish
during Ramadan, the holy month of fasting. Each evening
when the fast breaks, a feast is held. Then the meat had

been succulent and tender. The she-camel's flesh in Afar couldn't have been more different. It was tough and sinewy, as if the long treks across the desert laden with salt had drained it of all moisture.

We did not sleep until late that night. All the meat and the entrails were cooked, and much was eaten. What was left over was packed up in sackcloth next morning and stowed on the back of the last camel. The blocks of salt were then redistributed, all the animals sharing the load of their dead sister.

Samson rose early that morning to read the Bible.

Like me, he'd been touched by the camel's death and its effect on Kefla Mohammed. I watched from a distance as he tied two sticks together and planted them in the cleft where the camel had caught her foot. It was a marker to warn others of the danger, as well as a tribute to the dead animal.

The morning's departure was delayed, and we didn't start walking until some time after eight. Sensing a slackening of the pace, I asked Samson if he thought we were nearing our destination. He was reluctant to find out, but he winked at me. He could smell civilization, he said.

Four hours later, after crossing a ridge of hills, we saw a cluster of houses on the horizon. As we drew nearer we made out people, goats and a few cars. Kefla pointed to the distant settlement.

'That is Kwiha. We will be in Mekele this evening.'

Inside I was jumping for joy. The novelty of trekking through Afar had long since worn off. I slapped Samson on the back and promised to treat him to the softest bed and the biggest meal the Tigrayan capital had to offer. He smiled, his cheeks dimpling, but before he could reply, Kefla came over.

'We will sell some of the salt in Kwiha,' he said. 'The market there is good.'

Soon the caravan was making its way through the dusty lanes of the small town. The camels seemed awkward now that we'd escaped the desert. They did not belong in a town, just as cars don't belong in the desert of the Danakil.

We went straight to the market, which was in full swing.

There was the usual assortment of green plastic buckets, piles of dirty bottles, polythene bags, old clothes, worn-out tools, grain and butchered meat on sale. Women haggled for food, and their children rummaged through the heaps of old clothes in the local equivalent of window shopping.

The camels were led to one side and relieved of their loads. About a third of the salt was taken off to be sold, and what was left was then redistributed.

Danakil traders such as Kefla sell their salt to a central dealer. He in turn sells slabs to middlemen who saw it up into smaller blocks. Individual customers buy only a small block, a few inches square.

These days salt is brought from Afar to be eaten. But in more ancient times the salt bars, called amole, were also used as currency. The Egyptian monk Cosmos recorded their use, and a thousand years later the Portuguese priest Francisco Álvares said he saw salt being used as money throughout Ethiopia: 'He who carries salt finds all that he requires.' Even as late as the 1960s travellers to Tigray reported seeing salt being used for trade.

As I stood there in the market, listening to the rhythmic sound of salt slabs being sawn, it began to rain in great splattering drops. Rain is generally welcomed in the north of Ethiopia, but it is the curse of the salt business. The sellers scurried away to borrow plastic sheets from their neighbours to protect their precious inventory.

Within an hour we were ready to press on to Mekele. Somehow the camels knew we were close to our destination and the pace quickened. Kefla was pleased with the money he'd made from the sale at Kwiha and he stuffed a great wad of bills under his shawl. Before we started the last leg to Mekele, he had ordered Yehia to untie all the camel meat which was still uneaten. He had then approached a group of beggars dressed in rags, and offered them the food. Samson was touched by his generosity.

'Kefla is a good man,' he said. 'He may not be a Christian yet, but I think he will go to Heaven.'

From the moment we crossed Mekele's city line, it was obvious that the place was going to be different.

Not just different from the desert, but different from every other town and city in Ethiopia. Mekele was inexplicably modern. The tarmac under the camels' feet was newly laid and as smooth as patted butter, with cat's eyes in the middle, and gutters along the sides of the road.

The houses were large and imposing, with imported tiles on their roofs and satellite dishes the size of fish ponds in their backyards. There were large hotels and restaurants, and petrol stations where fuel was actually on sale. All the vehicles were brand new, running on flawless tyres.

Samson looked astonished at his first sight of Mekele.

'I have heard of this place,' he said. 'People talk about it in the bars in Addis. They are usually laughed at, though, because no one believes them.'

'Why is it so prosperous?'

'The president,' said Samson. 'The president's from here.'

Kefla said he and the others would spend the night in Mekele but that they would leave at dawn. They felt uncomfortable in the town and they were anxious to get back to their families with the proceeds from the trip. Since Mekele had grown in size and sophistication, there wasn't the same demand for salt as there had once been. These days, explained Kefla, the people of Mekele want refined salt, and they can afford to have it imported.

'It's not good for us,' he said. 'One day, everyone will want it. That will put us all out of business and we'll probably starve to death.' He paused and then, looking me squarely in the eye, he grinned. 'Maybe that's when God will have mercy on us and turn all the salt back into gold.'

That evening Samson and I invited Kefla and the others to a meal at a small restaurant. We had endured hardship and were ready to taste luxury. I ordered just about everything on the menu for my guests and made quite sure that they didn't catch sight of the bill. It came to far more than they had earned from the entire journey. That night Samson and I slept on soft mattresses and showered in hot water. I had thought of asking Kefla and the rest of the team to join us in the hotel, but Samson had insisted they'd be embarrassed. Instead I'd offered them some money, but they'd refused to take it, even when it was handed over by Samson. They were too proud. So, in the end, I'd presented each of them with clothing and pieces of choice equipment from my kit bags.

In the morning, after a good night's sleep, we went down to the reception desk. I wanted to send someone to find Bahru and the Jeep. The doorman said something had been left for me during the night. It was a package wrapped in sacking, about the size of a brick. I opened it. Inside was a neatly cut piece of grey salt.

After a long search we found Bahru in the back of the Emperor's Jeep parked in a lane off the main roundabout.

He was fast asleep, and the front of his shirt was encrusted with dried vomit. I banged on the door and he sat up like a zombie woken from death. Four days of debauchery had taken its toll. I wondered how he had funded it all. Despite his hangover, however, he seemed pleased to see us and said he'd been doing some research. He had heard that the Italians had dug a series of test trenches for gold about fifty miles north of Mekele. I was so surprised at Bahru's initiative that I gave him a handful of tattered *birr* notes almost without thinking. That seemed to cure his hangover instantly, and within minutes our bags were loaded aboard the Jeep and we were jolting along a rutted country road. The dust churned up by our wheels was like talcum powder and it got into everything, but the surrounding landscape made up for it.

The president was right to be proud of his homeland. The highlands of Ethiopia are beautiful, and I found myself staring in amazement at a vast sweep of land covered in lush vegetation. Never before in Africa had I seen such astonishing fertility.

Tigray's people seemed as fertile as their land.

Wherever we looked there were children herding sheep and cows with long horns, old men whipping their donkeys forward, women working in the fields and more children foraging for kindling. The Tigrayan people look quite different from the other Ethiopian tribes. They are fine-boned and svelte, and they stride about as if they are walking on air.

The road sliced through passes walled by great granite bluffs, so perfectly formed that they looked as if they had been carved by man. Then the granite cliffs gave way to sandstone and to open fields where crops of *teff* rustled in the breeze.

An hour out of Mekele, the storm clouds broke and torrential rain began. Almost instantly, the downpour turned the dust into a thick soup, and the Jeep began skidding about.

Bahru said his informant had given him directions to the gold trenches. Even though he was quite sure where he was going, I forced him to stop and get directions from a young boy who was out in the rain hurling stones with a sling shot. His teeth were chattering with cold, and his arms and legs were covered in goosebumps. I asked if he knew about the trenches. He said he did and would show us the way. They were at a place called Werkamba.

'That's good news,' said Samson. 'It means "The Place of Gold".'

Before we reached Werkamba, the mud became too deep for the Emperor's Jeep to continue, so Samson and I decided to leave Bahru in the Jeep and walk with the boy through the downpour. The mud was the colour of oxtail soup and as thick as porridge, and in places it came up to our knees. I had brought along a camouflage green army poncho and so kept reasonably dry, but Samson had no waterproof clothing and was soaked within minutes.

Werkamba was a village of about ten houses built of stone, each with a finely woven thatched roof. The boy said that a big mining company had been looking for gold in the area. I found out later that it was Midroc, the company that also operated the Lega Dembi mine. Villagers dread the discovery of gold on their land because then the government nationalizes it and they are forced to leave. Samson said that farmers do all they can to pretend that their land has no gold, though some of them mine illegally, digging narrow tunnels to reach the seam. I even heard of a farmer who built a hut over the entrance to his mine shaft. He managed to keep the shaft secret for more than a year, but word eventually got out. The government seized the land and he was thrown off it.

In the village we were given freshly roasted coffee by the boy's mother and she told us what had happened. Engineers had come the month before and taken soil samples. A foreigner had also come. She was worried, she said. They were all worried. I asked if they did any mining themselves. The woman held her son's head to her chest and looked at the ground, but she didn't reply.

The new test trenches were set alongside the old ones made by the Italians, a couple of miles east of the village. They were no more than a yard deep, suggesting that the gold was close to the surface. Samson pointed to the veins of marble-like quartz that ran through the rock. Where you find those, he said, you find gold. It was unclear whether the Italians had actually mined the area. When I looked the place up later at the Geological Survey in Addis Ababa, I could find no record, but I knew that significant mining was taking place across the border in Eritrea.

I had brought the Gold Bug metal detector along with me. At last there was no danger of being arrested by officials or being mobbed by excited hordes of illegal miners. We assembled the unit and swept the test trenches once the rain had started to ease off. The machine squealed piercingly wherever the head was pointed.

Samson raised his eyebrows.

Then he knelt down in one of the trenches, probed with his fingers and selected a lump of soil.

'Look at this,' he said, crumbling it with his fingertips, 'it's got gold in it.'

He suggested we spend a couple of days at the trenches looking for nuggets. Gold is one of the hardest metals to find with a conventional detector, largely because the machine picks up nodules of iron, known as 'hot rocks', but specialized detectors such as the Gold Bug can compensate for iron in the soil. The metal detector has come a long way since it was invented by Gerhard Fisher in the early 1930s. Fisher was a German *émigré* and a close friend of Albert Einstein. When he showed his first model of a detector – the 'Metallascope' – to Einstein, the great scientist reputedly forecast that it would be a commercial failure.

Though I was tempted by Samson's suggestion that we look for nuggets, I knew I couldn't. Before setting out in search of Solomon's mines, I had privately sworn an oath that I would not try to make a profit from the gold business. Instead we took a few soil samples to satisfy our curiosity and then we hurried back through the rain to the Jeep.

That evening, in the town of Adigrat, perched on the border with Eritrea, I planned the next stage of the journey.

I was more keen than ever to seek out Tullu Welel, and to locate Frank Hayter's mine shafts.

We took out the map and had a good look at the route. There was quite a distance to cover down the western flank of Ethiopia. But before we could find out the truth behind Hayter's claims, there was one more place to visit. A friend had told me about a monastery called Debra Damo. In its vaults there were said to be secret texts that told of King Solomon. I was happy to give the place a miss and head straight for Tullu Welel, but Samson said that visiting a monastery was an act of piety, and that it would bring us luck. I found Debra Damo on the map, right on the Eritrean border. It wasn't far from Adigrat.

We set off soon after dawn.

The rain clouds which had brought such discomfort the day before had vanished and now the landscape was bathed in sunlight. Bahru put his foot on the accelerator and the Emperor's Jeep hurtled along, swerving round potholes and bouncing over ruts. We were on the main road to Axum, but there was very little traffic. Instead the road was full of cows and sheep grazing the verges. After an hour of driving Bahru misjudged a turn and hit a sheep head on. The poor animal was trapped under the Jeep. Despite this, Bahru refused to stop immediately for fear of encountering a furious farmer. Only once we were some distance from the herd did he pull over and get out to cut the mangled carcass from the chassis.

Another hour passed, with similar near misses. Bahru seemed exhilarated by his recent kill and refused to slow down, smiling evilly when I shouted at him. Then we came to a village where the road was full of people and animals heading for the morning market. Bahru seemed to accelerate deliberately, and people and animals leapt for safety. One sheep was too slow and there was a sickening thud as our wheels caught it. The animal's owner managed to jump in front of the Jeep – a brave act in a country like Ethiopia where most vehicles have unreliable brakes – and we were all catapulted forward as Bahru slammed into first gear. Thankfully, the farmer wasn't injured, but before we knew it, the entire village was pressed around the car. They wanted blood.

I told Bahru that he was on his own. He would have to get out and face the mob. His perpetual grin wavered and his lower lip began to tremble.

The crowd peered in through the windows.

Some of them were arming themselves with stones. Others were trying to rock the Jeep from side to side. I yelled again for Bahru to get out. Gathering his courage, he climbed out of the window and on to the bonnet. Then he bowed his head and pleaded with the farmer. I could not hear what he was saying, but his body language was eloquent.

He was begging for mercy.

The villagers worked to free the sheep from the wheel arch. Then they daubed the Jeep's filthy white bodywork with the animal's blood. The farmer was shouting at the top of his voice. Samson said he was demanding compensation.

He wanted cash, lots of it.

Still standing on the bonnet, Bahru tried to talk his way out of the situation. He was the kind of man who could talk his way out of anything. Samson translated. First

Bahru blamed the sheep for its stupidity. Then he blamed the Jeep's brakes. After that he blamed the poor condition of the road.

The villagers said they were sick of dangerous drivers. The dead sheep was no more stupid than any other sheep, and the road was bad because of the government. They were, they said, going to make an example of Bahru. They'd make sure he never injured another helpless animal again.

I prodded Samson in the back. He stopped translating and, with great reluctance, climbed onto the bonnet as well. I watched them through the windscreen: two grown men, throwing themselves at the mercy of the crowd. Every so often they would turn and point to me. Instead of lessening the villagers' rage, this seemed to anger them even more. I began to wonder if my companions were offering my head in exchange for the dead sheep.

Then Bahru fished out his wallet from his back pocket.

Like a conjurer performing a trick, he demonstrated that the wallet contained no money. The only thing inside it was a driving licence. He offered it to the farmer, promising to leave it as collateral until he next returned to the village. The villagers talked among themselves, debating whether to take the licence. At length they agreed. The farmer put it in his top pocket and shouted a string of insults.

Samson and Bahru clambered back into the Jeep.

They looked very relieved.

Bahru threw the Jeep in gear, waved to the crowd, and sped off. Then he burst out laughing.

'What's so funny?'

'Those people are as stupid as their sheep!' he exclaimed. 'I've got lots of fake licences for times like this.'

A few miles from Debra Damo a wizened old man hailed us for a lift.

He was so frail that I feared he might die in the back seat. His curly hair was as white as bleached whale bones, and all his teeth were missing. He said he was eighty-five years old, and he had been to the monastery a thousand times.

'What about its treasures, the books about Solomon?'

The man ran a thumbnail down the ridge of his nose.

'Yes, there are books,' he said. 'They are written in Ge'ez, the old language. They are very precious and they are guarded by the monks.'

'Will they show them to me?'

'Of course, but first you must get to the monastery.'

I had heard that no women were permitted to set foot in Debra Damo, and that the ascent kept a lot of men out too.

Shortly before we reached the mountain Bahru stopped to wash the sheep's blood from the Jeep's bodywork. He said that if it hadn't been for me, he would have killed a lot more animals. It took his mind off the tedium of the drive. Like a Danakil warrior forbidden to hunt for testicles, he felt that his rights had been curbed by political correctness.

Debra Damo is perched on top of an *amba*, a flat-topped mountain, that rises 8,400 feet above the surrounding land. The track that leads to it is hideously rough, and when the Emperor's Jeep refused to negotiate a giant pile of boulders, we were forced to abandon it. The last stretch entailed crawling on our hands and knees up an enormous rockfall.

We eventually reached the foot of the mountain in the early afternoon, but I could see no way up it. There was no path, and the cliffs towering above us offered no footholds. I told Samson to ask our fragile passenger which was the best route. The man put his hands over his ears and laughed a great toothless laugh, which echoed around the rocks like the ripple of distant thunder.

When he could laugh no more, he sat down in the shade and fell asleep. I feared he was another madman and was about to give Samson more orders when a strange thing happened.

Someone whistled from halfway up the cliff.

We looked up, blinking into the light. A hand was waving and pointing downwards. We shouted up questions, but before they were answered the man up the cliff threw down a plaited leather rope. It was as thick as my wrist, and it stank of rotting meat.

Telling Samson that he was more athletic than me, I made him go first. He wound the rope around his waist, but before he could start to climb, he was lifted from the ground. I could only marvel at the strength of the men who were hauling him up. Samson rose higher and higher with jolting movements, his hands frantically clawing at the rock face as his head was battered against its walls. At first he whimpered with fear, but then, as the height increased, the whimpering turned to groans and then to a chilling scream. I called up to him, telling him to be brave. Then suddenly Samson vanished.

Shading my eyes, I tried to work out where he'd gone. There was no sign of life. I shouted to the old man asleep in the shade but he didn't wake up. So I called up to the rock face. A moment later the plaited rope reappeared. I'd brought far too much baggage as usual. How was I going to get it and myself up? As if in answer to my question, a second rope appeared, thinner than the first but also made of sinewy leather. I tied it round my bags' straps and then they too began to rise.

When the bags were no more than a speck in the sky, the voice called down again. Then the hand pointed at me and at the thick rope. I wound it around my waist, securing it in a reef knot. But before I could adjust it comfortably, I found myself being pulled upwards. As I rose higher and higher, the rope cut into my sides, squeezing me like a boa constrictor crushing its prey. I breathed out, gasping, and found I couldn't breathe in again. Then I began scrabbling desperately for finger-holds in the cliff. But every time I found a fragile purchase in a crevice, the rope tore me away, jolting me upwards. It was as if a group of enormous fiendish jinn were at work.

The walls of the cliff were polished and grooved where the rope had rubbed across them over the centuries. A few more minutes and I was nearing the top. I could hear voices now, a young child and a cluster of men. Then there was the sound of Samson urging me on. The last twenty feet were so terrifying that my hands still sweat at the memory. I felt as if I was being cut in half, and the sight of the ground far beneath me made me feel sick with vertigo. A minute more and it was all over. I was pulled into a doorway and lay there on my belly, shaking and whimpering.

A skinny figure was looming over me.

He was wearing dark green trousers and a royal blue overcoat, darned in places with white thread. On his feet were sandals made from rubber tyres, and on his head was a white cotton cap. His nose was long, his ears were pointed, and his mouth was hidden by a tuft of white beard. He looked like Asterix the Gaul, and like Asterix he obviously had a magic potion.

Samson introduced me to Asnake. His modest appearance belied his extraordinary strength. When I commented on his muscles, he roared with laughter.

'God gives me strength,' he said.

'He gives us all strength,' added Samson piously.

'Doesn't anyone ever fall down the precipice?' I asked.

'Oh, yes,' he replied airily, 'people die all the time.'

A child priest appeared.

He was huddled in a white shawl and his feet were bare. He said his name was Ebya and that he would escort us to the monastery. A narrow path led round the edge of the cliff and up to the plateau above. Still shaking, Samson and I began to worry about getting back down the cliff face, but Ebya simply smiled and told us to look at the view. We could see for many miles in every direction.

The afternoon light played on the hills, bringing them alive.

Beneath us there were dry riverbeds, copses of trees and farmsteads, and in the distance we could see a mountain range veiled in mist. I could even make out Bahru asleep on the roof of the Jeep. Ebya pointed to a crest of hills in the foreground. He said they were in Eritrea.

Up on the plateau, a herd of fifty oxen were grazing in long grass. I was about to ask Ebya how they'd got there but Ebya had more important things on his mind. Had I been to America? he asked. I replied that I had.

'I am going to America,' he said earnestly.

'But aren't you a monk? Surely you'll spend your life here.'

The boy sniffed, then wiped his nose on his arm.

'In America there are Christians, aren't there?'

Samson answered for me.

'Many, many Christians, and many, many churches!' he exclaimed.

Ebya led the way through a maze of wattle and daub walls. As he walked, he foraged under his *shamma* and brought out a familiar sheet of paper. It was a Diversity Visa form for the United States.

I rolled my eyes.

'I think they will need me in America,' he said.

Debra Damo was supposedly founded by Abba Aregawi, one of the famous Nine Saints of Syria who fled persecution and arrived in Ethiopia in about 451 BC. A legend says that Abba Aregawi stood at the base of the mountain, wondering how he could ever climb it. But God called to a serpent which lived on the top of the mountain and told the creature to lower its tail and pull the priest up.

For fifteen hundred years a company of monks have inhabited the remote monastery. They are brought as children by their parents, who believe that good fortune will be conferred on the family if a son devotes his life to God. Until recently, Ebya said, there were also three hermits who spent their lives in silent prayer. No one ever saw them, but when they died, their bodies were taken to the far side of the mountain and thrown into a cave.

'I will show you the bodies,' he said.

I was impatient to look at the secret manuscripts which spoke of Solomon, but I knew it would be discourteous to refuse. So we made our way to the edge of the plateau and down a narrow track that clung to the rock face. Ebya cheerfully clambered over a tree growing out of the cliff. Samson and I followed, not daring to look down. Then the young priest gestured to a narrow cave entrance and, before I could stop him, he slipped inside, calling out to us to follow.

At the back of the cave lay several skeletons. One still had black and rotting flesh attached to it. The stench was appalling. Ebya picked up a femur and waved it around.

He said big birds flew into the cave and fed on the rotting bodies.

After another terrifying clamber back along the path, we reached a cistern. Over the centuries the monks have carved a number of them out of the plateau, some as deep as sixty feet, to collect water on the rare occasions when it rains. Ebya said the water was very fresh. He scooped up a cupful for me to drink. Just in time I noticed that the water was alive with maggots and I hastily passed it to Samson.

It was early evening by the time we were taken to the church. The building was square in shape and made of small rectangular stones. It stood behind a wall and was surrounded by trees and patches of dried grass. It is said to be the oldest church in Africa.

As we took off our shoes outside a monk waited in the doorway. I pushed Samson forward to begin the lengthy salutations. The monk welcomed us in a whisper. He said he had been waiting for our arrival for many months, and he thanked God for delivering us safely to Debra Damo.

The antechamber of the church was decorated with wooden panels carved with images of elephants and giraffe, camels, gazelle, lions and snakes. There were paintings, too, vividly coloured. One showed Abba Aregawi being pulled up the mountain by the serpent. Another depicted Saint George dispatching the dragon. In a third the Queen of Sheba was arriving at the court of Solomon.

'Solomon,' I said.

The monk's face lit up.

'Ah, Solomon.'

'A wise king,' I chirped in.

'Yes, wise, very, very wise.'

'And rich.'

The monk smiled.

'*Very* rich,' he said.

I instructed Samson to ask about the secret manuscripts. The monk gazed at the floor.

'There were many books,' he said, 'but recently there was a fire in the library. Only a few now remain.'

'Where are they?'

He pointed towards a door leading to the back of the church.

'In the Holy of Holies.'

'I'm looking for King Solomon's gold mines,' I said. 'And someone told me that you might be able to help me in my quest.'

The monk turned to a wooden lectern standing in the middle of the anteroom and pulled off a mottled green cloth. Beneath it lay a very large book bound in scarlet leather.

'Is that the *Kebra Negast*?'

The monk opened the book at random, revealing neat handwritten columns of rounded black letters. The script was Ge'ez, the ancient language of Ethiopia. He did not answer my question, but he did speak.

'God appeared to Solomon in a dream,' he said, 'and asked him what special power he wished for. The young king replied that he yearned for wisdom so that he might be able to distinguish between good and evil. God blessed him with wisdom. Then Solomon built his great temple in Jerusalem, layering the walls with the purest gold, Ethiopian gold.'

He paused to turn the page with both hands.

'Word of Solomon's wisdom and fortune spread across the oceans and the seas,' he went on, 'and it came to the ears of Makeda. She wanted to look into the wise king's eyes and to hear of his learning. So she travelled with a great caravan through the desert, from our land to Judah.'

'Where in Ethiopia did Solomon get his gold?'

The monk did not reply but he continued to talk.

'And Makeda came to Jerusalem and rested in Solomon's palace, which was also fashioned from gold. She gave him precious beakers and fine objects and much gold, pure gold. And she asked him hard questions, and he answered them. Makeda was stirred by the king's wisdom and power. And Solomon was moved by the queen's beauty. So he held a banquet and sprinkled the food with salt. Makeda ate much and that night she slept in a bed beside Solomon's own.

'Between their beds was a jar of water. Solomon said he would not touch Makeda if she agreed not to use what belonged to him. But in the night the queen was overcome with thirst. She reached for the jug of water and drank from it. Solomon jumped from his bed and took the queen, for she had stolen what was his. Makeda returned to Ethiopia, where their son Menelik was born.'

'But what of the gold, Solomon's gold?'

Again, the monk turned the pages of the book.

'I will tell you of the gold.'

'Where did it come from? Which part of the country?'

'From the west,' said the priest, 'from the land of Shangul.'

'*Beni Shangul*?' I repeated, remembering that Dr. Pankhurst had spoken of the place and had remarked on the quality of its gold.

The monk nodded.

'Yes, that is right. I myself come from Beni Shangul. The people who live there know about the mines of Makeda.'

'You mean the mines of Solomon?'

'No, they were not the wise king's mines. They were the queen's, for this was her kingdom.'

I asked him to tell me more, but the audience was at an end.

'It is time to pray,' he said.

Without another word, he disappeared into the main body of the church. I called out, asking for more details of the gold, but there was no reply.

Ebya led us out through the enclosure and back to our shoes. It was dark now, and the air was flickering with fireflies. We stayed at Debra Damo for another day, but we did not see the monk again. Ebya said that the monks preferred to spend their time alone rather than speaking to visitors. If they had wanted to talk, he said, they would never have joined the church.

Before we plucked up courage to descend the cliff and make our way back to the Emperor's Jeep, I had to know the answer to a question. The herd of oxen grazing on the mountain still baffled me. As no women or female creatures of any kind were allowed to enter the monastery, it wasn't possible to breed cattle there. I knew, too, that there was no track or secret path up the mountain.

The only way to get to the top was by rope.

I asked Ebya how the oxen were brought up.

'That is very difficult,' he said. 'When we want to bring an ox up we lower down a pair of big ropes. Then we tie them around the ox and all the monks come out to pull it up the mountain.'

Ebya broke off to take a deep breath and his eyes widened.

'The ox makes a terrible noise.'

From: *In Search of King Solomon's Mines*

On the Trail of The Sirdar

KAMAL TAPPED HARD on the driver's door. There was a rustling inside, sounds of commotion, then of fear, followed by urgent clambering. The passenger door was flung open and a girl of about fifteen leapt out. She was veiled in black and ran very fast. An oily, bearded face appeared at the window. 'It's me,' said Kamal hoarsely.

The man inside glared out at us with anger. 'I paid for her in advance!' he shouted.

'We've come for the sand.'

Kamal pulled the tarpaulin back and pointed to the load. 'Feel that,' he said.

I did. It was slightly moist, cool to the touch. 'Top quality,' said Kamal, 'and half the going price.'

When he set eyes on the sand, Hamza said it was the lowest quality he had ever seen. He boasted that he'd been born in the desert, a fact that enabled him to tell good sand apart from bad merely by the smell. The other two guardians were equally scathing when they saw the giant dark mound now sitting outside the house.

'It will give you trouble,' said the Bear.

'And it'll bring bad luck into the house,' said Osman.

It was obvious the guardians were disparaging because Kamal had brought the sand to Dar Khalifa. As far as they were concerned, anything my assistant did was part of a grand scheming plan to relieve me of all I owned. They hated everything about him. Most of all they hated that I listened when he spoke.

For my part, I really could not work Kamal out. He was an impossible person to pigeonhole – capable of brilliant thought one minute, but utterly reckless behaviour the next. While I had him working, I valued his know-how, his ability to get difficult things done. At the same time, I was still unsure of his real motives.

One morning in early December we drove back out to see the carpenter. It was the middle of the week, and we were going to check on the windows he was making. The carpenter kissed Kamal's cheeks, praised his ancestors and ushered us to sit down in the shade. A pot of mint tea was brought, poured out once into glasses, then poured back into the pot, before being poured out a second time. A team of boys fetched the windows and held them up like oils at a fine-art sale. They looked very good. The carpenter was pleased when I praised the work. He exclaimed something in Arabic.

Kamal translated. 'He said: "Through these windows, your eyes will separate reality from illusion."'

I pondered the comment as we drove back towards Casablanca. It was a dazzling morning, far cooler than previous days. The road was lined with hawkers selling cactus fruit and plums. Kamal didn't say anything on the way home. His mouth was clenched tight. He breathed through his nose, huffing like a stallion before the race, as if he were overcome with anger. I asked if something was on his mind. He didn't reply. Then, suddenly, he swerved off the main road onto a dirt track, dust enveloping us. I was taken by surprise.

'Where are we going?'

'Short cut,' he said.

We drove for thirty minutes in the opposite direction from Casablanca. On either side of the track there was open farmland, rich red African soil, peppered with crows. I kept silent. As far as I was concerned, it was the middle of nowhere.

At a place where the tracks converged and then crossed, Kamal hit the brakes. The Jeep skidded to a halt, sending dust sideways like talc cast into the wind. Kamal got out of the car. He said he wanted to check the exhaust. At that moment, two men appeared from behind a bush. They looked like labourers from the city. Kamal greeted them as if they were old friends. A surge of adrenalin welled through me. For the first time, I was frightened of Kamal. I thought he was going to kill me right there and then. The car key was still in the ignition. I was about to jump into the driving seat, throw it in gear and charge away. But at that moment, he ambled back to the car, started the engine and headed for town.

'Who were they?' I asked.

'They wanted a ride to Casa,' he said.

'It looked like you knew them.'

Kamal turned to face me. His distant brown eyes locked into mine. His mouth was tight shut, jaws clenched. He stared at me for so long as to be uncomfortable. It was not the time for speaking. He could feel my fear, I was sure of it. I hoped he would burst out laughing, slap me on the back, or let me in on a secret. But he didn't speak.

In the same week, I received another postcard from Pete. The writing was more obscure this time, as if it was written by someone who had come to know pain. It said: *Had the chop. Now I'm learning the Path to Allah.* The note was followed by an address in Chefchaouen, a small town south of Tangier. I showed it to Rachana.

'I think you'd better go and see if he's OK,' she said.

'But I hardly know the guy.'

'So what?'

There was a far stronger reason to venture north. I wanted to track down the house in which my grandfather had lived for the last decade of his life.

Kamal's team of artisans were about to turn up at Dar Khalifa. I couldn't face them, I don't know why; perhaps it was because I was so sure they would create more problems than they solved.

I took the morning train from Casa Voyageurs and was soon trundling north along the coast. Leaving Casablanca and the Caliph's House behind filled me with new energy. It was as if a mantle of burden had been eased from my shoulders. I stared out at the groves of cork oaks and breathed in long and hard. If I could keep standing a little longer, I thought to myself, we would have a chance of weathering the storm.

I planned to go straight to Tangier, to spend a night or two ferreting out the riddle of my grandfather's last years. After that, I would head down to Chefchaouen to find the newly circumcized American.

My grandfather was The Sirdar Ikbal Ali Shah. He was the son of an Afghan chieftain, raised in a tribal fiefdom in the Hindu Kush. As is traditional in our family, he was encouraged to master many fields of study, to live many lives in one. He was a medical doctor and a diplomat, a professor of philosophy, an expert on folklore, mysticism and political science. He was an adviser and confidant to half a dozen heads of state, and the author of more than sixty books – on poetry, politics, biography, literature, religion and travel.

At twenty-three he was sent to Edinburgh to study medicine. He was very taken by Scotland and wrote later that the mountains, the castles and the strict system of clans reminded him of his Afghan homeland. It was 1917 and the Great War raged on. A generation of young men were being slaughtered in the trenches of Flanders and France.

One spring day, my grandfather was invited to a charity tea, where a group of young women were raising funds for the war effort. Across the crowded room, he spotted a prim Scottish girl standing alone, china cup poised to her lips. Her nickname was 'Bobo' and her family came from the Edinburgh elite. She was only seventeen. Her brother had just been killed fighting in France and she was distraught at his loss.

Bobo spied Ikbal gazing across at her. She stared back with nervous anticipation, and they fell in love. The next day she asked her father if she might meet the Afghan chieftain's son for tea. The request was refused and she was locked in her room. Allowing her heart to rule her mind, Bobo escaped, eloped with Ikbal, and together they travelled to his ancestral fortress in the Hindu Kush.

Their marriage endured more than forty years, until the day of Bobo's death. They lived in Central Asia, the Middle East and in Europe. Then, in 1960, Bobo died suddenly of cancer, weeks before her sixtieth birthday. My grandfather could hardly contain his grief. He vowed that he would not return to any place they had been together, or to look at anything that would remind him of his beloved wife.

Morocco was a country where they had never travelled. My grandfather had heard of the kingdom's mountains, its *kasbahs* and the proud tribal traditions. The sound of such a place was alluring. So, that summer, he packed his sea trunk with some books and a few clothes and set sail for Tangier.

There is no better way to travel through Morocco than by train. The journey from Casablanca to Tangier takes about six hours, sometimes longer, depending on whether the driver takes a long lunch or a short one at Sidi Kacem. In winter, the travellers are bundled up in heavy woollen *jelabas*, worn as overcoats, as if a searing arctic wind is about to tear through. But it never does.

The man sitting opposite me in the compartment noticed the calfskin amulet round my neck. He was in his sixties, dressed in a pale *jelaba* with black trim, and brown *baboushes* on his feet. His face was swollen, scattered with patchy beard and sores. I explained to him that the amulet was given to me by a friend.

'What for?'

'For the jinns,' I said.

The man scratched his face. 'Let them into your head and you'll have trouble,' he replied.

'They're not up here,' I said, tapping my temple, 'but in my house.' I laughed. 'Anyway, it's not the jinns who are a problem,' I said, 'but the people working for me.'

'What's wrong with them?'

'They believe in the jinns,' I explained. 'That's the problem.'

The man didn't say anything else for a long while. I stared out of the window at the ploughed fields edged in cactus plants. I thought our chat was at an end. But a traveller's conversation can be disjointed, strung out along miles of railway line. The man cleared his throat.

'Across from me,' he said, 'I see a sheet of white paper. There is no writing upon it, nothing at all. The paper has just been made. It's new. There's great hope for it. A beautiful poem could be written on it – something inspiring, something wonderful. Or a fabulous picture could be drawn on its surface, the face of a child perhaps.'

I looked at the man, and took in his sores and his tired face, and I wondered what he was going on about.

'But the great shame is that the sheet of paper will never know beauty,' he said. 'Why? Because it doesn't believe.'

My only clues were a few letters written by my grandfather to my parents during the last years of his life. They were always composed in dark-blue fountain pen on lightweight writing paper, in a precise, sensible hand. They spoke of a life of solitude, of modesty, a life waiting to be reunited with Bobo. At the top of each was printed the address: 21 rue de la Plage.

Once in Tangier, I bought a street map from a tobacconist and found rue de la Plage running inland from the port. The nearest hotel was Cecil's. I was acquainted with it from my grandfather's letters. He waxed lyrical about the place, suggesting it was palatial in the extreme, an outpost of true luxury. I walked from the train station down the waterfront. A group of children were playing marbles on the pavement in the yellow light of afternoon. I asked them for the direction of Cecil's. Without looking up, one of the boys pointed over his shoulder.

I had not noticed the whitewashed hotel perched there behind him, set back on the far side of the esplanade. It was easy to see its original appeal. The building was wide but not high, two storeys clinging to the ground floor's roof. There were steps up from the street, a sheltered entrance, above it an expansive balcony. All the windows had slatted jalousie shutters; some were blown open by the wind, others bolted shut. The place resembled one of those solid, compelling gems found in the novels of Graham Greene.

Time had not been kind to The Cecil. Even in the sugar-sweet light of late afternoon, it was hard to lavish praise on the current condition. Washing lines crisscrossed the balconies and the whitewash was dirt-grey and blistered with damp. I walked up to the entrance and climbed the steps.

Inside, the receptionist was watching television with his left eye; the other was covered in a home-made patch. Holding the TV antenna in one hand, he was jiggling it to make sense of an Egyptian soap opera. Beside him, a squat man was smoking hashish. Both figures looked up in amazement. It was clear that no one had ventured there in years.

The entrance was gloomy, the walls waxy and damp. The only decorations were tourist posters from the 1970s and a cardboard cut-out of an Aeroflot stewardess. There was a sense that at one time, perhaps long ago, something very evil had taken place within the walls.

I enquired if there was a single room for a night or two. The hashish-smoker cackled with laughter; his friend dropped the antenna and shuffled over to a desk diary. His fingers began in January, turning over a week at a time. They made their way through many months of blank paper, until they arrived at December.

'*Oui*, monsieur,' he said hesitantly, 'I think we have space.'

He led the way up an attractive double staircase, no doubt quite a feature in its day. On the first floor were yet more mildewed posters of Moroccan highlights, and innumerable ice buckets on stands, filled with cigarette ends.

After wrestling with a Chinese padlock on door number three, the manager swung the door inwards. He winked with his one good eye, as if to prepare me for the opulence inside. I stepped across the threshold. Not since my travels in search of India's underbelly had I seen such impressive wear and tear.

All the windows were cracked or missing entirely, half-concealed behind rotting curtains. The linoleum floor was mottled with dark spots where previous guests had stamped out their cigarettes, and the bed was a ramp, collapsed at one end. There was no bathroom. It was explained in a mumble that the hotel had a problem with its water supply.

'There are no toilets at all?'

The manager replied in the negative. He suggested the place was far better off without the toilets, sticking his nose up at the very thought of them. Then he held out a palm and asked for payment in advance. I counted out some banknotes and passed them over.

'Where can I take a shower?' I asked.

'In the kitchen of the restaurant next door.'

The last time I had come to Tangier was thirty-five years before, aged three. My strongest memory of the city was the scent of orange blossom. I can smell it now. It was pungent, intoxicating. I had spent days running through the public gardens, dressed in my itchy camel-wool *jelaba*, sniffing the air. I remember, too, the warmth of the sun on my back, the crowded cafés and the people. There were so many people then.

In the 1960s Tangier was famed for the foreign writers who took refuge there, away from the more rigid conventions of Europe and the United States. The most celebrated was author Paul Bowles, who moved to Tangier after the war and resided there until his death in 1999.

Wandering the streets, it seemed to me that the vibrancy of Tangier had been replaced with gloom, a melancholy, as if the party had moved on elsewhere. The buildings reflected it. They were no longer loved. Fabulous villas and theatres, hotels and cafés, were all boarded up, or fallen into a limbo like The Cecil.

It was dusk by the time I reached rue de la Plage. I stood at the bottom of the hill, staring up at the narrow street. I admit it – I was apprehensive. I was fearful, too. I am not certain why. Sometimes it's like that, when you have travelled far to be somewhere or to meet someone very special. You pause at the last step. There was a temptation to turn on my heel and take the next train back to Casablanca. My grandfather had been a figure of inspiration, an example, as well as a myth. And this was reality – the place where he lived and where he died.

Keeping well to the side of the road, I started walking up the hill. There were small shops on both sides, each one offering the same selection of knick-knacks and razor blades, toothpaste, boot polish and canned cheese. I checked the square enamel numbers outside the shops. As I did so, I felt my heart in my chest. There was 17, then 18, 19 and after it 20... one more to go... 21 rue de la Plage.

I had arrived. My feet were pressed together outside the doorway, on the very spot my grandfather had been struck by the reversing Coca-Cola truck back in 1969. The road was two-way then: astonishing, as it was barely wide enough for a single car. It was so steep that vehicles were challenged to get all the way up to the top. The local taxis had perfected a way of revving their engines, racing headlong, swerving from side to side so that their bald tyres could maintain traction.

I turned my back to the lane and stared up at the building. The outer wall was made from large, square blocks of stone. It went straight up and gave no sign of what lay behind. The doorway was arched, filled with a blue wrought-iron gate, backed by a sheet of steel. Above it was a modest marble plaque inscribed with the words 'Villa Calpe'.

I took a deep breath and rang the bell. I waited. No answer. I rang again. Still no answer. I was about to leave, and walk back down the hill to Cecil's, when a woman arrived at the front door. She was in her fifties, with a mass of grey hair knotted up in a bun. Her face was kind and motherly, dominated by wide-rimmed glasses. I was struck by a warmth, a generosity of spirit. It seemed to radiate all around her. She was carrying a basket. In it was a Siamese cat.

It was a difficult moment. I began to explain in my limited French that I was the grandson of an Afghan chieftain's son who had once lived at Villa Calpe.

'Do you speak English?' the woman asked in an American voice.

'Yes.'

'Then you had better come inside.'

A steep bank of steps ran up to the villa. It was cobbled at the edges in rounded pebbles, stone slabs in the middle.

A nervous old Alsatian charged down to the door and was called sharply to heel. On the right of the entrance was an outbuilding. It looked down onto the street. The American woman, whose name was Pamela, lived there. At the top of the steps was the villa itself; the walk up to it was shaded by a canopy of vines.

Pamela said that the landlord lived in the villa. She offered to arrange for me to meet him the next morning. We chatted about books for a moment or two. Pamela was well read. She knew my book on Ethiopia, my quest for King Solomon's Mines, had read my grandfather's books on Afghanistan, and she even knew my grandmother's autobiography – the tale of how she abandoned Scotland for the Hindu Kush.

Twenty minutes after our doorstep meeting, I was sitting with Pamela in a small café, eating barbecued fish. I asked how long she had lived at rue de la Plage.

'It's been twelve years,' she said.

'Do you live alone?'

'No,' she replied. 'I share it with my cats and with five hundred kaftans.'

'What brought you here?'

Pamela stared into a glass of local red wine. 'The wanderlust of youth,' she said, her gaze unflinching. 'I was living in Brooklyn, in 1965, when I heard a Yugoslav cargo ship was about to leave for Eastern Europe. Without giving it a moment's thought, I talked my way aboard. The first stop was Tangier. For me it was the exotic East. I planned to be on shore two days, but stayed two months. The smells and sounds, the blaze of colour – I was knocked out by it all.'

Pamela said she had spent years living and travelling through the Mediterranean and north Africa. Much land passed beneath her feet, but her first love was always Morocco. She returned to the United States and opened a Moroccan restaurant in Los Angeles, but even that wasn't enough to satisfy her heart.

'One morning I packed it in,' she said quietly. 'I bought a one-way ticket and arrived here with a pair of suitcases and my favourite travelling cat. I have never looked back.'

I told her about my grandfather, who had come to Tangier after the death of his wife.

'Whoever you are,' she said, 'Morocco takes you in. Before you know it, you have a home and friends, and you've forgotten your troubles.'

I asked Pamela what her friends had thought when she had set up home in Tangier.

'They tried to hold me back,' she said.

'Why?'

She looked across at me and sighed. 'Because of their own fear,' she said.

The next morning, I was up early. Sleeping at forty-five degrees had been uncomfortable, but nothing in comparison to the desperate nocturnal urge to pee in a hotel without toilets. I sponged myself down as directed in the roach-infested restaurant kitchen next door. It is a memory I hope, someday, to forget.

Pamela had told me to come to the villa at nine-thirty to meet the landlord. She had set up the rendezvous and gone off to work with her favourite travelling cat.

The doorbell was answered by a slim, straight-backed man, aged about sixty. His hair was dyed black and glistened in the light. It was combed carefully to the left side of his square head. He introduced himself as David Rebibo. He said he was one of Morocco's last remaining Jews and that his family had owned Villa Calpe for more than a hundred years. I asked if he remembered my grandfather.

'How could anyone forget such a man?' he replied swiftly. 'It was a long time ago, and I was much younger, but we would sit together on the balcony and he would tell me of his travels.'

Mr. Rebibo led the way to the villa. As I passed under the canopy of wisteria vines, I first set eyes on the building's extraordinary facade. It was arranged on two floors, linked by a curved double stairway rising from a patio in front of the house. Wherever I looked, there were flowers and ferns erupting from terracotta pots.

I was led inside. The rooms were small but well appointed. There were long mirrors to give an extra dimension, and a great many pictures – some Indian, others European and Chinese. On every windowsill and table there were orchids. I found it intensely moving to be in the house where my grandfather had spent his last years. I took in the details, which his own meticulous eye would have treasured – the cornices and ceiling roses, the sconces on the bedroom wall, and the patterned brass handles on the doors. But my delight at being there was tinged with sadness, for it was here that he lived a life waiting for death, pining for his beloved Bobo.

We went back out onto the patio and sat at a wrought-iron table, the winter sun quite dazzling above. The landlord pressed a hand to his glistening hair, unsure perhaps whether the dye could take the sun.

'Your grandfather would sit here in the mornings,' he said. 'He would read and write letters. He used a fountain-pen, on onionskin paper.'

I pulled out a clutch of the letters. 'Here are some of them,' I said.

Mr. Rebibo leant over and glanced at the sheets. 'That's his hand,' he said calmly. 'Look at the precision. He was the most conscientious man I have ever met.'

A maid descended from the first floor, a headscarf knotted at the back of her head. She set a silver tray with tea on the table.

'Did he ever have visitors?' I asked.

The landlord poured me a porcelain cup and slid it over. 'Oh, yes,' he said. 'Some very important people indeed. He knew the late king, and his father, too. And, of course, I remember you and your two sisters coming. You were very small. Your father brought you.'

I stirred my tea and breathed in the steam.

'The first time I met your father,' he said, 'he had recently returned from Arabia, where he had been the guest of King Ibn Saud. He was sitting where you are sitting now. I remember it so clearly.'

Mr. Rebibo called his elderly Alsatian to heel.

'He told me a story that has stayed in my mind,' he said.

I asked what it was.

'Your father was welcomed at the palace in Mecca,' he said. 'He had forgotten to bring a gift. Suddenly he found himself in the throne room before the old king. He bowed low, kissed Ibn Saud's right hand and said, "Your Majesty, I would like to present you with a gift. Here it is before you. It is I. I give myself to you as your servant until the end of my days."

'Ibn Saud looked down and said: "I thank you for your fine gift and I give you back to yourself. Now, come and sit here and we will talk."'

The landlord laughed, sipped his tea and laughed again.

'I can't tell you how sad we were when the accident happened,' he said. 'Your grandfather had just walked back down the hill from Café de France, as he did each morning. He had reached the door and was taking out his key, when the truck reversed. He was knocked unconscious.'

'Did you see it happen?'

'No. I was away on that day. When I returned, your grandfather was dead.'

We sat in silence for a few moments. The vines round the villa's door were alive with shadows and birdsong.

'Now,' said the landlord in a serious voice, 'I'll give you what you came for. I am surprised that no one from your family has come to collect them until now.'

'Come to collect what?' I said, confused.

'Your grandfather's diaries, of course.'

From: *The Caliph's House*

Buenos Aires

NASRUDIN ENTERED A competition for profound observations.

One by one the contestants gave voice to a deep matter. It was evident the standard was very high indeed.

When it was Nasrudin's turn to make a profound observation, he clapped his hands, and begged everyone to listen well, declaring that his observation was wiser than anything spoken by any man in history.

The judges, the other contestants, and the audience clustered around.

'The moon is more useful than the sun,' the wise fool said.

'That doesn't make sense!' someone called out.

'Of course it does,' Nasrudin responded. 'Because you need the moon's light to see at night, don't you?!'

*

The first time I heard the word 'Argentina' was as a child, when a troupe of puppeteers came to Langton House.

They had read bootleg Spanish translations of my father's books, and were feverishly excited at having arrived at our home in a quiet corner of Kent. Even though they were

283

from Argentina, they were dressed in sheepskin coats from Afghanistan – something that made no sense to me at all.

But then I was only four and a half.

They showered my sisters and me with gifts they'd made themselves from scraps and junk. Sequinned bags and tie-dyed waistcoats, lamps fashioned from old tin cans, spinning rainbow discs, mobiles, and stained-glass wigwams lit by tea lights.

The thing I liked best of all was the stuffed toy one of the Argentinian visitors brought me. His name was Rudolfo and he said he'd made it himself...

A soft toy of Nasrudin on his donkey.

Skewed awkwardly to the side, it was stuffed with second-hand stockings, and it smelled unlike anything I had experienced before. My mother grimaced when she saw it for the first time. She said it was how Argentina smelled, and that I ought to wash my hands after playing with it.

When the puppeteers left, my father slumped in a low leather chair, and seemed lost in despair. Even though I was young, I could see something was wrong.

So I asked what the matter was.

My father sat up, his head bowing down to my level.

'Show me your Nasrudin,' he said.

I held the stuffed toy up by the donkey's foot.

Pressing his nostrils into the fabric, my father breathed in, lids lowering over his eyes as though he were experiencing the most delicious perfume.

'Smell it,' he said.

'I already did. Mummy says I have to wash my hands after touching it. She thinks it smells like dirty old socks.'

'She doesn't know what she's talking about.'

'Why not, Baba?'

'Because she's never been to Argentina.'

'The place the puppet men come from?'

My father nodded.

'That's right. Argentina.'

Pulling the toy away from him, I hugged it tight and nudged my nostrils into it.

'That's right. Smell your Nasrudin,' he said, 'and never forget that smell... because one day you'll go there.'

'To Argentina?'

'Yes.'

'What will I do there?'

My father grinned.

'You'll go in search of Nasrudin,' he said.

With time all dreams come true, and I finally got to Argentina.

The first time I went, forty years had passed since my father had lived there, reaching the Argentine capital by boat. About my age at the time of his arrival, he had accompanied my grandfather on a humanitarian mission on behalf of the India Office, to source halal meat for Muslim soldiers. As ever, they were shadowed by spies, who regularly filed disparaging dispatches to Whitehall.

After several months in Argentina, they made plans to leave, their mission completed and their funds spent. The day before the ship set sail back to Europe, my father was sitting alone in a café on Avenida Santa Fe when a young man stumbled in, touting lottery tickets.

Spotting a foreigner, he made a beeline for him.

'Señor, your last chance to buy a ticket!' he announced breathlessly. 'The national lottery is to be picked this afternoon!'

'I won't win. You know it as well as I.'

The ticket-seller clicked his tongue.

'No, no, señor, on the contrary… I am absolutely certain you are going to win!'

'How can you be so sure?'

The vendor selected one of the paper squares, holding it in his fingers as though it were treasure.

'Because this is the winning ticket, that's why.'

My father sipped his coffee.

'If it is, then why don't you buy it yourself?'

The young man sighed.

'If I did as you suggest, and buy the winning ticket for myself,' he answered, 'I would be robbing you of your destiny.'

So, my father handed over a coin and bought the lucky ticket.

That afternoon, he won the lion's share of La Grande de la Nacional, the Argentine National Lottery.

Next day, my grandfather set sail for Southampton, leaving my father to spend a bale and a half of *peso* notes. Had he taken the money out of Argentina, it would have been devoured by tax.

From time to time in our childhoods, he would reminisce,

describing the suite in the Plaza Hotel where he lived, the cut of the suits he'd had made, or the parties he attended at the invitation of Evita and Perón.

Only after his death did I learn another side of the story.

Six months after my father's fatal heart attack in November 1996, a letter arrived at my London flat. The front of the envelope was plastered with large postage stamps, my name and address written in a precise cursive script.

It was from Rudolfo, the puppeteer who, thirty years before, had given me my beloved home-made Nasrudin.

Through pages of handwritten text, he described how he'd been selling lottery tickets on Avenida Santa Fe one morning, and how he had sold a winning ticket to a young foreigner sitting alone.

'You must think me mad to write this,' he wrote, 'but I saw something in his eyes – something I had not encountered before. It was as though they were burning with anticipation: a most desperate and urgent need to complete a body of work.

'Selecting a lottery ticket, I informed him it was the winning one. As I said the words, I felt deep in my heart it was true. Next day, after the massive win, I found him looking for me on Avenida Santa Fe. On seeing me trudging up and down with the tray of lottery tickets hung around my neck, he said he needed to speak to me urgently.

'So we went to a café nearby. Not one of the grand haunts on Santa Fe, but one that was a little more comfortable, and we drank coffee together. I had no idea that he had struck gold. The tickets were just numbers to me – numbers to sell so that I could pay my family's debts. When he told me of his success, I was happy. As I said, I felt his need – and a destiny far greater than mine.

'The next thing I knew, he'd paid my family's debts, given us savings, and even bought us a car. In the following weeks and months, we became firm friends. Your father was invited to all the fashionable receptions, where he made a name for himself – he was unlike anyone high society had encountered before.

'Early one morning he came to my apartment on the edge of Buenos Aires, an attaché case under his arm. He said it was full of banknotes – money he wanted to give away to change lives. Over a period of a year, I helped him to locate people in need. A baker who required money to open a shop. An artist who couldn't paint because he had three dead-end jobs. A young mother who had no funds with which to send her children to school. One by one, he helped them, always making sure the gifts were made anonymously.

'We continued in this way for a full year. At the end of it, there were several bricks of *peso* notes left. A year to the day of the lottery win, your father packed his bags, and put the remaining money in a cardboard box. Having given me a hug, he passed me the box and an envelope "These are instructions on whom to help with this money," he said. We hugged again, and then he was gone.'

The Buenos Aires of 1988 was not the same Buenos Aires of 1948.

The glitz and the glamour of the post-war days when

Argentina was the richest country on earth were long gone. The military junta and the Falklands War were recent memories. Distraught mothers paraded through Plaza de Mayo in front of the Casa Rosada, clasping enlarged photos of their disappeared sons. The streets were filled with rubbish. The currency had just crashed – yet again.

Soon after my arrival, overland from San Paulo, I found myself strolling down Avenida Santa Fe in the flat light of late afternoon. Without thinking, I was drawn into a café, the doors open wide to the street.

Taking a table at the front, I ordered an espresso, and smiled.

'I'm here, Baba,' I whispered. 'I'm in Buenos Aires at last.'

At that moment, as though cued to do so, a young man swept in, a tray of lottery tickets suspended around his neck.

He strode over.

'Will you choose one for me?'

He picked out a number. I took it and paid.

'Is it a lucky one?' I asked, as he turned to leave.

'Yes, of course it is,' he replied.

Unlike my father, my fate was not to win a share of the Argentine National Lottery. Despite this, it was my destiny for a long-anticipated dream to come true…

…but not for another twenty years.

I longed to meet Rudolfo, the puppeteer who'd made my Nasrudin – the tatty old toy stuffed with stockings and my first scent of distant Argentina.

Even though I returned to Buenos Aires again and again, and roped everyone I met into the hunt for him, there was still no luck. He'd long since moved from the address on the front of the envelope, and no one could even say whether he was alive or dead.

In the winter of 2008, I rented an apartment in the suburb of Palermo Soho, and hid myself away to write a novel, *Casablanca Blues*. The short days were packed with long writing sessions, as they always are when I'm working on a book.

A week passed; then another.

I rarely left the apartment, and only then to buy provisions. For, as every writer knows, nothing is so important as getting past the mid-point.

On the night of the fifteenth day, I had a dream.

A fabulous and fantastical dream.

I dreamt I was seated with Nasrudin on his donkey, flying through space and time...

Back to a bright spring morning in 1948.

Peering down through the cloudless sky, I saw Santa Fe curving round to where it met Avenida 9 de Julio. We soared past an open-air café where my father was scribbling notes, and on to the magnificent Teatro Colón.

A performance was about to begin.

The great and the good of Buenos Aires were streaming urgently from limousines in sable coats, white tie and tails. Inexplicably, my father was there as well – strolling towards the steps, Rudolfo at his side.

On waking, I found the dream waiting in my mind. However hard I tried to forget it, it hung there, like a curtain, as if begging me to observe it.

Condemning myself for slacking, and uncertain quite what I was in search of, I grabbed my overcoat and hurried down to the street.

Fifteen minutes later, I stepped from a taxi outside the Teatro Colón.

Unlike in my dream, the *grande dame* of Buenos Aires was silent, shrouded in scaffolding, as the restoration struggled on.

I stood there for ten minutes, my coat keeping out the wind.

'Where are you, Rudolfo?' I asked, the words lost on the breeze.

Then I remembered something... a stray comment my father had once made. It was so trivial that my mind had hoarded it away in a thick file marked 'insignificances'.

'Argentina is one of the most civilized nations on earth,' he'd told me many years after the puppeteers had come and gone. 'They treat creative people like kings. In Buenos Aires there's even a sanctuary for actors and those connected to the arts. One day you may see it for yourself.'

Pacing fast, I wove my way through the backstreets to Avenida Santa Fe, pausing at number 1243.

La Casa del Teatro – 'The House of Theatre' – had been established in the thirties, as an Art Deco refuge for retired performers down on their luck. It featured guest rooms for residents, and even its own theatre. High above the grand stone edifice, the masks of comedy and tragedy peered down at those hurrying by – landmarks in their own right.

Eaten alive by guilt for escaping my desk, and yet refusing

to give in to doubt, I pulled the door open and initiated the kind of doomed enquiry that has characterized my life.

Even when certain there's no chance at all, a trident jabbing inside me always goads me to ask... just to be sure.

It can be credited with most of my successes, and for reuniting me with Rudolfo Fernández Peña... the puppeteer.

As soon as I mentioned his name, I was rewarded with an ear-to-ear grin.

'He's like my father, and I am like his son,' spouted the doorman.

'Does he live here?'

'Yes, of course.'

Sighing, I exclaimed joy.

Calling a lift finished in hardwood and brass, the doorman dispatched me to an upper floor. A well-dressed orderly met me there and enquired if Señor Fernández Peña was expecting me.

I responded in the negative.

'Does he know you?'

'He did at one time.'

Not wishing to put the puppeteer on the spot, I wrote a message, folded it, and asked for it to be passed on.

Three days slipped by in which I burrowed deep into my unlikely plot in far-off Casablanca.

A watched kettle does not boil, so I slipped my phone into the desk drawer and forgot about it.

On the morning of the fourth day, the phone rang, and a distinguished yet elderly voice spoke my name.

An hour later, the same voice was greeting me face to face.

Since selling the winning lottery ticket and ensuring the proceeds went to the needy, Rudolfo had lived a life of high adventure.

He'd cycled overland to Afghanistan; had sailed across the Pacific in a boat he built himself; and had got lost in the Sahara in a home-made hot air balloon. The journeys were mapped out on a face shrouded by a wind-chapped sheet of leather.

As soon as his mouth had spoken my name, Rudolfo pulled me to him in one of the longest and most satisfying hugs of my life.

When at last it ended, my neck was damp with his tears, and I was left feeling as though I'd been baptized and born again.

Rudolfo took me to a splendidly shabby café on Avenida Santa Fe five minutes' walk from La Casa del Teatro. The walls were stained yellow from decades of cigarette smoke, the light fittings smashed, and the floor re-laid in the cheapest lino.

Two or three elderly regulars were sitting at the bar staring into space, no doubt reminiscing about the glory days.

As soon as the heels of his shoes were through the door, Rudolfo's mood changed. While overcome with emotion when we hugged, he was now overcome with passion for the room.

'Every time I come in here I weep,' he said. 'Can't help it. The more I try to stand tall, the greater the cascade of tears.'

'Why does it make you sad?' I asked.

The puppeteer held up a hand, the fingers as leathery and wind-chapped as his face.

'No, no...' he said fast. 'There's no sorrow. Only joy. You see, this is where I began my first incarnation.'

'Which incarnation was that?'

'As the lad who stumbled from one end of this great avenue to the other, selling lottery tickets from a tray hanging around my neck. The incarnation in which I came through those doors over there one bright morning, and sold a young man in a rather crumpled linen suit a rectangle of paper.'

'*My father?*'

Rudolfo blinked.

'I can see him sitting at this very table, making notes.'

Unable to reply, I sat there profoundly moved, staring into Rudolfo's eyes.

After a long expanse of silence, I explained that I still had my beloved stocking-stuffed Nasrudin, although he was a little worse for wear.

The puppeteer seemed pleased.

'In stuffed toy years he's an old man, and his donkey's even more ancient,' he said. 'But then, I suppose, everything has its time.'

As my ears took in the words, I cast an eye around the café, wondering how long it had left.

I spent all afternoon chatting to Rudolfo, listening to his life's narrative, played out in extraordinary detail. The episodes continued over many more days, until it was time for me to leave Buenos Aires.

The first draft of my novel done and dusted, and my

luggage packed, I went to meet the puppeteer for the last time.

'I'll be back soon,' I said, knowing full well that I would not.

'Then I'll wait for you,' he said.

Three years later, arriving once again in Buenos Aires, I made a beeline for Avenida Santa Fe.

To my great sorrow, the café was gone.

So was Rudolfo Fernández Peña...

Ticket-seller, raconteur, adventurer, puppeteer, and maker of the most unusual soft toys the world has ever known.

From: *Travels With Nasrudin*

Beyond the Devil's Teeth

Then they rose and followed Lingo,
Followed onwards to the forest,
From the mountain Dewalgiri,
Followed on till night descended.

Jesús poured himself a beer and blew the foam from the top.

The corners of his mouth were turned up, so that it seemed that he was smiling even when he was not. Before drinking from the glass of the Polar lager, he tipped a little liquid onto the dusty café floor.

'Are the flies bothering you?' I asked.

'No,' said Jesús, 'it is for the saints.'

We sat on the veranda of a Café Popular in Ciudad Bolívar on the southern banks of the Orinoco. The sky suddenly turned inky black and the Venezuelan rains gushed down.

I had come in search of Macumba.

The cult's existence had intrigued me since Wood had first spoken of it on his roof in Mumbai. And I was eager to learn more and understand the mechanics of a society whose roots were imbedded so interculturally.

The route from East Africa had been straight-forward enough. A cheap courier flight had taken me from Jomo Kenyatta International Airport, at Nairobi, to Amsterdam. From there, I had flown standby to Miami, in time to catch a direct, discounted flight to the Venezuelan capital.

Brazil was my target, in particular its Amazonian capital: Manaus. I was careful not to reveal the reason for my quest to anyone. Previous experience had shown that esoteric matters are either derided by most people, or else tend to scare them.

Even from Oswaldo, whom I planned to visit in Patagonia, I had kept secret my thoughts, my deep fascination for Macumba.

A child selling cigarettes crawled under an amphibious army truck and kept his chin high, waiting for the rain to cease. His friend pushed a tub of purple ice cream under one of the wheel arches and climbed in after it.

Jesús took a gulp of the lager, and continued with his stories.

We had met on the bus from Caracas, the Venezuelan capital. He had pressed his tanned fingers tightly into mine, laughing through a bearded mouth, exclaiming that our friendship would last forever.

Giant moths fluttered above the crowded café life, taking refuge from the tropical storm. One landed on the pelt of a dead cat, which hung high up on a wall: its wings matched perfectly with the cat's matted fur, and it was invisible for a moment.

Jesús cut me a piece of *cachapa*, a maize pancake filled with white cheese. It had been, he said, a favourite dish of the country's liberator, Simón Bolívar. He offered the rest of the pancake to a table full of soldiers who sat next to us.

One stood guard, his hands gripped around a nine-millimetre UZI machine-gun, while the others drank beer and played draughts. It all seemed so like Africa: the beer and the tropical rains, and nature's domination of the land.

Jesús talked for hours about his country.

'Yes, of course there is corruption here,' he said, 'but there is corruption everywhere. God gave Venezuela all the minerals it would ever need: he gave us oil and aluminium, mangrove bark and tonka beans. Education is free and there are ten universities in the country. Bolívar would be pleased if he came back now. My father wants me to join him in business. He has a little land that farms balata gum. You must come and meet him and stay with us.'

Putting down my drink – a tall glass of coconut milk – I broke in: 'Jesús, I have to go southwards. I am heading for Belo Horizonte, in Brazil. My friend Oswaldo Rodríguez Oswaldo gave me a letter of introduction to his cousin who lives there. Then I want to go south, to Buenos Aires and beyond: to walk amongst the ice mountains of Patagonia.'

'Where have you come from?' Jesús enquired.

'From the east.'

'Did you go to that place… "India"?' asked Jesús.

'Yes, I stayed there for a long time.'

'What are the people like?'

'Well,' I began, 'the first thing is that there are so many of them... well over a billion.'

Jesús looked at me as if I were mad.

'In Venezuela,' he said, 'we have nothing like that!'

'They're fine once you get used to them. But they have some unconventional customs and traditions.'

'What do you mean?' said Jesús, pouring himself another beer.

'Hindu people revere cows as sacred... they worship them.'

'Worship them?' Jesús yelled. 'In Venezuela, we don't worship cows, we barbecue them! India must be an amusing place: tell me more!'

'There is a God called Ganesh,' I began. 'He has the head of an elephant and the body of a man. He's got four arms and rides upon a mouse.'

Jesús started to roll about, crippled with laughter.

'These customs might seem peculiar but they are very ancient. People have worshipped cows in India for four thousand years. I find such ideas strange as well, but I respect them, if only for their longevity.'

The Venezuelan nodded in agreement and wiped the tears from his eyes.

'We may not have as many people, but this is a big continent. And, remember, the map might look very pretty, but its colours can deceive!'

I promised that I would return to talk with Jesús again after leaving Patagonia. It all seemed so easy. Jesús' watery green eyes rolled, perhaps in awe at my naive confidence. Then he fell off his chair. For he was very drunk indeed.

As I walked back to the Roma Hotel, winged insects of all types buzzed around the street lamps, and wide-bodied lizards scuffled around my feet. The hotel's owner was asleep in the garden, stretched out on a rope bed. I opened the door of my room. There was no lock, and the hinges squeaked as I pressed the door inwards.

Since my travels in West Africa I preferred not to turn on the light before I slept: it only revealed where the biggest of the insects were and attracted more creatures around the bulb. The bed was large and the pillow moulded around my head as I lay down to sleep.

There was the sound of a cricket moving restlessly on my bed. I edged away and was just about to drift into sleep, when a hand lunged down against the sheets and squashed the insect and its noise with a single blow. I leapt up and ran to the light switch. A stubby figure was sitting up. He had almond eyes and one-inch bristles radiated sparsely from his face in all directions.

'Hello,' he lisped. 'My name is Kiato.'

He stared at me and blinked, almost as if telling me his name explained why he was sleeping in my bed. Fumbling for a pair of wire-framed glasses, he slowly unscrewed his eyes which had been blinded by the light.

'The manager said I could stay with you, I am from Japan,' he said, with an American accent. 'Does that bother you?'

'No, since you're here you might as well stay.' I was too exhausted to argue, and made a mental note to claim half my money back in the morning. 'I have to leave early, anyway. I am going to El Dorado and then towards Brazil,' I said.

'Really? That's where I'm going. The bus leaves at six,' said Kiato.

I turned off the light.

No sooner, it felt, had my head touched the pillow, than Kiato shook me and said that it was time to leave. When travelling alone it can sometimes be hard to refuse company.

At the bus station people lounged around eating purple ice cream and drinking pineapple juice. There was a shout: a man was running towards me through the damp morning air. He waved a piece of paper and moved with wide athletic strides.

'*Amigo* Tahir, *mi amigo!*' he called.

It was Jesús. He gave me his address so that I could find him on my return. It was time to get on the bus. As I stepped aboard, Jesús handed me a leather pouch.

'They are tonka beans,' he gasped, 'they will bring you your fortune.' We shook hands and the bus moved away towards El Dorado.

Oil processing plants and nodding donkeys, for pumping oil to the surface, mingled with the jungle and lined the route. The landscape was identical to that of Uganda. Berries and fruits of all colours weighed down the branches of rubbery trees, which sprouted from the brick-red earth. Kiato whistled and took pictures of all he saw with an autofocus Minolta. He was, he said, from Kyoto, the ancient Imperial Japanese capital.

'I studied at the American school in Tokyo,' he explained. 'My father wanted me to work for his company. So I went to the airport and took a flight to Guatemala. It's best not to argue with him, just to leave.' Kiato stopped speaking.

We both stared in horror at our first encounter with serious deforestation. One hillside after the next lay barren, like shaven scalps. The oncoming lane of the newly macadamized road carried massive tree-bearing trucks towards the ports. It was as if the very soul of Venezuela was being exchanged for yet another petrochemical processing plant. A receding line of jungle was the only witness.

Kiato was now too shaken to take photographs. He moved about uneasily, put the camera on his lap, and said, 'My country buys the wood and gives Venezuela technology to exploit its minerals in exchange. I'm ashamed of what I see, knowing that my people are to blame.'

The bus's brakes were slammed on and we all trooped out at a military checkpoint.

Our passports and malaria tablets were scrutinized by an officer with two red shoulder-stripes – attached with safety pins. Another soldier touch-typed in triplicate and handed the bus driver a permit to proceed.

More than a hundred butterflies were squashed against the radiator grille. Some were still moving like dying soldiers on a battlefield, their pink and blue wings twitching in minute movements.

Eight hours later we reached El Dorado.

It was a place surpassed by its reputation and would have been easy to miss. Surely this was not El Dorado, the lost city of gold? I suspected that it was not: a lost city would be more glamorous, of that I was certain.

Two men and a dog lay out asleep in the full scorching afternoon sun. I had the feeling that I was stepping down onto a film set. The dog woke up, barked at Kiato, and waddled away to sit in the shade. We moved into a hotel with no visible name, off the main square.

The room, which was despicably filthy, had a defective fan and was divided in two by a spotted plastic table covering. Yet, curiously, I was surprised to find that the bathroom down the hall was immaculate.

Paintings of romantic French landscapes hung on the walls, freshly laundered towels were waiting to be used and the shower emitted a geyser-like jet of water. Puzzled that such a dingy rest-house should offer impeccable bathing facilities, I made enquiries.

An assistant to the manager confided the reason. He said that when the gold-miners arrive back to El Dorado – city of sin – the first thing on their minds is a long, soothing shower. After spending weeks without washing, the bodies of these gold-miners or prospectors are awash with traces of the precious metal. Conniving landlords install filtration systems and high-pressure showers to relieve them of the grains of gold.

Kiato wanted to see one thing more than anything else: the Angel Falls. They are said to have the longest drop in the world: over three thousand two hundred feet, and are on the Churun River, a tributary of the Caroni.

Kiato's guidebook said that an old German and his Guyanese wife led expeditions to the Falls. The weather-worn trailblazer, however, was asleep on the veranda of his house when we found him. And he had led no trips into the jungle for over ten years.

At the town's small airport a hammock had been slung between a six-seater Cessna 206 and a tree. Inside was Roberto, the pilot. Although he had no map, he said that he knew the route and agreed to take us to the Angel Falls.

But the problem was the weather.

Lightning storms were forecast for the following two days; Roberto would contact us at the right time. Thanking him, we went to eat spaghetti.

The café in the centre of town was square-shaped and trapped the heat, as if designed by an oven-maker. Those around us gulped down glass after glass of warm, dark lager. It was almost as if a spell had been cast to ensure the room was always baking hot, inducing the clientele to consume ever larger quantities of alcoholic liquid.

Waving my arms about, I tried to distract the unnaturally large population of flies which were swarming above my plate of over-cooked pasta. The insects were certainly breeding well in the damp café heat and lived long, robust lives on Bolognese sauce.

A man at the next table passed me a part of his newspaper to swat the insects. One fly, larger than the others, had landed on the wall next to where I sat. Rolling up the paper, I aimed, then lunged with all my strength.

The fly met a sudden end.

As I scraped its remains from the cement, I noticed something curious. An almost spherical object, like a gourd, dyed blue and decorated with etched vertical lines, hung from a nail in the wall. I took it down to inspect it closer.

The man who'd given me his newspaper was watching me. I glanced at him, half expecting an explanation of the object. He folded the remaining pages of his paper and laid it down, and said slowly:

'Macumba.'

I sat up, startled by the word.

'I want to know more on this Macumba; can you advise me how I might learn more?' I asked eagerly.

'What you are holding comes from Brazil,' said the man, in excellent English, 'although Macumba does exist in Venezuela. That comes from Manaus, in Amazonas, it's designed to give protection to everyone who comes here, and to make sure that no catastrophes happen in this little café.'

'What actually *is* Macumba?' I asked.

'It's a belief that developed in Brazil, although much of what it counts as sacred originated in Africa. When slaves were taken to South America by the Portuguese, they brought with them their ancient gods. Those gods, and their knowledge of magic, herbs and nature, are at the centre of what is called Macumba now. Macumba concentrates on spirit possession.'

The man lit a cigar and sucked hard on it. I invited him to sit with me. And, as soon as he had sat, he began to speak again:

'I became interested in Macumba, Umbanda and Candomblé when I was living in southern Brazil. Many of my friends took part in the ceremonies at the time, and one of my closest colleagues at work was a medium.'

'Who or what possesses the mediums?' I asked.

'Usually the gods of the Nigerian Yoruba tribe. They are known as Orishas, and it is thought that they control everything that happens to us and around us. You must pay homage to them and worship them, and then they will be happy and make circumstances favourable towards you. If you want to make them very happy you can let them enter your body.

'There were problems when the slaves came to Brazil, because the Portuguese wanted to make them Catholic. The Africans did a very ingenious thing. They pretended to be worshipping the Catholic saints, yet really they were praying to their own gods. Each of the gods was assigned the image of a Catholic saint.'

'Is Macumba used to cause harm?' I asked.

'Are you referring to Black Magic?'

'Yes, that type of thing.'

'No, Macumba itself is rarely used to inflict pain. That isn't the nature of it. It has come to be used very widely throughout South and North America – often known as Santería: for it does something very important. It acts as a system that gives social, psychological, and even medicinal aid. It also helps people relieve themselves of stress.

'But there is a cult which is known for its evil practices. It exists mainly in Cuba and is called as Mayombero. Its spells can maim, or put an end to life: they are designed eventually to destroy. Mayombero works in league with the Devil, whilst Macumba works with God.'

'I want to find out more about Macumba,' I said. 'Where can I find a group that practises it?'

'I heard recently that Manaus has a lot of ceremonies going on; why don't you try there? Failing that, Belem is famous for its special kind of rites.' He pulled a visiting card from his pocket and clicked it down before me. The gentleman nodded politely and, as I scanned the card's neat italic script, he left the café.

It read: *Professor Francisco Fernander.*

Kiato took pictures of a little boy who was dressed in a colourful Hawaiian shirt. His mother sat down next to us and began to chat. Her name was María. She had long, jet-black hair, alabaster-white skin, and eyes the deep-blue colour of the finest lapis lazuli.

At thirteen she had been married in Caracas, then had left her husband and settled in El Dorado. I asked what she did all day long.

'I take care of people,' she said. 'You know, this town revolves around mining gold. That's the only reason anyone's here at all. At night the prospectors would spend everything on beer and prostitutes, so I take care of their money for them. They trust me.'

Every few moments she would wave or turn to greet someone: she seemed to be very popular. We walked around the town with María as she collected money and noted down figures on a blue pad. She would introduce us to people, slipping in a side comment like, 'he killed his wife' or 'watch your wallets'.

One man, known to all as 'Princess', was delighted that María had brought two strapping young men for him to meet. He winked and removed his shirt so that I could admire his biceps. Kiato shuffled to the door uneasily.

Princess said his job was to wash the prison guards' uniforms and darn their socks. Sometimes he made dresses in his spare time. María whispered that he performed other duties too. He blushed, and we left.

I had read Henri Charrière's masterwork *Papillon* and been moved by his story. Papillon had been incarcerated at El Dorado prison after leaving Devil's Island in Guyana. When I asked María if it was possible to get into the prison, she became serious all of a sudden.

'Do you *really* want to go?' she asked.

I replied that I did.

'Then I shall see what I can do.'

By the end of the afternoon we seemed to have met everyone in El Dorado. There was not much to do, so we went to eat more spaghetti. Kiato set up a solar charger to replenish the batteries for his camera. Eventually I heard María calling my name, and turned around. She was sitting in a black Mercedes. Such a splendid car – easily capable of one hundred and fifty miles an hour – looked very peculiar in such a dilapidated place as El Dorado.

Kiato and I climbed into the back and breathed in the odour of the cool leather seats. A young man was at the wheel. He pulled up in front of a bar at the edge of town.

María went inside, and soon returned with a fat, bald man who was very drunk. He was pushed into the back with Kiato and me, his face slouched against the window. He writhed and muttered as if in a state of delirium.

'OK, now we can go to the prison,' said María.

'Who's the drunk?'

'He's the head of security.'

Five miles from El Dorado we tore across a wooden truss bridge, as the young driver demonstrated the full capacity of his machine.

'This is *La Colonia*, as the prison is known,' said María. 'It's surrounded by the Man-Eating River: there are so many piranha in these parts. Fall in there and you'll be stripped to the bone.'

At the checkpoint, the police chief was prodded and he managed to salute with his left hand before throwing up over the white leather upholstery. A row of uniformed guards saluted back and raised a barrier.

Eight hundred men were serving sentences at the prison. They hung about, chatting and making souvenirs to be sold to the few tourists who visited El Dorado.

Some cheered when they saw María and she blew them kisses. Various sections of the prison were pointed out. One wing was set aside for gay inmates, another for the most dangerous men: that was where Papillon had been. A couple of rather unenthusiastic offenders were painting the high-security area bright yellow.

María said that one man in particular would like to speak to us. We walked through gates with iron bars and locks that clicked behind us. Under the wide branches of a tropical tree we met Leroy. He had been sent here thirteen years before, convicted of murder, and was the only prisoner who spoke English. His voice wavered as he spoke to us. Now and again he chuckled loudly and his head shook from side to side.

'You can't imagine how it is for me to speak English,' he said. 'To use these words is like being able to breathe again. At first when I was locked up, away from my home country, Trinidad, I used to talk to myself in English. Even, oh, until a few years ago, then I gave it up. There's seven more years left, but I should get out before that for good behaviour. The guards here like me and are kind. I brew them fermented drinks and they sometimes give me cigarettes.'

'Is there anything we can send you, Leroy?' Kiato asked.

'Nothing I need, I'm used to it here.' Then he thought for a moment and said gently, 'But there is one small thing that I've been craving for a very long time.'

'Anything. What is it?' I asked him.

'It might seem strange, but could you say the word "melodramatic" out loud?'

Giant moths flapped like bats above our heads at El Dorado's most popular bar. The insects tried in desperation to obtain camouflage on the walls. Music blared from two colossal speakers. I hoped it was below the decibel level necessary to perforate eardrums. The habitat had been created by the ruthless clientele native to El Dorado.

When a teenager of a more refined aspect sauntered over, declaring that he knew a quieter place, we needed no further persuasion to follow. He was called Hubert.

El Dorado seemed an unlikely place for luxury of any kind to exist. The last thing I had expected was for the door of a discotheque to be swung open by a white bouncer in a dinner jacket.

He stood square in the door frame like a peg in a hole, taking the last drags from a very pungent cigarette with no filter. The room was dark and insipid. Air conditioning units rumbled in each corner, producing an arctic environment.

Hubert, Kiato and I made for a corner booth and sat. Hubert snapped his fingers and a forty-dollar bottle of Bacardi arrived on a silver tray.

Kiato and I glanced at each other in surprise as Hubert threw down a wad of new *bolívar* notes and motioned the waiter away. We had been living on no more than two dollars each a day. Hubert swallowed a glass full of the neat white rum and left. He said that he was going to get some women. He never came back.

The elite crowd of El Dorado swanned languidly about on the disco dance floor which dominated the nightclub.

Kiato started talking to a man at the bar, whose friend was also out hunting for women. We offered him some of Hubert's rum and he sat with us. His head was bald; a thick red beard sprang from his face and bounced against his chest when he spoke. It impressed Kiato enormously as his own beard was very sparse.

The friend, who had been looking for women, returned. He looked like a desperado and dragged me out, telling me to keep an eye out for under-age girls.

My lungs seemed to seize up when we entered the humid evening air. Two whale-like creatures approached us. My companion kissed his fingertips and nudged me in the ribs.

I wondered for a moment if we were looking at the same women. They ambled up, both looking as if they might be suffering from the latter stages of some unpleasant, nameless and virulent illness.

Both had revolving, roving eyes.

The desperado leapt about with joy. He started to pull the heftier woman towards an overflowing gutter. Protesting, I returned to the disco.

A few minutes later the wild man returned to the icy air-conditioned atmosphere and came over to where I sat. The huge women loomed behind with unsure steps. Kiato and the red-bearded man were horrified, and blamed me for the desperado's choice.

The larger woman pulled me up to dance. As she acclimatized to the arctic surroundings – romping about – the nature of her movements began to alarm me.

But the dance ended very suddenly. The record was removed and the strobe turned off. Without any words, everyone from the disco moved outside. The time was exactly three a.m. People were walking towards a dark back street from all over town.

A man shepherded everyone into one of the shops. I recognized him: it was Princess, the laundry-man. An audience had assembled, all eager to get a glimpse of the action. Still not understanding what was going on, I asked the bald, red-bearded man.

'Don't you know?' he said. 'You must be from far away; Princess's fashion shows are famous.'

'Are they always held at this time of night?' I asked.

'Of course they are!' said the mouth swamped in red bristles.

Girls worthy of a Paris catwalk paraded about in dresses of red and green. As they twirled around, the crowd clapped and whistled and Princess beamed with pride.

When I was leaving the shop, María came over to me and whispered:

'Now you have seen El Dorado. Now I think you know why I stay here.'

We were woken late. A little urchin girl brought word from Roberto, the pilot, that the weather had cleared and he was ready to fly to the Angel Falls. Kiato and I entered the bright sunshine and the innocence of day. There was no sign of the prostitutes and alcohol. Princess was darning socks again; and pots of spaghetti were being brought to the boil at the café.

At the airport Roberto slipped from his hammock and stretched.

'It's a great day for flying,' he said, pulling on a pair of worn Levi's jeans.

We spoke for a while. I asked how he came to speak such good English. In El Dorado, few seemed to know the language.

'I'm from British Guyana. Started flying in Canada back in sixty-six. There isn't much call for a pilot these days. I ferry gold-miners around mostly, to the less accessible areas of the jungle.'

'Have you seen the Angel Falls before?' Kiato asked.

'Yup, but not for about twenty years. They're beyond the Devil's Teeth, shouldn't be too hard to find.'

We walked to the plane.

Three men were hoisting two forty-gallon drums of petrol up into the fuselage.

Roberto put out his cigarette and muttered, 'Probably best not to smoke around those babies. You don't mind if we drop them off at the Mission along the way?'

There was no choice.

I climbed into the co-pilot seat, which was jammed at the most forward position. This made it impossible to use the foot-operated rudder controls if I had wanted to. Kiato was wedged in the rear of the aircraft, his face squashed against the window, and with a slow-leaking oil drum between him and the exit.

We exchanged looks of dismay as Roberto turned into the wind, pushed in the throttle, and slid back the stick. The Cessna 206 felt very heavy indeed. As my seat soaked up the petrol like a sponge, I forced myself to stop imagining a gloriously explosive end.

Kiato hummed.

His face was tight and paralyzed with fear.

The Cessna's controls were still familiar. When I was seventeen, my father had sent me off to learn to fly. Biff, the most relaxed pilot in history, had taught me to solo a similar Cessna over the swamps of northern Florida. The one hard rule Biff had ground into me was that one must always have an emergency landing-spot in mind. Roberto set the direction indicator and adjusted the altimeter.

Two thousand feet below, the jungle sprawled out in all directions. One tree's canopy merged into the next. Where would we land if there was a crisis? I plucked up courage and asked Roberto. Pulling out a silver hip-flask from his back pocket, he opened it with his teeth and drained it dry. Then he cackled with deranged laughter.

The flying bomb proceeded for more than half an hour over dense jungle. From time to time palaeozoic rock formations jutted from the jungle floor. The Cessna buzzed like a moth between giant flat-topped cliffs, sprouting like mushrooms from between the trees. Roberto pointed to a clearing in the distance where a large white building stood. It was the Mission. Circling twice, we landed into the wind. The forty-gallon tanks were carried away.

A native dialect was spoken by the people who lived at the Mission. They had become used to the insects which infested everything. Slapping one's legs would leave a pair of blood-streaked hands.

Soon the irritation of insect bites was a memory. Roberto pushed the throttle in again and we soared high above the bumpy grass strip.

Little mining communities could be spotted on the banks of some rivers; their panning turned the water yellow. Roberto pulled the stick further back and we climbed to six thousand feet.

The crumbling mountains, covered in green forest, gave way to spectacular gorges.

Roberto put his hand on my knee. His voice trembling, he shouted,

'We are above the Devil's Teeth, the entrance to the canyon of the Angel Falls.'

It was as if we were venturing into a primeval land where dinosaurs and extinct monsters still roamed. The stone walls of the canyon were grey and crumbled with age. Our Cessna soared like an eagle round and around. Then, whilst banking steeply, we caught a first glimpse of the Angel Falls.

They plunged from the Caroni River down to the jungle floor. The distance of their vault was so great that the water turned into mist halfway down. I could understand how the American aviator, Jimmy Angel, might have felt on discovering the Falls in 1935.

Kiato's camera clicked. He, Roberto, and I whooped with wild exhilaration. We circled around the canyon four times.

Roberto was now, for some reason, very relaxed. He took his hands from the control column and fumbled for his own camera. The Cessna's nose began to fall. The altimeter's hands started to wind downwards. The trees grew bigger and bigger. As the engine made a tortured, droning noise, I grabbed the stick, gently easing it back.

Roberto banked left, and we flew through the Devil's Teeth and out from that prehistoric land – back into our own time.

On the return flight to El Dorado we stopped at a mining village to collect some prospectors. A cut-throat looking bunch of men, they were hardened by the gruelling conditions of their jungle work. Their hands were rough and calloused, and their burnt, worn faces were mostly hidden beneath tattered beards.

Each clutched a little nugget of gold.

Rubbing their palms together in their relief at escaping the jungle for a time, they chatted of their favourite prostitutes who would be awaiting them in El Dorado.

When we landed, Kiato and I left Roberto and walked back into town. We were both silent. Our minds had been captured by the force of nature.

There was time for one last bowl of spaghetti before the bus bound for Kilometro 88 arrived in the square. I glanced round at El Dorado – that most extraordinary place – and climbed aboard.

Kilometro 88 was about as exciting as its name suggests. The town was almost an exact replica of El Dorado. Kiato and I took shelter from the torrential rain in a cavernous drinking house.

In the bar, which was hung with bunting, I pulled up a beer-stained chair. Just before sitting, I noticed the beer stains were moving. A pair of eyes amongst the stains blinked.

Almost every free surface in the room was covered with giant moths, which were perfectly camouflaged in the sordid atmosphere. The floor seemed to be littered with piles of decaying brown leaves, which twitched even though there was no breeze.

Kiato ordered a large steak with macaroni piled on top. The bus to Santa Elena, at the Brazilian border, arrived as he sucked up the first pieces of pasta. There was no hurry to bolt the food. The driver and passengers waited courteously until we were ready to leave.

For fifteen hours the silver bus laboured towards Brazil. When it rained, water drenched us, seeping through a thousand holes in the ceiling. When it became dark we ploughed on at three miles an hour. The driver's friend walked in front, guiding the way and forcing all wandering animals to clear the road.

Just before noon the next day the bus pulled into Santa Elena; the town had a sense of greater social cohesion than El Dorado or Kilometro 88. It seemed as if people resided there because they really wanted to be there.

Old crones sat in doorways knitting, and their grandchildren played in the dirt at their feet.

The previous week had seen the heaviest rain in the region for a very long time. A major bridge en route to Manaus, the Amazonian capital, had been washed away two days before. It would be at least a month before repairs were completed.

Under a magnificent statue of Simón Bolívar, an assorted group of travellers had gathered. Kiato sat down and waited for them to introduce themselves. Like us, they were heading towards Manaus. And, like us, they had heard of the bridge which had been washed away.

The tallest was an aristocratic chap: Rudolf van den Bosch-Drakenburgh. Standing six foot two, he had a Daks tweed jacket slung casually over his shoulders, and wore a paisley-patterned silk cravat, knee-length breeches, and what looked to me like handmade riding boots.

'What's all this nonsense about?' he began in a light Dutch accent. 'Luigi, go fetch my brogues!'

A monstrously large creature unpacked clothes from an antique sea trunk. Although taller than the Dutchman, he lacked any air of sophistication. His clothing was tattered, his hair was oily and unkempt, and his severely sunburnt face was peppered with grotesque sores.

'The suede ones or the black pair?' he asked gently, ducking with subservience.

Luigi was a batman and general factotum to den Bosch-Drakenburgh. Foamy saliva filtered through one corner of his mouth, dripping onto his torn shirt front. He had not adapted to the climate well.

Originally from Galway, in western Ireland, he was now living in Shepherd's Bush, London, where, he assured me, a good pint of Guinness was to be had.

It remained a mystery why an Irishman, even though resident at Shepherd's Bush, had a traditionally Italian name. Yet perhaps even more mysterious was the reason for his utter subservience to Rudolf, who had gained complete domination over the Irishman. Luigi seemed to crave a sadistic master.

Kiato demonstrated how to use the solar battery-charger to another man, who sat beside him. He was thin and his face was drawn and white. He was a Russian named Yuri.

We spoke for a long time and, out of the three, Yuri's comments and expressions were by far the most interesting to me. He had been born in Volgograd, the only son of Orthodox Jewish parents.

'My father died when I was eight,' he said. 'And for my mother there was great prejudice against her for being Jewish and a widow.' He lit a cheap cigarette before continuing in his poetic English. 'I studied English and German in Moscow.

'It was so wonderful to be in that city, you can't imagine. My mother was very proud, I think. Then, in 1982, when I was twenty, the Red Army sent me to Afghanistan. The initial eagerness soon evaporated. They told us lies, they said that we would be fighting the Americans! Can you believe that?'

'Where were you stationed?' I asked.

'At first near Kandahar. I thought that was bad. The rations would often be cut in half because the Mujahedin had hit the supply convoy to our base.

'Then one spring morning my unit was moved to fight in the hopeless offensive against Commander Ahmad Shah, at the Panjshir Valley. Many of my friends were killed. Others committed suicide, or went mad because of bad treatment or drinking engine coolant: there was no alcohol. We were like rats in a cage, shaking with terror whenever the rockets fell like rain.

'I vowed that when I got free I would see something of this world. Twelve months later I was sent back to Moscow. There had been no news from my mother for over half that time. Then I found out that she had died from depression a month before.'

✳

RUDOLF THE DUTCHMAN held still as Luigi's clumsy hands fumbled, trying to tie the plaited leather laces of his brogues.

Having acquired exit stamps from a small police outpost, we walked towards the Brazilian border. A truck with no doors or windows picked us up and dropped us at the frontier army post. Rudolf spelt out his various titles to an officer who wrote them all in the register.

The officer's face was three inches from the page. Crouching with concentration, he formed each letter individually, using a blunt pencil. A gust of wind shook the tree above, and an avocado fell to the ground. The officer dropped the pencil and scampered over to the fruit. Another produced a knife and they split it in two.

Luigi hauled Kiato off to look for toads, saying that toad-spotting was a popular sport in his native town. The rest of us took shelter from the evening rains and slept our first night in Brazil.

At six the next morning clouds of blue smoke drew closer with a noise like an approaching tank. A truck with no exhaust-pipe trundled up. Two blonde German girls were riding in the back. They pulled us up and we set off for the bridge which had been washed away.

All but Kiato and I were strong swimmers, and were confident that we would be able to cross the water. Luigi passed around handfuls of toads, and snuggled up to the Germans, who were called Elaine and Seline. They looked uneasy as the Irishman jerked something from his jacket pocket. He pulled out a creature, as large as his palm, with eight furry legs which moved in opposite directions.

The girls screamed and Elaine punched Luigi, who – recoiling from the force of the blow – dropped the spider on Seline's lap. Rudolf stretched out and struck Luigi on the other side of his face. Wrapped in gloom, Luigi edged over to where Kiato sat.

The truck pressed on, deeper into the jungle.

Snakes slid across the road, monkeys and colourful birds moved amongst the greenery and called out from the forest. The pot-holed track ended where the water began. A hammock had been slung from one petrol tanker to another, and a workman was cradled in it, asleep. At the river's bank the current was fast moving. Forty metres separated us from the other side.

Luigi crouched on all fours without being instructed to do so. Rudolf sat on his arched back and removed his shoes. It seemed natural for the Irishman to assume this position, leading me to suspect that the two men had been together for a long time. Kiato and Yuri went off to look for something to use as a float. Somewhere in my saddle-bags I found a hundred and fifty feet of parachute cord.

Rudolf took charge.

Handing the line to Luigi, he told him to swim across the river and tie it to something on the other side. The Irishman, who was evidently embarrassed at removing his clothes in public, dived in – the cord in his mouth – and swam to the other side completely dressed.

The German girls looked at him as if he were mad. In an easy movement, each stripped off all her clothes and leapt naked into the water.

A mechanism for hoisting the packs across the water was slowly developed. Yuri had found an inner tube.

It was attached to the line. Rudolf commanded Luigi to swim across with every pack. As always, he was compelled to obey. The two complemented each other perfectly: one was a sadist, the other resigned to a life of masochism.

Each was dependent on the other.

The inner tube, which had a slow leak, was pressed deep into the water by the weight of Rudolf's trunk. The Dutchman removed his cravat, but refused to undress. He said that he was light enough to ride aboard the trunk. We all watched. Rudolf's twitching lips strained to be confident.

The Irishman tugged gently at the line.

Tube, trunk, and master glided across the choppy surface of the river.

Halfway over, Rudolf began to shake.

He scrabbled to keep level. But the well-travelled sea trunk, which had begun to list badly, slid into the river like a sinking ship.

The Dutchman went with it.

Kiato, Yuri and I cheered. The German girls whistled and shrieked with laughter. Only Luigi seemed sad. Either he sincerely cared for Rudolf's safety, or – as I suspected – he knew that he would be beaten.

Elaine and I walked ahead of the party.

We both wanted to keep at a distance from Rudolf, who was in a very bad mood indeed.

Along the red sand track we strode, splashing through the puddles of rainwater. Elaine talked of her life. I was impressed by the great strength of her character. Sweat dripped into her eyes as she spoke.

'I don't understand weakness,' she said. 'I've always believed that if one person in the world can achieve something, then there's no reason why I, or others, can't do the same. I don't know how someone like that Irish guy can put up with being treated that way.'

We both glanced round to see Luigi stumbling slowly under the weight of Rudolf's sodden trunk and his own pack. Foam oozed from both corners of his mouth, and his thick mop of black hair stood on end. The Irishman was like an animal trained by a lion tamer, but in a distressing way had become addicted to the torture.

Exclamations of joy broke the monotony of Luigi's groans.

Yuri had spotted a small round hut at the point where the straight red sand road met the skyline. Rudolf was complaining that he had blisters and was thirsty. Indeed, we were all utterly exhausted, having walked for five hours.

The evening air was thick with mosquitos and great speckled moths.

The owner of the round hut gave us some hot water and pointed to a group of trees from which we could sling hammocks. Rudolf ordered the proprietor to give him a chair. When comfortably seated, he made Luigi bathe, bandage, and dry his blistered toes.

Yuri and I stared up at the night sky. His voice trembled in awe as we watched shooting stars cascade across the galaxy.

'In Volgograd, I had a telescope,' he said. 'It was the only escape from a childhood of oppression. Every night I would sit and watch satellites spinning through space. It's strange that here, far from Russia, I see the same stars. It's wonderful to think that people all over the earth stare up and see the same planets, the same constellations. Yet at the time you feel a very personal sensation, as if they are invisible to all but you.'

He pointed at the constellations, slowly naming each in turn, and speaking of the new ones – of the southern hemisphere region – which he had not seen before.

A generator rumbled in the background. The man in the hut moved in the flickering light of a black-and-white television. A broad satellite dish fixed to the top of a tree trapped pictures beamed from Boa Vista. *Dallas* – the American soap opera – was starting, and the Amazon night had just begun.

Kiato had mastered the art of sleeping perfectly still in his hammock – something which I was incapable of doing. As I floundered about, experimenting with random positions, Kiato had analyzed the problems. A colony of ants shared my hammock. They climbed around my body and explored the creases of my skin.

In the middle of the night, my hammock turned inside out and I was thrown face down onto the ground. The grass was warm and smelt of liquorice, and I felt closer to nature than I had ever done before.

I dreamt of Papillon's tale, and of the Angel Falls.

As the sun rose over the jungle treetops, I sensed a snout snuffling up my trouser leg. At first I tried to ignore it, but the probing persisted. I opened one eye, then the other. The spiny nose of an ant-eater was foraging up my trousers for breakfast. It was very happy. I could feel the warmth of its mouth and the lapping of its rasping tongue, sucking up the insect colony to which I had become host.

A little girl with bright blonde hair ran out of the hut shouting, 'Oscar! Oscar! You are so naughty!'

Grabbing the ant-eater's snout, she dragged the creature away to play with her in a ditch.

The jungle turned into low-lying green savannah as we continued pacing deeper into Brazil. The landscape bore an uncanny resemblance to that of Africa. People waved and whistled, and had the same air of open hospitality as the friends I had left from Dakar to Ngong. Once joined to Africa, now thousands of miles away, this was the last segment of the puzzle that had formed Gondwanaland.

We entered Boa Vista in the late afternoon.

Kiato, who had drunk stream water the night before, was feeling very ill. Cramps stunned his abdomen every ten minutes and he was drenched with sweat. He started a course of antibiotics, swearing he was strong enough to continue to Manaus.

Yuri and the two German girls decided to rest in Boa Vista for a few days.

The road southwards to Manaus had only been recently completed, yet it was already washed away. Nature had reclaimed it for herself. The fastest way to the Amazonian capital was by boat – which left from Caracaraí – on the Río Branco.

Yuri shook my hand as Kiato and I mounted a bus bound for Caracaraí.

'Never forget,' he said, 'that we inherit the world and all her problems. Walk softly upon the earth and you will achieve great things.' It seemed a very philosophical, very Russian, departure.

Kiato lay down and slept most of the way until we reached Caracaraí. He seemed to be getting a little better. Rudolf fed us with red boiled sweets, as the Irish batman sat and sulked.

The bag of sweets passed him by.

'Doesn't Luigi like sugary things?' I asked.

'No,' was the reply, 'they're bad for his teeth. I don't let him indulge. You'd expect him to thank me, but he was brought up without manners.' Luigi's eyes were as wide as fish bowls. His lips were cracked and swollen, and a coarse rash had developed under his chin. He looked at Rudolf, then a single tear ran from the corner of his left eye towards his lips.

A lone riverboat bobbed up and down on the Río Branco. She was called the *Río Uaquiry*. We climbed up a steep plank from the shore onto her dull boards. The captain said he was leaving that night for Manaus. The journey would take three days. He could provide food along the way for a small price.

A pair of cockerels were fighting in the street which ran to the jetty. A huddle of dogs sat gnawing at a buffalo's head outside the butcher's shop. Hammocks of all colours were displayed on a fence: a boy with a kite was their salesman. I bought a yellow hammock for myself and a packet of chicken soup powder for Kiato.

Back at the boat three blond men were ascending the gangplank. Each had an athletic build and carried a surf-board. I recognized them immediately as native Californians of the surfer variety.

'Hey Pops, is this tub heading for Manaus?' one of them called out. Rudolf donned a blue cravat, slipped on his riding boots and came to introduce himself.

'My name is Rudolf van den Bosch-Drakenburgh… I am from The Netherlands, and this is Luigi, my assistant.'

'Oh man, that's great. I'm Marvin, this is Leo and Pete.' The men shook hands and the Californians told their tale.

'We came overland from Los Angeles. We bought this great car in LA for fifty bucks and started to drive south, but after thirty miles she caught fire and burnt out. So we left her and hitched through Central America as far as here.'

I slung my hammock and asked Marvin why they had brought surf-boards to central Brazil. Marvin looked at me, then at his two friends. I had the feeling that I had asked an idiotic question. Pete swept back his long blond locks of hair and replied earnestly:

'Dude, we've come to surf the Amazon!'

'Awesome tub!' shouted Leo and Marvin simultaneously. They set about making a pirate flag. A skull and crossbones were sketched out on an old shirt, which was hoisted up on the flagpole.

The boat had two decks. It was forty feet long and half as wide. At nine that evening, diesel fumes belched upwards and the engine gave out a spluttering groan.

A single low-watt bulb flickered above the captain's dining table and he invited us to come and eat. A dish of hard-boiled eggs, dried beef and rice was passed around. Kiato threw up as soon as his eyes saw food.

Marvin sat beside me and began to tell of grotesque diseases endemic to Amazonas. Disease – in particular bubonic plague – was his only interest other than surfing. As there was one plate and only a single spoon, we took it in turns to eat. The glass was passed from one hand to the next, like the witch sisters sharing a single eye.

After the meal, the captain, whose name was César, offered to take me to the bridge.

César relieved his eight-year-old son at the helm.

As the craft broke through new waters of the Río Branco, César made jokes and drew long breaths through a cigarette.

'I have never left Amazonas,' he said. 'But I want my boy to travel when he is older. He must see the wonders of the world.

'You know, I sent my son to school in Caracaraí and they tried to tell him about all kinds of imaginary animals. One, they said, was a wild striped horse! Can you believe it?!' he exclaimed, spinning the boat's wheel through his fingers. 'I was worried his teacher was telling him lies, so

I went to meet the man. "What's all this rubbish you're telling my son?!" I demanded. "Have you ever seen such creatures with your own eyes?" I asked him. He had not, so I brought the boy to live with me on the boat. When he's old enough I'll give him money and send him away to see the world. Then he can come and teach proper knowledge, not fairy-tales, in the school at Caracaraí.'

From: *Beyond the Devil's Teeth*

Duel of Miracles

At Gulbarga, the American couple shook my hand, clenched their faces in courteous smiles, and stepped off the train. I would have enquired why they were taking such an unconventional route to Bangalore, but I had asked enough questions already.

The Minar Express rumbled across the border into Maharashtra, Mumbai's state. Drifting off to sleep, I filled my mind with images of Mumbai. I saw Churchgate Station and the Chateau Windsor Guest House, the Eros Cinema, and my cherished restaurant, Gaylord's. As I slipped into a deep slumber, I felt something tugging my earlobe. Without even opening my eyes, I knew who it was.

'Bhalu, go and sell your damn soap bars and leave me alone!'

'Sorry,' said the Trickster, 'unexpected stop. We're getting off at the next station… Solapur.'

'What are you talking about? What about Mumbai? Only ten hours to go now… let's go on to Mumbai!'

'Hurry and get off the train – it's slowing down for the station.'

'I'll meet you in Mumbai,' I said. 'I've got nothing to do in Solapur.'

But the Trickster had already made the decision for both of us. He was hauling his grubby pillowcase sacks down from the luggage rack and pulling them to the door. With great reluctance I followed him down on to the platform.

After hiring a convoy of taxis at enormous cost to bear our combined luggage to Hotel Khajuraho, Bhalu disappeared, leaving me to pay off the drivers. It was unlike him not to pay his way, and was even more unusual for the Trickster not to insist on supervising his loot himself. Without giving his irregular behaviour much thought, I checked into the hotel.

As it was late I was forced to pay an eighty per cent surcharge.

*

NEXT MORNING THE door of my room arched inwards as a fist struck its outer side.

The overly zealous bellhop announced that a guest was waiting for me in the reception. I wondered who it could be. It certainly wasn't Bhalu, who had not yet reappeared – he would have come through the window.

After the taxi ride and hotel surcharge, word would surely spread through Solapur that the world's most gullible man had come to town. My curiosity piqued by the prospect of an unexpected guest, I hurried down to the reception.

Before I could ask for the visitor, a man sidled up and shook both my hands. Aged about forty, he was of average height, average build and average appearance: except for a rather splendid Van Dyke beard.

'Hello, hello, hello,' he said, continuing to waggle my hands in his, 'I have come to meet Mr. Shah.'

'I am Mr. Shah.'

The Van Dyke beard twitched with delight.

'Can we sit together?' asked the man, gargling as if there were marbles in his mouth.

'Excuse me for being so forward... but do I *know* you?'

Van Dyke twitched again.

'I am Goad Baba,' he said.

I ran the name around my mind. Even with my inexpert grasp of Marathi – the language of Maharashtra – I could decipher the name.

'That means Mr. Sweet,' I said.

'Precisely!'

Goad Baba lured me out on to the terrace of the Hotel Khajuraho. A contingent of gardeners and their lackeys were watering plants, scrubbing the flagstones and repotting seedlings. With the monsoon well underway, it was a busy time in the garden. Goad Baba and I sat in silence under a large parasol, shading our eyes from the bright morning sunlight.

A waiter pranced over, laden with a tray of tea. He unloaded the teapot, spoons, two cups, slices of lemon, and a jug of milk. As he stooped to place the sugar bowl at the centre of table, the man with the Van Dyke beard brushed him away.

'Do you mind?' I said pertly. 'I'd like some sugar.'

Goad Baba wrung his hands together. I had the feeling I was about to learn the reason for his visit.

'How many spoons do you take?' he asked.

'Two... I like two spoons of sugar in my tea.'

Without hesitation, the self-invited guest dipped the thumb and forefinger of his left hand into my tea. In the East, where it's important to observe conventions of courtesy, a guest can get away with a lot more than in the West. But in the East, there's another convention that's followed rigorously. Everyone wipes their posterior with the left hand. This second custom led to distinct misgivings. Where had Van Dyke's left hand been?

As his fingers were withdrawn from my tea, I craned my neck to inspect the man's fingernails. An ebony-black crescent of dirt was concealed beneath each one.

'Go on!' sniffed Goad Baba. 'Try it. Taste your tea!'

I mumbled a range of feeble excuses. The guest lifted the cup to my lips like a chalice of Eucharistic wine. I gulped down half a mouthful of the straw-coloured liquid.

'Darjeeling,' I said. 'I like Darjeeling very much.'

'But what about the sugar?' said the stranger.

'You're right: it tastes very sweet – maybe it's a freak batch.'

'No, *Sahib*.' Goad Baba sniffed again. 'This is not freaky, this is my *talent*.'

'What talent's that?'

The man dried his fingers on his beard.

'I make things sweet!' he said.

My fears had been realized. Word had spread that Tahir Shah – the most ingenuous person in the world – had arrived in Solapur.

Goad Baba touched everything on the table and begged me to verify his skill.

'Taste this spoon,' he said, 'or taste this, the cup, or the table itself!'

I licked a couple of random objects. Sure enough: they were all unusually sweet.

'So, how did you acquire this *talent*?'

Goad Baba pressed his magic fingertips together and explained:

'I was an office clerk here in Solapur. Last year, after a big meal, I picked something from my tooth. To my surprise, I tasted sweetness. Suddenly I realized that anything I touch goes sweet.'

'What other things have you touched?'

'I have touched so many things,' he said innocently. 'I touched a bowl of rice, a loaf of bread, a cigarette, my friend's shoe, a wallet, a car...'

Goad Baba's list was certainly extensive.

'And?'

'And... they all went sweet... like sugar.'

Mr. Sweet pulled up his sleeves in the middle of the conversation. He was keen to prove there were no sugar cubes hidden up his arms. This put my mind at rest. I had expected the talent to be nothing more than a sleight-of-hand illusion, like *vibhuti* pellets.

'Thank you for sharing this,' I said. 'But what do you want *me* to do?'

Like the man with the Midas touch, Goad Baba stretched up and pressed his thumb to the parasol... turning it sweet.

'I was hoping you could take me to London,' he said optimistically.

'Whatever for?'

'I want to prove my skill to *The Guinness Book of Records*,' said Goad Baba, breaking out into a broad smile. 'I am thinking they will be liking me very much!'

Not again, I mused. Why can't I get away from the Indian preoccupation with *The Guinness Book of Records*? Every other person one meets in India seems to be perfecting an outlandish skill, in the earnest hope of getting their name into the venerated book.

One fifth of all Guinness's mail comes from India. The records book is deluged with material from the subcontinent on a daily basis. One can only sympathize with the chaps at Guinness. What could life be like at an office bombarded day and night with letters from deserving Indians? One single 'greetings' fax sent by a Delhi man to the Guinness headquarters was supposedly a hundred metres long. There's so much interest that *The Guinness Book of Records* is published in four Indian languages.

But whereas many nationalities concentrate on breaking the more sombre records, Indians prefer to perform extraordinary feats. The obsession may, I suppose, have resulted from the tantalizing records of endurance set by the nation's holy men.

Dozens of ordinary Indians are world-record holders. Surendra Apharya, for instance, has the record for inscribing a grain of rice. He burned 1,749 characters into a single grain using a magnifying glass. Others hold records for limbo dancing on roller-skates ($5^1/8$ inches); for crawling (870 miles); for milk bottle balancing (more than 64 miles); for continuous standing (17 years); and for needle threading (11,796 times in two hours).

Conmen tour small Indian towns masquerading as agents from the sacred *Guinness Book of Records*. For a steep charge they judge the applicant's entry, promising to include it in the book.

I told Goad Baba I would inform Guinness of his exceptional talent. He was thrilled and, clenching my hand in his, shook it up and down vigorously. When he was gone I licked my palm. It was very sweet indeed.

Soon after my meeting with Goad Baba, I was talking to an Indian journalist.

When I mentioned the queer skill, the reporter cited half a dozen other Indians claiming the same ability. He told me how the trick was done. Most Goad Babas, he said, were nothing more than copycat illusionists. They wash their hands in a strong solution of saccharin – which is five hundred times sweeter than sugar.

Within seconds they go from being ordinary people to men with the Sweet'N Low touch.

*

BHALU HAD STILL not reappeared.

He often vanished for a day or two at a time. But this time he was gone much longer. Six days passed. Each day

I became more and more irritated, especially as he had coerced me into stopping at Solapur in the first place.

At dawn on the seventh day, I rose early to get ready to take the bus to Mumbai. As I emerged from the shower a rustling noise startled me. I spun round. It was Bhalu. He was climbing in through the window.

'Come on and follow me,' he called, climbing back outside and shinning down the outside of the hotel.

'Bhalu, where have you been?'

'I'll tell you later. Just follow me.'

With great unwillingness, I followed the Trickster out of the window. My room, which was on the third floor, enjoyed a fine view across the southern portion of Solapur. But as I grappled for a handhold, the city's sights were the last thing on my mind.

'What the hell are you up to? You don't just turn up after a week away and get someone to risk life and limb scurrying down a drainpipe. Why don't we use the stairs like everyone else?'

'Don't be lazy,' he retorted, lighting up a *biri*. 'There's something you'll want to see.'

Bhalu led me at breakneck speed through the main area of the town.

As we hastened past boarded shops, standpipe bathers and tea-stall attendants, I wondered what the scam *du jour* was to be. The week without Bhalu had been a welcome break from my new role as a conman's accomplice. Every day, the Trickster encouraged me to turn my hand to another and more unlawful activity, hissing that such knowledge might be useful to me in the future. But when would I need to concoct beauty products from lavatory bleach, spent tea leaves, and grease scraped from the door hinges of a first-class railway carriage? Or, for that matter, when would anyone ask me to create aphrodisiacs from dried mango skins, turn all-purpose miniature bars of Lux soap into medicated suppositories, or pass putrescent drainage liquid off as holy Ganga water?

Bhalu's childhood had moulded him into an incorrigible con-artist. He may not have known the key dates of Indian history, or the correct way to eat peas with a knife and fork, but he had no need for such profitless information. A professional scammer requires far more practical expertise. The Trickster's qualifications were unsurpassed for life on the street. He had a salesman's tongue, a forger's fingers, a gambler's nerve, the million-dollar smile of a chat-show host, and the mathematical artifice of a Nobelist. He spoke faultless English, passable Italian and German, and could communicate in a dozen Indian languages. On their own, none of these attributes may have been enough to survive on the streets of Kolkata. But Bhalu had been blessed with a far scarcer virtue – natural charisma.

And so, as on many other occasions, I found myself hurrying behind him, wondering what depravity was to be next on the agenda.

Twenty minutes after being bundled from the window of the Hotel Khajuraho, we were walking on grass. Bhalu had brought me to a wide hockey pitch on the outskirts of Solapur.

As I was about to declare my disapproval, I heard voices coming from the far end of the hockey ground. To be more precise, I heard what sounded like a gargantuan, bloodthirsty demon. Screeching as if its baby demons had been snatched by another monster, it was severely distressed. Bhalu said to take no notice of the noise. We had come for a far more important encounter. More important than a female demon robbed of her babies? The Trickster nodded ominously. The demon was trifling in comparison to what he had arranged.

The monster's shrieks did not subside. Instead, they became louder and more aroused. I peered over to where the sound was coming from. Even when narrowing my eyes to focus better, I could see no demon. The pitch was flat, with a large, dense bush bordering it. Telling Bhalu to send for help if I were attacked, I went over to investigate.

When it comes to bewilderment, India has its own scale. No other country on earth can mystify a foreigner so utterly. Sometimes, when travelling in the subcontinent, one has no choice but to concede total defeat. This was one such instance. I leant forward to peer round the shrub, prepared for anything. Standing behind the bush there was no weeping demon, but something far more unexpected.

Ten men and women, each dressed in sports clothes, were exercising.

Yet instead of performing familiar training drills, they were laughing. It was no timid tittering… rather, it was a puissant, hostile form of laughter.

'Excuse me,' I said, 'what are you doing?'

Hearing my question, the leader of the group abruptly stopped guffawing. He pulled up his white cotton ankle socks.

'We're members of the Solapur Laughter Club,' he said grandly.

'Members of what?'

'The Laughter Club... We meet here every morning to laugh.'

'Forgive me for my ignorance... but *why* do you laugh?'

The team leader gave me a stern look.

'For exercise, of course! Laughter is the best way to keep the heart and lungs in trim. A powerful spate of early-morning laughter is equal to a three-mile jog.'

'Is that so?'

'Yes, it is,' replied the class in unison.

'Who tells the jokes, then?'

'We don't use jokes,' called out a scrawny woman at the back of the group. 'They're forbidden.'

'Forbidden? That seems a bit hard going – especially if you're doing laughter exercise.'

The team leader seemed keen to get on with the routine.

'Sooner or later a joke would offend someone,' he said. 'So we've outlawed them. In any case, we can laugh on cue.'

He clapped his hands twice. Within an instant, the sound of the wailing demon echoed out across the hockey field. I would have thanked the fitness fanatics for their time. But they were too busy laughing.

AT EIGHT O'CLOCK the first spectator arrived.

'Is *it* going to be here?' he asked.

Bhalu dipped his head in a nod. He pointed to the centre of the hockey pitch. The man handed the boy two rupees, then sat down in the middle of the field.

'Is *what* going to be here? Why did that chap give you two rupees?'

The Trickster told me to be quiet.

By nine o'clock the sun was high. Five hundred people had turned up to watch the mysterious spectacle. On arrival, each dropped two rupees into a large empty paint can held by Bhalu. Whatever it was for, the audience seemed to feel it was money well spent.

An hour later, a thousand people were loitering about on the hockey pitch. More were turning up all the time. Each obediently dropped their two rupees into the tin. I had never seen Indians so willing to pay money for anything before.

'Bhalu,' I snorted, 'what are you up to? You could get into a lot of trouble for this.'

The Trickster waved me out of the way. He had entrance fees to collect.

At ten-thirty, an official in a tattered uniform accosted Bhalu. A weighty pouch was handed over. The man turned on his heel and hurried away.

I was growing increasingly alarmed. Always at the cutting-edge of fraud, my travelling companion was now navigating in uncharted territory of deceit. I warned him of the consequences. Again, he brushed me aside.

Then, promptly on the stroke of noon, a man and a woman pranced over to the hockey pitch. Both were heavily laden with accessories and equipment. They appeared to be ignoring each other. Their arrival was greeted by a resounding cheer from the audience.

'You've got to tell me what's going on,' I hollered at Bhalu, who appeared relieved at the couple's arrival.

'Prepare yourself for a fantastic show,' he said. 'I heard two gurus were trying to "control" a group of villages near Tirth – just west of here. Both claim supernatural powers. I went to meet them on your behalf.'

'Why didn't you take me along?'

'Because,' said the Trickster, running his hand through the paint can of coins, 'they wouldn't have agreed if a foreigner was around.'

'Agreed to what?'

'Agreed to a duel.'

'Are they going to kill each other?'

'Of course they aren't,' snapped Bhalu. 'They're going to have a duel of miracles.'

'How ever did you get them to trek all the way over here?'

The Trickster stuck his nose in the air haughtily.

'They're letting me referee,' he said. 'As the judge, I said the duel must be held on neutral ground.'

'And what about your tin of cash?'

'Well,' he replied derisively, 'you wouldn't begrudge me my wages, would you?'

THE CROWD WAS getting agitated.

They were ready for the duel to commence. Bhalu had taken great care to advertise the special form of combat. He had hired an army of street children to spread the word in the villages surrounding Solapur. Potential spectators had been advised that one of the godmen would undoubtedly suffer terrible humiliation. There is only one thing an Indian villager enjoys more than a miracle, and that's to see someone publicly embarrassed. The Trickster had made a considerable cash profit on the entrance fee alone. But one would not expect a fraudster from Kolkata to stop at that.

To Bhalu, the crowd was not merely a potential audience, but a captive market in itself. The *avatars* had been ordered to delay for as long as possible. That is, until the referee gave the word. As the spectators waited for the singular blend of miracles and humiliation to ensue, the army of street urchins scurried about selling wares from the Trickster's pillowcase sacks. Soap bars and shower caps, hand towels and sachets of French perfume: all were touted at knock-down prices.

Even after the entrance fee, and snapping up a few bargain toiletries, Bhalu noticed that some of the spectators still had money left. And so he turned his hand from soap-bar magnate to bookmaker. The ability to swap one profession for another in a split second is a gift which turns humble entrepreneurs into billionaires. Bhalu had that gift.

I went over to have a look at the godmen. They were both unquestionably odd.

On the left was Sri Kasbekar. Probably in his fifties, he had the appearance of someone who had been dragged round the keel of an eighteenth-century sloop. His features were gnarled, his apparel bedraggled beyond description, and his hands crudely tattooed with indistinct symbols. Yet there was something far more unusual about the guru. He was polydactylic: he had six fingers on each hand. Polydactyly is not uncommon in India. From time to time one sees people with a sixth digit protruding from another finger. Sri Kasbekar's condition was far rarer – for his two extra digits were perfectly formed.

Without counting his fingers individually, one might not have noticed the difference. Rather, without counting them, *I* might not have noticed them.

The other two thousand bystanders observed them immediately.

While in the West people are wary of genetic mutations, in India an extra appendage has an uncanny significance. Hindu deities are frequently portrayed with an additional set of arms and hands. To many in the Solapur district, a perfectly formed sixth finger on each hand suggested miraculous powers.

On the right side of the makeshift arena was Srimati Kulkami. Svelte in a butch kind of way, she had long auburn hair, a square mouth filled with square teeth, and alluring midnight eyes. She was dressed in a vibrant fuchsia cotton *sari*. But it was her ears which first attracted one's attention. Their outer edges were thick with neatly clipped hair. The bristles were about the size and shape of an eyebrow. It looked as if a hairy caterpillar was crawling up into each ear.

The Trickster addressed the gathering, whipping them up into a frenzy. He announced the ground rules. Each seer would be permitted to perform four miracles. No member of the audience would be allowed to participate, although props were admissible. The referee could disqualify either dueller at his discretion. The guru with the best miracles would be permitted to offer divine salvation in the villages near Solapur.

Seething with anticipation, the spectators swayed forward. I sensed that many villagers' fortunes were riding on the contest. Bhalu curled two fingers around his tongue and whistled.

The duel of miracles began.

First up was Srimati Kulkami. Brushing back her hair, she addressed the audience in Marathi. She told them she did not like to use her abilities frivolously, but she had to prove her competitor was a fraud. Indeed, she claimed he was worse than a mere con-artist – he was *Shaitan*, the Devil.

Srimati Kulkami's oration went down very well. Bhalu paused from translating for me, and noted down half a dozen last-minute bets.

Without hesitation, Kulkami began to weave her magic. She pulled a hundred-rupee note from her blouse, dipped it in water, and then set it alight. Remarkably, the paper did not burn, although it was engulfed in flames. This was the first miracle.

Feroze had taught me variations on the illusion. It can be done with most kinds of paper, cloth, or even wood. In this case, the paper was probably treated with a solution of carbon disulphide and carbon tetrachloride.

For her second act of wonderment, Srimati Kulkami announced that the *Shaitan* had created an unfavourable atmosphere. If she, a divine being, did not alleviate the hex, a plague would strike the audience down. Such side-comments of impending destruction proved very popular with the assembly. Delighted, they nudged each other in the ribs, and jostled a little closer to the godwoman.

To assuage the evil forces, Kulkami took up a large brown coconut, and held it above her head. Wailing incantations, she called for the demons to stir from their hiding places and flow into the body of the nut. No place, she said, was safe for them but the confines of the coconut. Then, crouching over, she crimped the nut between her *sari*-covered legs. As two thousand pairs of eyes scrutinized her, the mystic held the coconut at arm's length, towards the gathering. A minute passed. The same thought went through everyone's mind: had the miracle failed? Such failure would spell divine disgrace. Another minute passed. As the audience held their breath, the end of the coconut blew out. Like some kind of schoolboy's bomb, a jet of flame and oily smoke issued from the hole.

We all stared in wonderment: this was clearly impressive stuff.

But there was more to come.

Seizing the nut in both hands, Srimati Kulkami flung it at a stony patch on the arena. It split open. A quantity of what looked like blood soaked into the ground. Raising her frame to its maximum height, the godwoman cried that the villagers were safe now from her competitor's evil: for the blood had been that of the demons.

Only later did I work out how the illusion had been achieved. Coconuts have three eyes at one end. One of these is soft, and can easily be bored out. The guru perforates the soft eye and fills the nut with a saturated solution of potassium permanganate. From a distance, this resembles blood. The hole is sealed with wax. For the explosion, the mendicant surreptitiously inserts a pellet of sodium through the soft eye. As it reacts with the water in the potassium permanganate solution, it causes a violent eruption.

After Kulkami's two miracles, the spectators were beside themselves with enthusiasm. A live display of what they considered to be real magic was even better than the special effects of Bollywood movies.

To further heighten the sense of tension, Bhalu ordered that Sri Kasbekar should now present two miracles. This was a popular decision. The godwoman was led away to the sidelines, and the polydactyl addressed the villagers.

He told them he was not their god, but their servant: he would heal them, not dictate to them. If they selected his opponent, they would live below a sky made dark with malevolence. The recitation, which carried on for about fifteen minutes, sounded like a party political broadcast.

Cautioning both duellists to refrain from bad-mouthing the other, Bhalu commanded Sri Kasbekar to get on with his routine.

Before the performance began, the polydactyl waved his fingers at the crowd. Titillated like old women at the sight of a naked man, they edged forward for a closer look at the mutation.

For his first miracle, Sri Kasbekar carried a bucket full of greenish lemons into the centre of the arena. Next, he held up a needle and thread and removed his shirt. Grabbing a chunk of flab on his stomach, he stabbed the needle through it, and sewed on a lemon. The audience watched nonplussed as the *yogi* sewed one lemon after the next on to his belly. Instead of grimacing with pain, he chanted mantras, and maintained an airy smile.

'Isn't that hurting him?' I asked the Trickster.

'Don't be so stupid,' he replied. 'Watch how he's pinching the fat tightly with his fingers before jabbing in the needle. Do that and it doesn't hurt... it hardly even bleeds.'

Bhalu was right. There was no blood. Within ten minutes, Sri Kasbekar had a dozen fruits hanging from his abdomen like spiders on silk. He seemed in no discomfort at all. Fluttering his fingers once more, with the lemons still dangling, he moved on to his second feat.

With great care he pulled a three-foot viper from his bag of props. Dazzled by the sunlight, the snake reeled about as its owner explained to the bystanders that this was an extremely poisonous reptile. The serpent, he told them, came from the wastelands of the Great Thar Desert. One drop of its venom would bring an agonizing death.

The spectators listed backwards. Twisting the viper about his twelve fingers, the godman induced a brave villager to come forward and try his luck with the snake.

The referee shouted out from the perimeter of the arena that volunteers were prohibited under the rules. A communal sigh of relief swept through the audience. The macho villagers had had their pride saved by officialdom. For Bhalu's part, the rule had been a shrewd calculation. If one of the spectators had been struck down by a Rajasthani serpent, he would have had hell to pay.

With no takers allowed, Sri Kasbekar waved the snake around his head like a lasso. Then he prised its mouth open and forced its fangs on to his neck. A stream of blood issued from the *swami*'s jugular. He then threw the viper on the ground and stamped on its head. It might have been a harsh move, but the reptile could have killed the godman, who was none the worse after the encounter.

From where I was standing, the snake bite was plausible. The crowd had also been impressed by the stunt. As they applauded wildly, I remembered something Feroze had told me in Kolkata. Standing one morning at the window of his study, he had declared that ninety per cent of Indian snakes are non-venomous. Ignorant of the many species of serpent, most villagers assume that any snake bite is fatal. For his illusion, Sri Kasbekar had used a harmless snake. It didn't actually have fangs. As its mouth was pulled from his neck, he had squeezed a blood-filled sponge over the area.

Two miracles each. The score was even. Anxious to keep up the tension, Bhalu called for Srimati Kulkami to perform her next feat.

Taking her place in the circle, she informed the audience that her twelve-fingered rival had used an innocuous species of serpent for his demonstration. The godwoman had hoped to secure victory through denouncing the opposition, but the villagers were far too astute to declare a winner halfway through. Having paid two rupees each to watch the duel, they expected value for money. In their eyes, value meant quantity.

For her third miracle, Kulkami pulled up the hem of her *sari* and washed her feet in a bucket of water. As she sloshed about, she emitted a series of shrill gasps. The spectators were unimpressed by the woman's manner. I sensed the tide was turning against her, largely for her outbursts against Polydactyl Man.

After three or four minutes of washing, Srimati Kulkami jerked her body about as if it were being entered by angelic forces. She then pushed the bucket away, and walked calmly down a long piece of dusty yellow cloth. Moments later the miracle was visible. Distinct rusty-red footprints had been left where her feet had stepped. The material was held up to the audience. Their reaction was sober. The miracle had none of the anguish of snakebite or of sewing fruit on to the skin.

As with so many other illusions I had seen on my journey of observation, Feroze had accommodated me with a faultless rendering of the trick at his mansion. The deception is very simple. The feet are not washed with ordinary water. It's a mixture of slaked lime and water. Shortly before use, the cloth is dipped in a light turmeric solution and dried. As the seer's holy feet press against the fabric, a chemical reaction occurs. A red mark is left where the turmeric and lime meet.

Sri Kasbekar's third miracle was one I shall not readily forget. It wasn't that the feat was so remarkable; but the response it drew touched me. Like a stage magician of the old school, Polydactyl Man walked into the arena in silence. He had removed the lemons from his belly and replaced his shirt. A thousand people surrounded him, but none said a word. I sensed that they were now truly awed by his presence.

Frivolously, he withdrew something from his *lungi* and placed it on the ground. It was a thick black ballpoint pen, with four small buttons up the side. Chanting a cryptic mantra beneath his breath, the godman walked around the pen in a figure of eight. When he had completed the circuit in one direction, he repeated it the other way. He did this seven times. Only then did he pluck the pen from the ground.

I was ready for the implement to squirt blood, or to write with invisible ink. But what happened was totally unexpected. Polydactyl Man held the ballpoint out before him in the way a fencer holds a foil. Then, as the mystic closed his eyes in concentration, the pen began to speak. It was no random voice, but that of the godman. Sri Kasbekar was speaking through the pen.

The audience went apoplectic. This was surely proof that he was a higher being. Even Bhalu recoiled at the feat. By chance, I could explain the miracle. About a year before, I had been glancing through an airline's in-flight magazine when I spotted the same ballpoint 'Memo Pen'. Advertised as the gadget that every weary executive needs, the pen has a microchip which stores a few seconds of one's voice. Perfect, the ad had claimed, for the businessman on the move – make a note of that brilliant idea when driving, in a lift, or when out and about. I wondered whether the American manufacturers had dreamt their executive toy would ever become a divine object.

The villagers had already made up their minds. They liked the oracle pen and Polydactyl Man. But a heckler at the back of the crowd was calling for the last two miracles.

The referee clapped his hands. As he was riding on a high of public adulation, Sri Kasbekar was allowed to go first.

A shallow pit had been dug in the hockey pitch and filled with red-hot coals. I had warned Bhalu that he could get into trouble for defacing city property, but he waved my outburst aside. Calling out a fantastic set of magical words, Polydactyl Man approached the coals. Then, with great self-control, he stepped on to them. Halfway across, his face seemed to buckle from pain. But he continued, without giving voice to his discomfort.

Firewalking has occurred in the East for thousands of years. It's recently been introduced in the West, too. Tired Memo Pen-carrying executives now hurry across hot coals as part of special bonding seminars. Contrary to popular belief, firewalking is dead simple. The skin on the soles of the feet and the ash which covers the coals are both poor conductors of heat. Anyone can do it. But the villagers didn't know this. For them, Polydactyl Man was the hero of the day.

A quick glance at his feet proved he was indeed the hero, but for another reason – sabotage. While his back was turned, the godwoman had stealthily sprinkled sugar on to the coals. The sugar melts and sticks to the feet, burning them.

Determined not to be beaten by subversion of any kind, Sri Kasbekar took the pain. After all, he was passing himself off as a living god. As more and more godmen earn a living from healing and performing miracles, an increasing number are falling victim not to Rationalists, but to sabotage from their own kind.

When the time came for her last miracle, Srimati Kulkami crawled beneath a heavy blanket positioned at the centre of the arena.

I could sense the spectators wishing her to fail.

Very slowly, her head, and then her body, began to leave the ground. An inch at a time, it rose above the grass. The seer paused at about three feet, her body quivering slightly under the blanket. This was the first time I had seen a full levitation performed.

Just as I was going to ask Bhalu how he thought the illusion was done, something rather embarrassing happened. Embarrassing, that is, for the godwoman. The thick wool blanket which had covered her slipped away. In an instant the secret of full body levitation was revealed. The secret was that there was no levitation. Srimati Kulkami had been standing under the blanket, her arms outstretched, holding two chipped hockey sticks by the handles. The sticks' blades had been pointing upwards, giving the impression of feet.

Her face red as a beetroot, she proclaimed that Sri Kasbekar – the Devil – had bewitched her with a curse.

But no one listened.

The villagers were far too preoccupied with something else to pay attention to a fraudulent goddess. Besotted with Polydactyl Man's miracles, they yearned for more revelations from his miracle of miracles… the sacred oracle pen.

From: *Sorcerer's Apprentice*

Southward Bound

AN HOUR BEFORE I set off on the long journey to the Sahara, Ariane tied a pink ribbon round my wrist. She said that each time I touched my hand to the ribbon, or looked at it, it would mean she was thinking of me.

In a small bag I had packed a few essentials and a letter of introduction from Dr. Mehdi. I pulled the door of the house closed. The guardians were standing to attention in a kind of shambolic royal guard. They saluted and Rachana drove us out through the shantytown, up the hill, to the railway station at Oasis.

We crossed the tracks and I waited for the train to Marrakech. Rachana was standing against the light, Timur on her hip, Ariane between us. There was a blast of a horn in the distance and the train rolled in, steel wheels grinding against the tracks. I kissed Rachana and the children.

'I won't be long,' I said. 'I'll be back as soon as the favour is done.'

'This isn't about a favour,' said Rachana, leaning forward to hug me.

I climbed up, turned back to wave, and the train jolted away out of Casablanca towards the south.

There is nothing like a train journey for reflection, and the passage from Casablanca to Marrakech is one of the most inspiring I know. Movement has a magical effect on the mind. It stimulates the eyes, distracts them, allowing real thought to take hold. I stared out of the window at a landscape changing by slow degrees from urban to farmland and then to a desert panorama – baked terracotta-red.

My mind jerked from one memory to another, scraps of people, places, smells and sounds. A single minute of recollection can be a rollercoaster.

I thought of the scent of summer flowers, drowsy with bees, at my childhood home.

Soaring above the Amazon in a two-seater Cessna.

Toes in the sand on a Brazilian beach.

For more than a decade I have travelled with two books.

They are always with me, a part of my hand luggage. The first is my father's *Caravan of Dreams*. The other is Bruce Chatwin's *The Songlines*. They are my travelling companions, a source of stimulation on a dark night, or on a train journey south.

I value *The Songlines* for the notes in the middle. Each one is a polished jewel, a splinter of wisdom, a piece of something much larger, but complete in itself. I dug out the book, opened it at random as I always do and read a line which says that a Sufi dervish wanders the earth because the action of walking dissolves the attachments of the world, and that his aim is to become a 'dead man walking', a man whose feet are rooted in the ground but whose spirit is already in heaven. I have read *The Songlines* so many times. My eyes have scanned that passage again and again but, until then, I had not really pulled it through the machinery of my mind.

As the train grumbled south over the first miles of brick-red desert, I absorbed it for the first time. It made absolute sense. I slipped the book back in my bag and gazed out at a herd of scrawny camels standing at the bottom of a low hill. My eyes took a mental photograph of them.

But my mind was far away.

That evening I retraced my steps through Marrakech's medina, in search of Murad. I wanted to rebuke him for running off with Osman's wife. I have no sense of direction and it took me three hours to find the corridor at the end of which he lived.

Once there, I stood at the bottom of the ladder and called out the storyteller's name. There was no answer. I called again, and a third time. Then a muffled sound came from the chamber above. I crept up. Murad was sprawled on a heap of rags. I thought he was drunk at first, because he was lying back, in a kind of stupor. I greeted him frostily and asked about Osman's wife.

'She was unhappy,' he said, 'so very unhappy that I agreed to help her escape.'

'Where is she now?'

The storyteller shrugged.

'As soon as we reached Marrakech, she left,' he said. 'She was going to her relatives near Ouarzazate.'

'But why did you do this? If Osman wasn't so depressed, he might have come to kill you.'

Murad coughed hard.

'A woman is a flower,' he said. 'And the saddest thing of all is for a beautiful flower to bloom unadmired.'

That evening, I paid a visit to the Maison de Meknès, to have a chat with its owner, Omar bin Mohammed. I turned up quite late, but expected to find him reading in the lamplight near the door, or chatting to friends out in the street. To my surprise, though, the shutters were drawn. I banged on them. No reply. I assumed he must have gone home for the night. Then the owner of the next shop along rode up on a moped and held up a hand.

'He's shut down, closed, gone away,' he said over the sound of the engine.

'Why, where, how?'

The shopkeeper shut off the fuel and his vehicle conked out.

'In Marrakech there is a merchant tradition,' he said. 'We are proud of it, proud to be shopkeepers. Our Prophet – peace be upon Him – was a trader himself. But every moment you are in business, there is a clock ticking.'

'So what happened to Omar and the Maison de Meknès?'

The shopkeeper unlocked his front door.

'His time ran out,' he said.

The next day I was up at dawn. I wandered down to Jma el Fna, the great square. It was empty. No one. Not a bird, not a beggar, not even a storyteller. I stood there, right in the middle, and I thought of the history and the power of that place – the executions, the stories, the performances. Even when it was empty you could feel the energy. It almost knocked you down. I closed my eyes, shut my nostrils and put my fingers in my ears. Instead of feeling alone, I felt connected to every person who had ever traipsed across it. When I finally moved on, it seemed as if I was leaving with something new inside me, as though the soul of Jma el Fna had slipped in through my skin.

I went to the bus terminal and bought a ticket for the first bus south to Ouarzazate. There was a sense of great expectation. Families hustling aboard with bundles of cloth and bags of dried fruit, packets of dates, blankets in plastic bags, and buckets tied up on strings. The driver tore the corner of my ticket and wished me peace. I took a seat at the back, behind a large wicker crate filled with chickens. They were alive but very silent, as if they hoped their owner might forget about them. Across from me sat a man with a striped kitten on his lap. The animal had smelled the birds, and was clawing to get nearer to the crate.

We left Marrakech and thundered out into the open country, on what is one of the most scenic roads in the kingdom. The man with the cat said he was a schoolteacher and that he didn't trust his wife.

'She hates animals,' he said. 'If she had her way, she would have them all poisoned – everything from the birds in the sky to the foxes in the forest.'

He had a don't-mess-with-me kind of face, angry eyes and a wild, frantic mouth packed with jumbled teeth. I glanced down at the kitten. The hand smoothing back its fur was gentle beyond description. It was hard to believe such a tender hand could be attached to the same body as the face.

'She must have had a bad experience with an animal,' I said.

The passenger clicked his mouth.

'She doesn't see their beauty,' he said. He stared down at the kitten, his angry eyes melting. 'But I hope she will change now.'

The bus hit a pothole, rocked to the side and the chickens lost their cool.

'Tomorrow's her birthday,' said the man. 'I've brought her this kitten from Marrakech. It's from an expensive pet shop. I spent a fortune on it.'

'Do you really think your wife will change after a lifetime of animal hatred?'

The man held the kitten's head up to my ear.

'Can you hear that?'

I listened.

'The purr?'

'It is the sound of an angel,' said the man. 'When my wife hears it, purring in her own ear, how can she resist?'

Dr. Mehdi had told me to head south from Marrakech to Ouarzazate, and then on past Zagora, until the small town of M'hamid, the end of the road. Once I got there, he said I was to make contact with his nephew Ibrahim, who would take me to the source of the salt. He gave exact instructions how much salt to bring back and how to pack it up.

At Ouarzazate, I found a small hotel where the rooms were little bigger than the beds and where the owner spent his life in the kitchen, beside a huge cast-iron pot filled with lamb stew. He was called Mustapha. He had scars on his hands from decades of stirring the pot, and a way of talking that was very pleasing to the ear. His sentences flowed like syrup, one pouring into the next.

The walls of the hotel were adorned with paintings of scenes from the High Atlas. I recognized one as the Berber bridal festival of Imilchil. There were no other customers, except for a pair of nervous Swiss tourists, who were travelling with their dog. I went into the dining room, where there was a single table. The Swiss were sitting there, tensely. When they saw me, they got up, apologized politely and left.

Mustapha stepped out of the kitchen and said the stew was fresh. I ordered a bowl. He brought it to my table and blew the steam off the top.

'It's very hot tonight,' he said.

I tasted it. 'Delicious.'

'I call it Morocco stew.'

'But stew is not typically Moroccan.'

Mustapha licked a fresh scar on his hand.

'There are a mixture of fine ingredients,' he said, 'prepared with care, over just the right heat. The flavour is subtle, a little delicate, but a delight to the senses.' Mustapha licked his hand again. 'Just like Morocco,' he said.

I pointed to the painting of a Berber girl in the traditional black and white striped robe of the Atlas.

'I come from Imilchil,' he said. 'We are a famous Berber family.'

When I had finished the stew, I ordered a second bowl.

He refused to charge me. 'Your mouth's appreciation is payment enough,' he said.

As I ate the stew, I told him about the favour I had been asked to do. I said that I was searching for the story in my heart.

'We are all searching for that,' he said.

'How can I find it?'

Mustapha pressed his palms together and touched them to his nose.

'I cannot tell you,' he said. 'But I can offer you something.'

'What?'

'A story that was given to me by my grandfather at Imilchil.'

He pulled up a chair, took off his apron, and began.

'There was once an island kingdom far away from here, where all the camels were tall and proud, and the men were skilled in making pottery, from the soft clay near the shore. The king was fair to his people and a state of harmony prevailed. No one went without delicious fruit, or fine cloth for their clothes.

'Although the kingdom was prosperous, it was cut off from the world beyond, in the middle of the sea. Whenever anyone needed something not found on the island, a boat would be sent to the mainland to bring it back. But the waters all around were so perilous that these boats often sank, drowning all on board.

'Now, there lived in this kingdom a man called Jumar Khan. He was young and he was handsome, and he had a boat that he used to ferry goods from the next kingdom, far away. He would brave the high waves and travel there often. And on one such journey he spotted a stallion for sale. It was the colour of newly fallen snow, with a jet-black mane and eyes that shone like coals.

'Jumar Khan had no wife or children to support and he had a bag of gold, the profit from many dangerous crossings. He asked the owner the price of the horse. He had just enough money, but the animal's owner said to him: "I will sell it to you on the condition that you promise never to sell it to anyone else."

'Jumar agreed and paid the money. The animal was loaded up on to the boat and, in rolling seas, carried back to the kingdom.

'A few years passed and everyone praised the stallion. Jumar Khan himself loved it a little more each day. Then, one winter dawn, he set sail as normal, but a giant wave struck and smashed his boat onto rocks. Jumar and the passengers were saved by the beneficence of God. But with no boat, Jumar lost his livelihood and was ruined.

'He might have sold his horse, but he had made a promise never to do so. In any case, he loved it with all his heart and could not bear to be parted from it.

'One day an important merchant visited the kingdom. He was known by reputation throughout the East and his name was Sher Ali. While staying on the island, he heard of Jumar Khan and the hapless circumstances in which he found himself. And he heard of the fabulous stallion and the promise not to sell it. But in the merchant's experience, every object had a value.

'He sent word to Jumar's home that he would like to view the animal, as it was said to be very beautiful. The next evening Sher Ali arrived.

'With no money to afford staff, Jumar received his guest himself and prepared a fabulous meal of succulent meat garnished with vegetables grown by himself. Sher Ali ate until he could eat no more and, after a glass of tea, he asked about the horse.

'Jumar Khan shifted in his seat. "Oh, respected guest," he said, "as you know, it is our tradition to provide a feast for a visitor. And the more esteemed the visitor, the finer the meal is required to be. In my state of poverty, I was unable to provide a meal fitting for a distinguished guest such as yourself," said Jumar Khan, placing his hand on his heart. "The only way I could keep my honour was to serve you my beloved horse."'

The road wended southeast down the Draa Valley. An ocean of palms rippled out on either side, emerald green in a landscape so dry it seemed miraculous life existed there at all. The local bus ran the route, transporting merchants and their fruit up to Ouarzazate and ferrying their purchases back down to Zagora.

On our childhood journeys to Morocco, we visited Ouarzazate time and again. It was little more than a hamlet then. But providence had delivered fortune in an unlikely way. Hollywood had discovered the stark beauty of the region and used the mud fortresses and adobe villages as backdrops in a thousand movies, from *Lawrence of Arabia* to *Gladiator*.

Film money had delivered to the local people the kind of wealth that fuels the most fantastic dreams. Once he had dished up a third helping of his stew and finished his tale, Mustapha gave me a single piece of advice.

'I cannot tell you what story is in your heart,' he said. 'But I can tell you that money earned with ease is the devil's currency. Everything it touches is cursed. If you want prosperity, work hard for it and don't take charity unless you are a day away from being drowned.'

'Drowned by water?'

'Drowned by life.'

As the bus grunted and wheezed between the potholes, my mind flitted back to the days when our Ford Cortina made the same journey south. My mother spent her time sorting through brocades and kaftans she had snapped up at the previous *souq*, and my father would be in the front with our gardener at the wheel. He never stopped talking for a moment. Conversation was a kind of lifeblood to him, a way to process his thoughts before he committed them to paper.

My school friends went on family holidays. We never did. We went on expeditions, journeys with a purpose. My father would use them to draw our attention to aspects of life we might otherwise have missed. He used to say that anything the senses showed you could be regarded in a different way.

On a journey down the Draa Valley a generation before, he had asked the gardener to pull over.

'I have to get something,' he said, opening the door. He crossed a patch of scrubland and made his way down through a grove of date palms to the stream. We asked our mother what he was doing.

'Wait and see,' she said.

Ten minutes later he was back. There was something in his fist. When we were all looking, he opened his hand and showed us. It was a smooth black pebble, with two veins of white running down one side.

'What is this?' he asked.

'It's a pebble,' I said.

'What else is it?'

We shook our heads.

'That's all. It's a pebble and that's that.'

My father put the pebble in my hand and told me to look at it carefully.

'Do you see anything else?'

'No.'

'Really look,' he said. 'Change the way you are looking at it.'

'Baba, I'm looking. Really I am.'

A few minutes passed. The gardener stepped out to stretch his legs. When he came back, we were still looking at the pebble.

My father weighed it in his hand.

'What you see here and you call a pebble is all sorts of things,' he said. 'It's a fragment of something else, but is complete as it is. It's been rounded smooth by the river, moulded by time. If it stays in the river for a few million years longer, it will become sand. To an ant it is a mountain and to an elephant it's almost too small to be seen. And to us it's an object of beauty, something that feels very nice to touch, but it's useful too.'

'Baba, it's a pebble,' I said, 'and it's not useful at all.'

'Tahir Jan, that's where you are wrong,' he said. 'You see, this little pebble has a thousand uses. You could put it in a pan of milk and the milk wouldn't boil over. Or you could throw it at a wild dog that's attacking you, or scrape it on the ground to draw a map, or use it as a paperweight. Or,' he said quietly, 'you could just keep it on a shelf and look at it from time to time, as a reminder of our journey and of this very beautiful place.'

That evening, the bus reached Zagora after three punctures and a quick stop to barter chickens at the side of the road. In the countryside of Morocco, there are tokens of modernity – transistor radios, colour televisions and plenty of mobile phones. But the essence of life has not changed in centuries. The man sitting beside me on the bus had five chickens, all trussed up by the feet. Oblivious to their evident discomfort, he pulled them down from the luggage rack and took them on to the road. He bartered them directly for other goods at a line of makeshift stalls.

One was swapped for a jar of honey, another for a bag of clementines; the third was traded for some pomegranates, the fourth for a bottle of olive oil, and the fifth for a rough wicker basket in which to carry his goods.

When I stepped down from the bus at Zagora, I was immediately attended to by a boy of about ten years. He was holding a fishing rod in one hand and a jar of worms in the other, and he swaggered when he walked.

'I will help you,' he said.

'How do you know I want your help?'

He shook the jar of worms and peered in to see if they were moving.

'I know because you are a tourist,' he said, 'and tourists have money but no wisdom.' He tapped his temple. 'Nothing in their heads.'

'Who told you that?'

'My father did.'

'What does he do?'

'He sells carpets over there.'

'What's his name?'

'Ashrafi.'

'And what's yours?'

The boy shook the worms again.

'I'm Sami,' he said.

A few minutes later, I was sitting in a cramped carpet emporium, across from Sami's father. The shop was a concrete box, airless and so dusty that everyone inside coughed almost all the time. Ashraf's face was hidden by a mask of scruffy beard and dominated by a long, hooked nose.

He poured me a glass of mint tea.

'They call me the Eagle,' he said.

'Are you cruel and eagle-like with your clients?'

'No, it's because of my nose,' he said.

I told him it had been fortunate that I had met Sami at the bus stop.

Ashraf flared his nostrils.

'He was fishing,' he said.

'For river fish?'

The carpet-seller coughed hard and gulped down a lump of phlegm.

'For tourists.'

'Oh, yes, he told me that tourists have nothing between their ears. Empty heads.'

Ashraf grinned. 'You are different. You are a man of intelligence,' he said.

He poured me more tea.

'Well, I am also fishing,' I told him.

'For what?'

'For a story.'

'Then you are in the right place,' Ashraf replied. 'You see, each of my carpets is a story, a window that looks into another world.'

Sami started coughing so violently he had to go outside for air. When he was gone, his father stood up and pulled down a fine tribal rug, alternating red and white lines, ivory tassels at the ends.

'Look at this one,' he said, kneeling again. 'It's a story of the desert. The sheep which grew the wool were nourished by the plants that were themselves nourished in the soil, on the banks of the Draa River. The dyes came from berries in the trees, and the knowledge to create this masterpiece came from an ancient wisdom, trapped in the memory of the tribe.' Ashraf coughed again. 'There are stories in all my stock,' he said.

'But I'm looking for another kind of story… something with a beginning, middle and an end.'

The carpet-dealer lit a cigarette and filled the cubicle with smoke.

'They do have a beginning, a middle and an end,' he said.

'Not in the same way, though.'

Ashraf exhaled, and coughed some more.

'Two things can look very different,' he said. 'They can be different shapes, different colours, made out of quite different things. But to the heart they are exactly the same.'

From: *In Arabian Nights*

Portable Food

The kinds of food that are the most portable
in the ordinary sense of the term are:
Pemmican; meat-biscuit; dried meat; dried fish;
wheat flour; biscuit; oatmeal; barley; peas;
cheese; sugar; preserved potatoes; and Chollet's
compressed vegetables.

The Art of Travel

A JOURNEY OF considerable hardship requires a strong team, a team with the physical strength to persevere in dreadful conditions, and the mental stability with which to stare danger in the eye.

Years of sawing down the jungle had given the porters muscles that would put body-builders to shame, but their reserves of mental strength were pathetically lean. Before the night had been tinged with the subtle blush of first light, I crawled out of my moist sleeping-bag to confront the men. Their spirit was broken, shattered by the fantasy conjured up by Eduardo.

Giovanni was stewing up the last of the tapir, along with an agouti he had found dead on the forest floor. He would not look at me. When I approached, he pretended to be inspecting the sores on his feet. I had always been touched by Giovanni's humour, his honesty. If any man would tell the truth, I felt it would be he.

'If we push hard,' I said, 'we will reach the Gateway to Paititi by late afternoon.'

The cook did not look up. He was poking at a slender white worm issuing from his thigh.

'Please make sure the men eat well, and fast,' I added.

Giovanni swallowed hard, his face tilting down. 'We are going back,' he said.

'We are going upriver,' I snapped.

'*You* are,' he retorted. '*We* are not.'

A moment later the men were gathered around Giovanni, standing shoulder to shoulder like planks in a fence. They were not smiling, and when I took a step forward, they shuffled back as if I would harm them. I didn't know what to do, what to say. Ordinarily I might have turned to Eduardo for his advice, but it had been he who had fanned the flames of mutiny.

I ranted on for a time about dreams and aspirations, preaching a sermon that a man must follow what is in his heart. The porters' heads were low and their spirits not bolstered by my discourse. I said that Paititi was the magic wand that could transform our lives. It was there, I exclaimed, to test us, to unite us towards a greater glory. The porters stood motionless as I raged with an invented philosophy. I threw my arms heavenward and promised them that the invisible, all-seeing force of nature was looking over us.

'It will kill us,' Julio quipped.

'*El Tigre*,' muttered Oscar.

'*No somos estúpidos*, we are not stupid,' said another.

I turned to gaze upriver, taking in the screen of *chonta* palms perched at the next bend. Six pairs of green macaws flew overhead, wings flapping, beaks tweeting as they went.

'What do you want to change your minds?' I asked.

The men looked at each other, swapping quizzical side-glances.

'There is one thing that will make us happier,' said Julio.

I readied myself for an appeal for more money or increased rations. 'What is it?'

'*Queremos una ceremonia*, we want a ceremony.'

The ritual was a crutch by which the porters could prop up their floundering spirits. I did not condone it, but if that was what it took to continue, I was powerless to stand in their way.

Eduardo flew into a rage when he heard the team's demand. 'It is the phantoms inside them,' he shouted. 'Don't you see it?!'

'Let them have a ceremony,' I said, 'if it will keep them with us.'

It had been the Maestro who had worked them up into such a state and now I was justifying the remedy. I strode over to where the porters were huddled, all cosy and warm, beneath shreds of coarse blanket. 'You can have a ceremony,' I told them virtuously, 'as long as you are ready to move out first thing in the morning.'

There were no smiles, no glimmers of cheer, just a gallery of scowls. I went back to my nest of damp clothing and attended to my feet. The full day of rest would allow me to dry out the rotting skin between the toes. Meanwhile, the diet of Pot Noodles and bad jungle meat had given me terrible constipation. In recent days I had become obsessed by bowel movements. I had once read that Livingstone was similarly preoccupied, and had been plagued by bad bowels throughout his great African journeys. In my diaries I noted each movement in increasing detail, with estimations of weight, notes on firmness and colour. It seems like a sordid preoccupation to mention, but in the jungle, close inspection of one's stools makes for valuable research.

The day progressed with little sound from the porters. They lazed about, leading me to suspect that the ceremony was merely a stalling device. But then, as the half-light of dusk turned into night, their ritual began.

Oscar had trapped a black pig-like creature in a net. From a distance, it looked like a *paca*, a solitary nocturnal rodent that was always a welcome addition to the evening pot. The others had cut one of the blankets into thin strips, put them into enamel mess mugs, poured in a little kerosene and set them alight. The effect was of a dozen impressive torches, blazing with secret light.

Once the mess mugs were burning, the porters called me over. They had gathered in a circle, stripped to the waist, their torsos washed in yellow and orange, their faces haunted by charcoal shadows. Carlos rapped the back of a spoon against a metal bowl, in a sharp Morse code. The rhythm rang out across the veil of trees, warding away the spirits and luring the attentions of superstitious men.

Eduardo, Pancho and the film crew watched from a distance. I was planning to do the same, but Julio pulled me from the sidelines. 'This ceremony is for you as well,' he said.

The first phase continued for an hour. The spoon-rapping was joined by a chorus of grunts, the kind a rugby team makes before a match. Then a sharp knife glinted in the moonlight, and the *paca*'s life ended. Its blood was drained into a Pot Noodle tub, which was passed round. We each rinsed our faces in the crimson liquid.

Then Julio hacked off the creature's feet.

These were passed around as the blood had been. In the uncertain atmosphere, the men spent a moment or two sucking a foot, before passing it on. I cannot accurately describe the sensation of sucking a rodent's foot. I wondered who had thought up the ceremony and how it could have anything to do with the placation of evil. Once the sucking was at an end, and our faces had been daubed with blood a second time, the men squatted on the riverbank and whined like sows being led to slaughter. I followed their example, for fear of being ostracized.

It was at that point that Francisco told me to go back and sit with Eduardo. I walked over to the tent and watched from a distance. The ritual continued for another hour, with each man addressing the others in a peculiar high-pitched tone. Then, each one threw something into a low fire, burning between a tripod of stones.

'What are they burning?' I wondered aloud.

'*Su honor,* their honour,' replied Eduardo, '*y su dignidad,* and their dignity.'

Next morning we rose early, packed up the camp, and set off before anyone could protest. It had not rained, but the river had risen mysteriously during the night, most probably caused by rain falling on the leeward slope of the ridge further upstream. The porters' faces were rusty brown with dried blood, and their hair was curiously matted. I had not stayed awake to watch them, but Marko told me they had continued long into the night. The ritual, he said, had involved rubbing silt from the river into each other's scalps. Whatever the details, the ceremony seemed to have had the desired effect. The men were moving upriver.

We walked all morning, and through the first part of the afternoon, carrying the equipment up one set of rapids after another. There was no more talk of ghosts. The porters fell into a fine routine, relaying their burdens a few hundred yards at a time. In the many weeks we spent in the jungle, I cannot remember a day with less moaning and groaning, and less dissent. Even Eduardo noticed the change of heart. 'The spirits are resting,' he said smugly.

'I don't believe in that rubbish,' I replied, as we greased our feet.

Eduardo reached out to grasp my arm. He held it tight, crushing the bones together. 'You will condemn us to death,' he said.

By late afternoon I spotted a wide bend in the river, a signal that the chasm was close. Despite the team's exhaustion, I pressed them to continue until we had reached the Gateway. That night we camped on the rocks above the gorge. In retrospect it was a foolish choice. A downpour upstream would have flooded the river and we would have drowned, unable to escape. The water flowing through the chasm was much lower than before, but it was a treacherous passage none the less. To get to the other side, we would have to negotiate a three-hundred-yard trench of white water and rocks.

After the usual Pot Noodle appetizer and the main course of suspect stew at dinner, I rallied the team, thanked them for keeping the faith and staying with me. They pressed around me, their meek faces reflecting the candlelight, like a choir at evensong.

'Tomorrow we will pass through the Gateway,' I said, 'and we will walk into the future, with our heads held high. Paititi is close now.'

The men might not have been impressed by the speech, but I raised morale by promising double wages for every day we spent beyond the great chasm. Julio led the others in a round of applause, and they broke into spontaneous laughter. Much had changed in a single day. The porters were back on my side, and we had reached the new ground. It seemed as if, once again, the expedition had a future.

Passing through the chasm required bravery and folly in equal measure. Looking back is easy, and of little help. If we had known the price of the toll, we might never have journeyed through the Gateway at all. We began at dawn, our minds lulled by a night of sound sleep, our bodies energized by a hot breakfast of roasted *caramacha* fish. I harangued the men for a few moments as they loaded up like pack mules. Most had bandaged their hands with tough white tape and some had wound bandages tightly round their knees. They said it helped them deal with the strain.

The procession left camp on the dot of nine, snaking its way through the pouring rain up to the rim of the chasm. I was somewhere in the middle, enveloped in a green British Army poncho, which did little to keep out the water.

Eduardo was at the front, as always setting an example to the others by carrying an impossible load. Pancho, who was supposed to be guiding us, was at the rear of the procession. He kept silent all morning, even when he walked into a wasps' nest. Like the other local people I had met, he cackled with laughter at the misfortune, and went on.

The best route through the chasm was a point of contention. No one could agree on which way to go, and each man seemed reluctant to trust his life to another's plan. In the end I overruled everyone, and insisted on the path with the least overt risk. Even then, it was necessary to clamber over a series of grotesquely large rocks, each more slippery than the last. After that we were forced to wade up through the white-water trench.

The ability to tell a good route from a terrible one is a valuable skill when leading an expedition. Unfortunately for us all, it was a skill I did not possess. I had failed to take into account the invisible currents. The first three men who stepped uneasily into the frothing water were instantly carried away, along with their packs. The film crew, whose precious equipment they were transporting, whimpered like distressed damsels, as their exposed film raced downriver towards rocks.

That morning Pancho had been of little use. But as soon as he heard the frenzied shouts, he glanced at the river and took in the situation. His experience of fishing near rapids had taught him the way water flows. Within a few seconds, he had ripped down a stave, calculated the route of the flow, barred the way and saved the bags.

For eight hours we persevered through the white water, gaining a few feet an hour. Rarely have I felt so drained, so wretched, as on that day. The torrential rain did not cease for a moment. There was water above, below, and all around us. It shrouded us, froze us, and almost drowned us all.

At the end of the experience there was a beach, no more than a few yards of oily, claylike silt. We lay on it outstretched, exhausted, tearful and triumphant. I thanked the men for their endurance, but my words were scant payment for their efforts. They disliked me very much, but we had bonded, whether any of us wanted it or not.

Those who had the strength raised their heads a fraction and peered back at the Gateway. The chaos of rocks, grit and white foam, the waves and the ferocity of nature were overwhelming. I marvelled at it, as perhaps a condemned man might be awed by the workmanship of his noose.

As ever, Eduardo read my thoughts: 'The executioner will get us on our return,' he said.

His words were to haunt me over the next weeks: each mile I dragged the team on was a mile further to be covered on the way home. Only God knew how we would ever get through the chasm again. But then, if I was to believe Eduardo, the Gateway to Paititi was nothing compared to the journey ahead.

That evening, as we all crouched around a great bonfire, set back from the river on a plain of needlegrass, the old man spoke again about the danger. His words drifted into the night with the sparks. 'Paititi will rob our souls,' he said. 'It will feast on our guts, spit them out and laugh at our inanity!'

'We are getting near,' I said.

Eduardo spat into the fire: an unlikely gesture for such a refined man. 'What do you know of Paititi?' he snapped.

'That we have a chance at finding it.'

'*Huh!*'

'We have Pancho,' I said firmly. 'He knows, you told me so yourself.'

'I said that long ago,' Eduardo replied, 'when the river was an angel.'

'And now what is it?'

The Maestro wiped a tear from his left eye. 'From here on, the river is Death,' he said.

The first night beyond the chasm was humid, despite the increased altitude. No one slept well. I heard the men talking to each other and shouting out in their dreams. I let them lie in until eight, to make up for the hardship of the previous day. They were uneasy at breakfast. I could sense that something was wrong.

'What is it?' I asked Julio.

'Oscar saw a ghost,' he said, 'in the trees... It's there whether you like it or not.'

'I do *not* like it,' I said curtly. 'Ignore it!'

We put on our clothes, loaded up and moved out. A tense, anxious air hung over the procession. I would have rallied the team and urged them with words of support, but my rallying talk was spent. I knew that, from that point on, no amount of coaxing would work. If I wanted the men to stay with me, I would have to drag them forward an inch at a time.

The way ahead was a monotony of shallow water, sandbanks and heavy rain. Every tree looked like the one beside it, and every bend like the one before. I marched on without thought. It was the most dangerous way to continue. When I could be bothered I worried about the threat of shattered ankles, but most of the time I didn't waste my energy.

Boris started to moan about deadlines. He said something about having shot enough film. He suggested camping at the edge of the river, and waiting for us until we came back. I wouldn't have it, and forced him to continue. On a harsh expedition there's no space for anyone who does not intend to finish. In the army such men are shot as deserters. I told Boris, jokingly, that I would have him shot. We looked at each other when the threat had passed through the air from my mouth to his ear. The Bulgarian's face was taut. 'You would do it, wouldn't you?' he said at length.

'Perhaps,' I replied.

We carried on and each day melted into the next. It was a routine of getting up, putting on damp clothing, eating stew, trudging in agony, eating Pot Noodles, more trudging, building camps, sleeping and getting up again. The days were filled with painful movement upriver and the nights with fever.

We all dealt with the hardship in different ways, and clung to obsessions, in the hope they would help us through. I sought salvation in preoccupation with my bowels, the Swedes were devoted to keeping the Arriflex dry, and Marko thought of nothing but the well-being of his cigars.

As for the porters, they became universally obsessed with collecting the spent Pot Noodle tubs, and invented a thousand ways to use them. Back in England, I had given little thought to the snack's flavours. Most of what I had brought were Chicken and Mushroom, and came in a standard white pot. But a few were spicy curry flavour, called 'Bombay Bad Boy', and came in a black pot. A black market developed between the men, in which the rare black tubs were regarded as equal in value to a pair of rubber boots. I would have stamped out the trade, but allowed it to continue because it kept them occupied.

On other journeys I had found myself craving the luxuries of home, but not in the Madre de Dios jungle. I did not miss having clean water to wash in, a flush lavatory or laundered clothes. As time passed, I rarely thought of home, except of my wife and our baby daughter, whose first birthday I had missed.

As time progressed, we all developed a crude routine. It enabled us to endure what might normally be considered unendurable. Each morning I would put on my wet clothing just before setting out, and stay wet until breaking for camp each evening. I had become obsessed with keeping a single change of clothes bone dry. I would wrap the sacred dry shirt and shorts in multiple layers of plastic when not in use. I never washed them; clothes hanging out to dry invariably got soaked in an unexpected shower. My dry outfit was black with dirt and it stank.

Personal hygiene was equally hard to maintain. Like most of the men, I washed in the river each afternoon. The cleanliness of the water depended on whether it had rained. If it had, then the river's silt would be swirled up into it like lamb broth, and rinsing yourself did more harm than good.

Despite the Vaseline, our feet continued to suffer. To make matters worse, a few of the porters developed alarming sores on their backs. They were as wide as coffee cups, with dead white skin round the edges and shiny pink in the middle, like an exotic species of anemone. I experimented with a range of treatments, but none proved satisfactory. I would have handed out antibiotics, but our stocks had been ruined in the rapids.

Ten days after he had passed through the great chasm, Eduardo ranted on about a curse. He was always going on about curses and sin, exclaiming how Adventism was a defence against evil, so I didn't take him very seriously. We were traipsing through the river, making adequate headway, Pancho at the rear, Eduardo somewhere near the front. For once it wasn't raining; the sky was a great canvas of indigo, ribbed with cirrus clouds. Better still, the plague of sweat bees had vanished. I was about to give voice to my satisfaction, but the old man suddenly shouted out from the front: '¡*Paren*! ¡*Paren*! Stop! Stop!'

'What is it?'

I ran forward, stumbling across the rocks, and passed the porters, who had come to an abrupt halt. 'What is it?' I repeated, in a low voice.

The old man wiped a hand over his mouth. 'We cannot go on,' he said.

'Of course we can!'

'And risk such danger?'

'*What danger?*'

'*Las líneas malditas*, the Curse Lines,' he said.

Rodrigo had often taunted me with talk of the lines. He had said that only an embalmed cadaver could reveal the safe path between them. Eduardo's knowledge of the Curse Lines took me by surprise, for I had thought they were a figment of the shaman's expansive imagination.

My worry was not for Eduardo and his fears, but for the men. If they got a whiff of the new invisible danger, they would drop everything and run back to their village. Again, I pleaded with the Maestro to keep the hazards to himself.

'If we cross this point,' he said, jerking his thumb at the ground, 'we may not return here alive.'

Danger is the companion of hardship. I was prepared to bear risks, but unwilling to be beaten by hysteria. Eduardo's greatest strength, his humanity, was now working against me. Whenever he spoke, the porters listened. They trusted his judgement and believed every word that slipped from his lips. But I sensed that his usefulness was coming to an end. He was invaluable, but his ability to incite mutiny made him worthless.

We camped early so that I could quiz Pancho and get the old man back on my side. Some of the men took advantage of the remaining light and went to hunt birds in the marshes that formed a floodplain to the river. They returned with a number of straggly-looking ducks, which they plucked and cooked.

I had stopped eating Giovanni's stews because of the fish bones. A great variety of fish could be found in the high jungle, some of which looked primeval. Their common feature was an astonishing skeleton, fragments of which would tear into your cheeks and gums as you struggled to get at the meat. All the others thought I was mad to pass up the nightly blend of fish, game and rodent.

While the men prepared the camp, I went over to where Pancho was sitting. His expression was calm, like that of a mannequin, neither happy nor sad. He was making flights for his arrows from bristly black feathers. I asked him for his opinion on the Curse Lines. He didn't reply.

'Do you know about them?' I asked, again.

'*Sí*,' he said, at some length.

'Do you believe in them?'

Pancho preened half a feather through his lips. '*No los puedo ver*, I cannot see them,' he said.

'But do you fear them?'

The warrior did not answer. In the world of the Machiguenga it was considered polite to ignore a foolish question. After several minutes of silence, he turned to me and, staring out over the river, he said: '*Paititi no existe.* There is no Paititi.'

Across from where we were sitting, I could see Eduardo rallying the men. I could not hear his words, but it was evident that he was whipping up their fears. I rushed over, and took him aside. 'We can find Paititi!' I said earnestly. 'You must believe… If we believe, we will find it!'

The old man shook his head. 'No, my friend,' he said. 'Paititi is a fantasy. It is a dream. It does not exist.'

I found myself incensed by Eduardo's inconsistency. The hardship was dragging him down. He was trying to come up with excuses to pull out, and to take the porters with him. The worst aspect was that we had no idea how far there was still to travel. I started to ration the Pot Noodles, encouraging Giovanni to serve up as much of his devilish stew as possible. There was still enough dried food for a few more days, but I had to take into account the return journey We had stashed supplies en route, but almost certainly too little.

During the night Oscar jumped up and ran off into the jungle, screaming and waking us all. I thought we were under attack. Before I could give an order or find my lamp, two or three men went after him. I could make out the sound of limbs ripping through the dense undergrowth, of panting, and shouts of desperation. Eventually they brought the boy back. He was sweating, and hyperventilating. There was pasty white spit around his mouth; his eyes were dilated, and he was trembling.

'What is wrong?' I asked sternly.

Oscar's mouth chewed at the air. He swallowed hard.

'He's gone mad,' said Francisco.

I asked Oscar again what was the matter. He said nothing. His eyes streamed with tears.

'I am sorry,' he said, weeping.

An hour later the disturbance was over and the team were asleep again, but I lay awake, worrying about Pancho, Eduardo and the men. They were all much stronger than I, much more at home in the jungle, but I had the solemn duty of pulling them all ahead. It brought out the worst in me, and they began to call me *el Diablo* behind my back.

I didn't like being the brunt of their jokes, the focus of their whining, but as long as they were with me, I didn't care what insults they came out with.

The more they jeered in private, the more determined I became to carry them with me to the very end.

From: *House of the Tiger King*

Jma el Fna

PLAYED OUT AGAINST a backdrop of vibrant cultural colour, the late Marrakech afternoon is like nothing else on earth.

The *souqs* are packed with bargains, bustle, and with people cloaked in hooded *jelaba* robes. Stacked up are bundles of wool carpets from the High Atlas, dazzling brass trays inscribed with the names of God, baskets of dried damask roses, mounds of pungent incense and sulphur, and endless shops, each one crammed with treasure from the remotest reaches of the desert.

For all the wonders of the medina, it's the great square of Jma el Fna that I find the most tantalizing spot of all. It lies at the heart of real Marrakech, the city of snake charmers, the *crème de la crème* of the Exotic East.

Most people hurry across it fast. Pause too long and you're sure to be sucked in deep. But to me that's the true magic... being pulled down through the layers like a man floundering on the ocean waves. Allow yourself to be free, and you glimpse the many facets of this mesmerizing stew of humanity.

The *Halka*

A circle of people stands in the darkness, shoulders pressed together tight, necks craning forward for a view... a great green parasol looming over them, and me as I push in closer. The outside world gradually fades away and then... is shut out. The sense of anticipation growing, palpable and electric.

I'm being sucked in... through the rows of onlookers to the source of this frenzied, primal rhythm. I'm descending back through time... to when this place, Jma el Fna, was no more than an oasis in the desert. Suddenly, I break into the centre of the circle, walled by shadows and men's faces, illuminated by the jolting, jarring flame of a gas-lamp. It's like the meeting of a secret fraternity.

In the middle of the *halka* – the circle of souls – leaps the riotous silhouette of a man, a violin grasped tight in his hand, the crowd gripped by the wild strains of his instrument. As he turns into the light, I catch his features... bearded, tight curly hair, smiling eyes upturned to the stars. Raw, energetic, hypnotic... a Moroccan Jimi Hendrix, a Berber master musician.

First Impressions
Anyone who's ever been to Marrakech remembers the first time they stepped onto the frenetic expanse of Jma el Fna. For me it was a searing afternoon back in June '71. I was four years old. My fingers were pressed tight in my father's hand, my eyes blinking in the dazzling light.

Despite the heat, the square was crowded beyond belief. There were snake charmers and tumbling acrobats, medicine men in Touareg robes, blind men and water-sellers, madmen and doped-out hippies crouching in the shade.

Stumbling forward through the waves of people, I was mesmerized. It was as if every man, woman, and child on Earth was right there. A seething stew of humanity set in random motion.

Watching over it all like a sentinel – the minaret of Jma el Fna itself, the mosque of the annihilation, the mosque of eternity, the mosque at the end of the world.

Over the years, and especially since I moved to Morocco, I have returned to Marrakech again and again, and always find myself crisscrossing the square, usually heading for the shade of the ancient medina, whose twisting lanes stretch out behind it in a great secret labyrinth.

Soaking it Up

My father used to say that the only way to absorb the atmosphere was to close your eyes. 'Listen to the sounds that go unnoticed,' he would tell me, 'and breathe in the smells that the nostrils try to filter out... concentrate, and the reality will reveal itself.'

It's a lesson that's never failed me. And whenever I venture into Jma el Fna, I do as he suggested, and find myself transported to a space on the edge of the imagination, a cross-section of medieval Morocco that's as real today as it's ever been... but one whose true form is truly elusive.

Facts and figures: My father, who was from Afghanistan, would scowl when I would ask for facts and figures... when I begged to be told how big the square was, or when it was laid out.

'You've been brainwashed by the West,' he would say. 'To understand Jma el Fna you must cut away Occidental thinking, release your mind, and absorb the place from the inside out.'

Zigzag

For my father, the zigzag approach was the only way to understand something. 'Throw yourself in at the deep end,' he would say, 'run free, bouncing around like a billiard ball on the baize, and you'll build up an accurate picture, a little at a time.'

Forty years later, and I'm back in the middle of the square, ready to step out, to zigzag. I'm itching to feel the waves of energy, to seek out the invisible, and to hear the sounds that are muffled to even the sharpest ears.

Day, Night

Just like the *halkas*, the circles of joy and entertainment which are born and die through the day and the night, Jma el Fna is a place without a beginning or an end. It's a circle of life, with its peaks and lulls, enacted from the first rays of dawn to the last strains of night.

Every day. Every night.

Fishing for Drinks

Every time I visit the square there's something new, a display of fresh ingenuity. This time it's the man over there with scarred hands and a limp. For the last half-hour he's been laying out spiraling rows of plastic bottles, warm fizzy drinks. Everyone's wondering what's going on. He's already pulling a crowd and he's not even begun.

Jma el Fna is all about piquing the crowd's curiosity, and one way to do that is to keep them guessing. When they can't stand it any longer, he unfurls a clutch of homemade fishing rods, long bamboo staves, dangling strings with what look like curtain rings on the ends. The local preoccupation with fizzy drinks, and eagerness for a bargain, has made it an instant success.

Secret Police

Everyone says that the square's crawling with secret police. Like a separate group of invisible performers, they're masters of disguise, watching every hand, purse and pocket. The entertainers, healers, and food sellers all claim to know who's who. But they're not telling me. It's one of many secrets here, I suppose, I'll have to decipher for myself.

Tourists

The tourists stick out because of their pasty white skin and their clothing, but most of all because of the way they reel forwards between the *halkas*, enthralled by it all. Some of them are grinning, others scowling, all clicking photos instead of watching what's really going on.

It's as if they're desperate to penetrate what is a secret society. Some of them think they've actually done it, that they've been accepted into the folds. But they never quite manage. They're oil on the water. And although they can get mixed up for a moment, they separate out as they're washed forward through the crowds.

Earning Marrakech

These days it's far too easy to get to Marrakech. Budget airlines touch down at the new international terminal day and night, from across Europe and beyond. Waves of tourists emerge and, like moths to a flame, they're lured by the mythical reputation of Jma el Fna, the heart of Marrakech, the heart of Morocco.

Feel the Fire

It's all too easy in a way. Until quite recently you had to struggle through the desert to get here. Sweat, thirst, heat, and even delirium. But you arrived changed by the journey, ready to receive something so magical that language can hardly convey. If I had my way, you'd still have to reach Marrakech by foot, for there's no better way to soak up its core than as a wayfarer, ripened by travel.

Cigarette Sellers

Some square-dwellers are almost invisible as they slip nimbly through the crowds. But you hear them. A fistful of coins jangling as they approach, an open packet of cigarettes, sold one at a time to anyone needing a nicotine fix.

Medicine-man

As the afternoon light peaks in intensity, a row of healers lay out their stalls in a line on the ground in a corner of the square. Drawing a crowd, they reel off numbers and cures. Dressed in billowing indigo robes, embroidered with gold, turbans crowning their heads, they claim to heal any disorder – of body or mind.

Their dusty old quilts are packed with wares: ostrich eggs and stork feathers, tortoise shells, dried reptiles, great lumps of sulphur, antimony and chalk. Phials filled with murky grey liquids, dried damask roses, aromatic seeds, and swathes of shocking pink silk.

Of all those making their living here, it's the magico-medicine men who are doing the briskest trade. Customers hurry up one by one. They spit out the name of an affliction, in no more than a whisper… a rash, an eruption of sores, a need for revenge on a neighbour, or the yearning for a son.

The healer nods, his fingers conjuring a cure from the treasure chest of ingredients before him. His sales patter is unbroken as clients and onlookers stand spellbound. He wraps the mixture in a twist of paper, hands it over fast, and snatches the customer's coins into the voluminous folds of his robe.

A desert lizard emerges from under the same robe, head held high, a string around its waist attached to its master's finger. It blinks, as if in approval of the transaction.

Dentist
Nearby, in the shade of the mosque, is a dentist, sitting on a stool… in front of him a platter overflowing with human teeth. He's got small darting eyes, a checkerboard smile, and confidence in his skill at bringing even the most

severe toothache to a swift end. Whatever the condition, the treatment appears to be the same… a quick, open-air operation with a pair of rusted iron pliers, and a plug of grubby cotton wool to stem the flow of blood.

Henna Women

It's true that most of those who make their living in Jma el Fna are men. But look around and you realize there are professions reserved exclusively for women. They are the sorceresses and fortune tellers. And cast an eye through the square during the quiet hours of the afternoon and you see the henna women perched on stools under parasols. As soon as they spot a pallid foreigner, they hold up their henna-filled syringe and grin.

A catalogue of pictures is at the ready… decorated hands and feet. Squat on a stool for a minute or two, hold still as the hand grasping the syringe weaves its magic, and you've been initiated into the ancient sisterhood of Marrakech.

Snake Charmers

There's no noise so alluring, so utterly hypnotic as the *rhaita*, the snake charmer's flute. A cliché maybe, but a mainstay of Jma el Fna, a backbone of sound and sight that bewitches tourists and locals alike.

Long before you reach the square, you hear its piercing tone. Riotous, fearful, yet somehow tamed, it cuts like a laser beam through the interminable din of the traffic, and the clip-clop of horses' hooves.

Draw near, enchanted by the rawest streak of sound, and the serpents are knocked from their rest beneath a clutch of circular drums. Dazzled by the sudden blast of light, a pair of spitting cobras rear up, poised to strike. Despite the heat, the snake charmer's wearing a thick woolen *jelaba*, a ragged strand of calico wrapped around his head. And around his neck a water snake, its tongue licking the afternoon heat, a desert accessory.

Food Stalls

Just after the muezzin calls the afternoon prayer, dozens of iron carts are propelled forward from all corners of the square. Like gun carriages made ready for war, they're positioned precisely on the east side of Jma el Fna and unloaded. Cast-iron struts and staves, pots, pans, tables, benches and stools, are knocked into place.

These days the food stalls are fed by electricity, illuminated by bare bulbs, bathing the diners in platinum light. As soon as you draw near to the battery of stalls, the hustlers are galvanized into action. They're paid to entice anyone with a few coins going spare, to eat at *their* stall.

Fingers jabbing at the hodge-podge of dishes on offer, they can recount the menu in any language you chose – there's sheep brains and lamb on skewers, octopus, squid, and fried slabs of fish, tripe, goat's head, snails, all of it washed down with miniature glasses of hot, sweet tea.

Denzel Washington

King of the Hustlers is a burly, fresh-faced man of about thirty, who goes by the nickname 'Denzel Washington'. Venture anywhere near his food-stall, number 117, and he careens forward with a laminated plastic menu at the ready. Like the other hustlers, he's skilled in working out where you're from, long before you utter a word. This sixth sense, which must have evolved over centuries, makes the difference between survival and extinction.

Change

Travel back and forth to a place you love and it's the change you notice first. It hits you side on, blurring your memories. Sometimes when I visit the square, I cry out in rage at the creeping gentrification. For me, Jma el Fna should be stuck in time, unaltered ever... a Peter Pan destination.

But the wonderful thing about the square is that change is quickly assimilated or undone. Here, nothing is set in stone. Efforts to introduce boundaries of any kind are thwarted by an ancient system far more powerful than the authorities who clamour for change.

A few years ago the orange-juice sellers were corralled into a row of mock calèche carriages. I jumped up and down in ire when I saw them for the first time. But these days I realize that they have a place, and that it's the content which is important, rather than the container.

Boxers

Another *halka* is forming. In the middle stands a rough-looking man with a woolly blue hat, a week's growth of beard on his cheeks, and the end of a cigarette screwed into the corner of his mouth. He's got a heap of third-hand boxing gloves beside him, and he's cajoling anyone to come forward and try their luck.

As soon as the crowd senses action, their numbers swell. More and more people are turning up, the atmosphere stoked by a hardened accomplice in a flame-red tracksuit. He's coaxing people to throw coins down onto the ground. He'll let the fight start when there's enough cash in the ring. The dirhams come slowly.

In one corner there's a desperate-looking contender, with a broken nose, ragged *jelaba*, and back-to-front baseball cap. In the other, a handsome teenager in a Barcelona football shirt. He's got curly, greased-back hair. They raise their gloves, spar for a moment, but the fight's short lived. The youngster dodges a few swipes, then quickly abandons his hopes and his gloves.

But now, a young woman steps forward, puts on the gloves. I can't believe it. Neither can the audience.

The secrets of Jma el Fna are only revealed to the patient, and to the observant. Turn up day after day and you'll find the same girl stepping forward into the ring and strapping on the gloves. She's the ring-master's daughter and, like the other boxers, she's in on the deal.

Gnaoua

The roots of Jma el Fna sink deep down into the sand beneath the entertainers' feet. The place may now be paved over but it's a square of desert, an oasis with a sacred soul. Most of all, it's African, the vast expanse of sky above, boiling with cumulus clouds, a reminder to anyone who doubts it.

And of all the life-forces that pour through you in the square, the truest and most vibrant is surely the Gnaoua. A brotherhood of African troubadours, dressed in brightly coloured desert robes with cowrie-shell hats, they're forming a semi-circle now.

Great iron castanets, clattering like cymbals. Their rhythm gives the square its endless beating pulse, day and night. The sound is more like a cohort of warriors heading to battle than a troupe of musicians touting for tourists' change.

Appeal of Jma el Fna

Pass a little time in the square, and you begin to see that it's peopled by ordinary Moroccans. It's not a place for the bling-bling set or the *nouveau riche*. They steer well clear, preferring the fashionable cafés of the new town.

Yet Jma el Fna's great enduring appeal is that it turns no one away. It's an ancient entertaining machine, a healer, a listener, a giver of sustenance, and a friend.

Flautist

A flautist has entered the square and sits without fuss in the centre, playing his wooden pipe, as at ease here as a shepherd on a mountainside. Hunched in his dark blue *jelaba*, the crowds move around him, unsure whether to dwell or linger, the cacophonous nature of the space pulling them in different directions, looking for other circles to join.

He plays, oblivious to the surrounding throng, his cap on the ground, upturned and coinless. He plays a tune which, to my ears, could have been played here a thousand years ago… as the camel caravans paused en route for sustenance and entertainment. A timeless witness, he plays and plays but no coins come.

Blind Musician

It's true that some of the entertainers rely on their hustling skills to get by. But there are players with extraordinary talent as well. As evening slips into night, an old blind musician with a microphone strapped around his neck twists up the volume knob on his amplifier, and begins to play. He's not doing it for the money, but because the square is his sweetheart, his theatre, his home.

Pinstriped Healer

The business of a specific *halka* tends to be clear from a distance. Glance at the faces of the audience and you see it right away, reflected like candlelight in a mirror. Most of the time entertainers keep the atmosphere jovial, because humour leads to laughter, and laughter leads to generosity.

But some performers have a far graver message. The darkest of all on this night is a man in a black wool pinstripe suit. He has a huge beard, like a great black inverted candyfloss. He's missing his front teeth, and his creased face is gripped with an almost maniacal expression.

He's ranting on about jinn, the spirits that Muslims believe exist in a parallel world laid atop of our own. The subject is greeted with terrified looks, especially when the pinstripe healer starts spewing numbers – the alphanumeric *Abjad* system, linchpin in a magician's repertoire.

Row of Blind Men

Jma el Fna has its own telegraphy. It knows about you long before you know about it. A row of blind men begging for alms are alerted to my presence by a woman sitting on a stool nearby.

She calls to them, explaining that I'm recording them. They stand up and, staring directly at me with wide glassy eyes, wave their sticks. Commotion ensues and suddenly confusion and ill temper reign in a corner of the square. But the pervasive natural rhythm of el Fna soon restores order.

Bike Boy

Fleeting moments in the dark: a boy before me is suddenly pushed down to the ground on his bicycle by an older girl. She makes sure she hurts him, and is then gone, away into the night.

Storytellers

The storytellers (or *hakawatis*) draw the largest of all the crowds even if their own numbers are dwindling... when they are out, their *halkas* are lined with listeners, both old and young.

Recounting tales from *Alf Layla wa Layla*, *A Thousand and One Nights*, and other favourite collections like *Antar wa Abla*, they tap into a communal obsession for the fantastic.

The best storytellers are good businessmen as well. They know when to stop their tale on a cliffhanger, appealing for a few coins before they go on.

Like so much of what takes place at Jma el Fna, the stories are understood by few foreigners, as they're recounted in Darija, the Moroccan dialect. The tourists might take pictures of the crowd, but they don't penetrate... or receive the ancient message being passed on.

Order

Spend some time soaking up the atmosphere through all the senses, and patterns begin to emerge. It's part of Jma el Fna's own form of magic, an alchemy that transforms disorder into order.

Fears for the Future

I used to worry that the square would one day be destroyed, built over, its revelers disbanded. But now I see how impossible that would be. As a cornerstone of life, Jma el Fna is somehow indispensable to Marrakchis, as vital to them as the air they breathe.

Zigzag Conclusions

Standing in the ocean of people, circles forming, flourishing, and dissipating likes ripples all around, I'm reminded of my father's words, that the best way to understand the square, and to experience it, is the zigzag way... zigzag back and forth for long enough, and you're touched by the sorcery of the place... from the inside out.

Pass through it long enough and it begins to pass through you.

From: *Travels With Myself*

Iquitos

IQUITOS IS THE capital of Loreto, by far the largest department in Peru.

It's the only city of any size in a state as large as Germany. The flight north-east from Lima slices across the sierra and the barren highlands of the Cordillera Azul. Peer out of the window again and the mountains are gone, supplanted by a carpet of green. Even from twenty thousand feet you can't help but be struck by its vastness. Millions of trees form a single, unbroken canopy. Rivers crawl east and west like colossal serpents, twisting with oxbow lakes. All of it vivid with life, in ten thousand shades of green.

The moment I got out at Iquitos airport, I sensed the jungle around me. The morning air was thick with heat, the sunlight filtered through cloud. Where the runway ended, the rainforest began.

I followed the jumble of passengers across the cracked slabs of concrete towards the arrivals hall. Like me, they all had good reasons for making the journey. Only wheeler-dealers and the most intrepid tourists bother with Iquitos.

The middle-aged Peruvian who had sat beside me on the flight said he'd come to buy spider monkey bones for a Chinese aphrodisiac dealer. I was surprised he was so open about his line of business. Slip a wad of cash in the right hand, he said, and you could smuggle anything out of Peru. He poked a finger towards a Customs display case, which featured the skins of animals facing extinction.

'I can get you any of those,' he boasted.

'But aren't they endangered?'

'Hah!' grinned the businessman. 'There are plenty of them left; thank God, as I've got lots of customers in China.'

Long before the first bags had arrived, the luggage carousel came to life. We waited obediently, as the conveyor belt stop-started forward. The baggage did not come. Instead, a bizarre ceremony began.

A procession of thirty figures emerged from a cluster of bamboo shacks at the far end of the hall. They were dressed in fibrous skirts, their faces painted for war. The men led the way, each of them holding a long blowpipe above his head. The women followed close behind, all bare-breasted; and the children were unclothed.

Some of the warriors wore crowns made from the bright feathers of scarlet macaws. They danced around the hall, incorporating the empty luggage carousel into their routine. The warriors would take it in turns to ride the conveyor belt, while pretending to use their blowpipes.

None of the other passengers from the Lima flight showed any interest. I asked the monkey-bone smuggler what was going on. Grimacing, he swished his hand at the dancers.

'It's a horrible tragedy,' he said.

'What is?'

'The Bora… or what's *become* of them.'

'What are they doing here?'

'They live in the airport,' said the trader, 'the government's trying to step up tourism – they thought having a warrior tribe resident in the arrivals hall would be a good idea.'

'They look quite pacified to me,' I said.

'That's the saddest thing of all,' grunted my confidant. 'The Bora used to be one of the most feared peoples on the Upper Amazon. They used to slaughter anyone they wanted. They loved killing… *now* look at them.'

A fleet of three-wheel passenger motorbikes, known as *motocarros*, fought to take me into town. The drivers were a rugged breed, their shoulders trimmed with tattoos, bandanas hiding their mouths. The leader of the pack snarled at the others, frightening them away. He wasn't tall, but stocky. Around his neck he wore the skull of a small bird. Spitting a razorblade from his mouth, he threatened to carve up the rest of the gang. My bags were loaded onto the back of his bike. The driver stashed the blade back in his mouth and pushed away down the patched tarmac towards Iquitos.

The undergrowth loomed up from either side of the road. As someone who's more used to city life, I felt unsettled by the blend of creepers, roots and spiders' webs, which hung in the trees like fishing nets. Unfamiliar sounds echoed from the jungle, over the noise of the engine. I wondered how I'd survive on the long journey into the interior.

I watched in the wing mirror as the driver flipped the razorblade on his tongue. It was an impressive stunt.

'Don't you cut your mouth?' I shouted.

'It's not as hard as it looks,' he said. 'None of the others can do it, so they're frightened of me. If you don't make a reputation for yourself in Iquitos, *te comerán vivo*, people will eat you alive.'

I thanked the driver for his advice.

'Where are you staying?' he asked.

'I don't have a hotel yet.'

'Iquitos is full of thieves,' he replied. 'I'll take you to my friend's hotel. It's off Plaza de Armas, on Calle Putumayo. Stay anywhere else and you may get your throat slit.'

*

ON MY TRAVELS I've stayed in some extraordinary places.

In Rwanda, I once put up at a hotel where the walls were drenched in human blood; in Delhi I once put up in an opium den and, in Varanasi, at a *dhobi*'s, laundryman's, shack.

But none of them could compare with Hotel Selva.

The woman at the reception desk asked if her husband could keep his chickens in my bathroom. It was, she said, the only place near the kitchen with direct sunlight. I agreed reluctantly. She pointed down the hall to room 102.

'What about the key?'

The woman shook her head.

'At Hotel Selva we trust each other,' she said obscurely.

The building harked back to a time when Iquitos was one of the most prosperous towns in the world, founded on the rubber business. Its walls and rounded arches were built from solid blocks of stone; the stained-glass windows must have been imported from Spain or France. But Hotel Selva had been ravaged by a hundred years of Amazonian wear and tear. The windows had lost most of their glass years before, the guttering leaked, and the roots of a nearby ironwood tree had lifted the flagstones.

The panelled door of room 102 had come away from its hinges. Taking it from the entrance, I propped it up against the wall. With unsure footsteps, I edged forwards into the dim chamber.

I tried the light switch, but there was no electricity. Nor was there any furniture, except for a bare, mildewed mattress. The walls were coated with a veneer of slime. One corner had been used as a *pissoir*. The sounds of female ecstasy flowed from the adjacent room, in time with the creaking of a bed frame. I nudged open the bathroom door. About fifty full-sized chickens were flapping about, agitated by my intrusion. The floor was peppered with excretions and dried blood. A bolt of sunlight lit up the birds. A glance up at the ceiling explained the brightness. There *was* no ceiling.

As I stood there, surrounded by chickens, a second door to the bathroom opened. It led to the kitchen. A hand reached into the sea of birds and grabbed one, as another hand ripped off its head. The chef called back, asking me to keep out of his chicken coop. I had no business to be in the bathroom, he said, as there wasn't any water anyway.

I sat on the flea-infested mattress and took in my surroundings. I would have looked for another place to stay, but, as someone preparing for a journey of certain hardship, I decided that a stay at Hotel Selva would be invaluable experience.

By lunchtime Iquitos was coming to life. *Motocarros* tore down the wide avenues in droves. Shopkeepers wiped down the rich arabesque facades, sheathed in *azulejos*, glazed tiles. A battalion of shoeshine boys slipped from the shadows and patrolled the streets. Their mothers would be waiting for them to bring money for food.

Glance at a map and you wonder how Iquitos can survive. Like Manaus, its sister city in the Brazilian Amazon, Iquitos is a quirk of nineteenth-century history. It ought not to exist at all. Nestled on the Amazon's west bank, it's more than two thousand miles from the river's Atlantic mouth. No roads lead to the town; it can only be reached by boat or by aeroplane. Every pot and pan, every tin of tuna fish, outboard motor and drinking straw has to be shipped in.

I wandered up Calle Putumayo and turned right a block before the waterfront. A hundred years ago the embankment must have been a formidable sight. Overflowing with rococo grandeur, the buildings still had their elaborate Doric columns and lead-lined domes, their cornicing and balustrades. The buildings reflected the men who had erected them: opulent, powerful, arrogant. Men with no fear. They mirrored the might of the great river which they overlooked. But, as with Hotel Selva, time had dealt them a terrible blow. The plasterwork had chipped off, the banisters crumbled, and the Portuguese tiles had fallen like scales from a great fish.

Cast an eye over the palatial buildings, block out the groan of the *motocarros*, and it's not hard to imagine how things must have been a century ago. In a handful of years the rubber barons had transformed themselves from destitute adventurers into some of the richest men on earth.

One traveller passing up the Amazon in March 1854 afforded Iquitos a single line in his diary: 'A sparse and miserable hamlet,' he wrote, 'consisting of 33 houses, a straw-thatched church.' By 1900, Iquitos was a town of 20,000, of which 4,000 were Europeans. Crates of English banknotes were regularly unloaded at the docks. The rubber barons spent their new-found wealth like water. They bought Italian furniture, satins, silks, the finest porcelain, and entire cellars of vintage champagne – all of it shipped in direct from London.

For centuries native peoples of the western Amazon have dipped their feet in liquid latex, before curing them over a fire. Columbus reported seeing Indians playing games with strange 'elastic' balls. Rubber had been known of in Europe for a long time, but it was always of limited use. In the winter it became too brittle and hard, and in the summer it grew soft and sticky. But everything changed in 1839, when Charles Goodyear invented vulcanization.

Paying slave wages, the rubber barons employed thousands of native people as *seringueizos*, tappers. Only they knew where to find the rubber trees, which grew naturally in the jungle. They tapped the latex into cups, coagulated it into thirty-kilo balls called *peles*, and floated them down the river. The latex could only be harvested in the morning and evening – as the sun's heat thickened it. Once he had a bucket of latex, the tapper would cure it a little at a time over the smoke of a fire.

For a period of about thirty years, Iquitos was firing on all cylinders. At the same time that gold was discovered at Klondike's Bonanza Creek, a new elite of millionaires were living it up in the Amazon. But the boom years came to an abrupt end when, in 1912, the first crop of latex was harvested from Oriental trees.

A few years before, during the height of the bonanza, Henry Wickham, an Englishman, had smuggled seventy thousand rubber tree seeds to Asia. No one noticed his precious cargo plying its way east towards the Atlantic. With no indigenous diseases to attack them, and arranged in neat plantations, rubber trees thrived in Malaya.

Success in the Far East spelled disaster for the Amazon. Boom-time was snuffed out overnight.

*

THE AMAZON RIVER was swollen, its waters much higher than usual.

From my vantage point on the embankment I could see dozens of miniature islands – the roofs of submerged shacks. The heaviest rain in living memory had forced thousands of people out of their homes; hundreds more had drowned. I'd heard that high water was good for Amazonian travel. The sandbars which lie beneath the surface – some as large as steam ships – make navigation a constant danger. The higher the water, the faster the current, and the less threat there is of running aground.

As I stood there, the heavens opened and the afternoon rains washed down. I sought refuge in a café called Ari's Burger, on the east side of Plaza de Armas. It was a South American version of Arnold's, the fifties diner from television's *Happy Days*. The floors were chequered, the chrome tables topped in raspberry-coloured vinyl. A jukebox hummed away in one corner. The young waitresses glided about, their feet forced into under-sized plimsolls. They wore a uniform: red skirts, ivory pinafores and matching sun visors. Each of them had the same pouting lips, highlighted with shocking-pink gloss. Spiralling down over the right edge of each sun visor was a tight brown curl.

A teenage waitress hurried over through the tangle of chrome chairs. Puckering her lips as provocatively as she could, she suggested I order a banana split. It was, she said, her favourite. After ordering one, I made the mistake of admiring her curl. She leant down to pick a hair from my shoulder, and puckered a little more.

In Iquitos, casual compliments are taken very seriously. The girl, who said her name was Florita, lamented that she hadn't a date for Gringolandia, the disco. She would wait for me at ten. I choked out a list of excuses, and got back to my plans.

There was still much to do before my search for the Shuar could start. No time for disco dancing. On a paper napkin I made a list: *(1) Guide. (2) Supplies. (3) Boat.*

Florita swanned over with a huge banana split. Its bowl was as big as a geranium's pot. I rooted around with the long spoon, hunting for bananas. There were none. I asked what was going on. Florita said the bananas had been blended up.

Back to the list.

Sourcing a guide was the main concern. I needed a man who knew the Pastaza region, where the Shuar lived. He would have to be adept at diplomacy as well as jungle survival; a knowledge of *ayahuasca* would be useful as well.

Florita told me that I shouldn't look for a guide. If you want something in Iquitos, she said, you wait for it to come to you. Hang around, she pouted, and a guide would turn up.

Exactly thirty seconds later a sleek young man slipped easily onto the chair beside mine. He pulled a Marlboro from a soft pack, slid his tongue down the edge, and lit the end.

'I heard you were looking for a guide,' he said.

'Yes, I am, but how did you know? I haven't told anyone but Florita.'

The man, Xavier, squinted as the smoke furled up into his eyes.

'It's my job to know what's going on,' he said.

If Ari's Burger was Arnold's Diner, then Xavier was its Fonz. His hair was a number one on the sides, sheared with electric clippers, an oily quiff crowning the top. He wore his own self-styled uniform – ripped jeans and a white T-shirt with the arms torn off. As far as Xavier was concerned, arms were for wimps. Under the shirt, he confided, lay a tattoo of staggering size and imagination: a dragon savaging a mermaid, surrounded by angels. The sting of the needle, he said, had been excruciating.

'Can I see it?'

Xavier swept back his quiff.

'Are you kidding? The girls would go wild.'

Florita tiptoed over and nuzzled a note under my glass. It declared her undying love for me.

'Let's get down to business,' I said. 'Do you know the Pastaza region?'

'No man,' said Xavier, 'I'm not a guide... I'm a fixer.'

'Well can you fix me up with a guide? I need someone who knows the Shuar tribe.'

Xavier's ice-cool expression cracked.

'*Shuar*?' he murmured, miming a round object with his hands.

'Shrunken heads,' I said. 'But they don't do that any more.'

'It's not going to be easy. No one goes up there.'

'Well, I'll have to get another fixer who can find a man brave enough for the job.'

Xavier thumped his breast.

'Give me until this time tomorrow,' he said. 'I'll find you a guide so brave that he could walk through fire.'

*

IN THE LATE afternoon I explored the streets leading onto Malecón de Tarapacá, the road which runs along the waterfront.

Tourism didn't seem to have taken off in Iquitos.

Despite this, the backstreets were littered with tourist kiosks. Each one sold the same range of curiosities. There were blowpipes seven feet long, spears and snuff pipes, feather headdresses and stuffed piranhas, jaguar teeth necklaces and masks made from caiman skin. Frames panelled the walls of every kiosk. In them giant insects were pinned out.

I sipped a tall blended drink on the porch of a restaurant called Fitzcarraldo. It had once been home to the legendary rubber tapper and explorer of the same name. Werner Herzog's film *Fitzcarraldo* had made a great impression on me years before. I never thought that one day I might be sitting in the rubber tapper's headquarters, looking out over the swollen waters of the Amazon.

Fitzcarraldo's story echoes the trailblazer spirit and the wild excesses of the rubber boom years. Born Brian Sweeney Fitzgerald, the eldest son of an immigrant Irishman, he was known in the jungle as Fitzcarraldo. He fled into the Amazon in his early twenties, after being accused of spying during the war between Peru and Chile. Two years later, in 1877, he'd made a fortune as a rubber tapper, and was one of the richest men in Peru. The money was soon spent.

After watching Enrico Caruso perform at Manaus's £400,000 opera house, Fitzcarraldo swore he'd lure the great tenor to the Peruvian jungle. His dream was to bring opera to the natives. What better way to entice Caruso, he thought, than to build an opera house to match the one in Manaus?

To raise funds, Fitzcarraldo came up with a plan. He would make use of the vast rubber-tree forest on the Ucayali River, where fourteen million trees stood untapped. To succeed, he first had to get a boat beyond Pongo das Mortes, the Rapids of Death. Everyone said he was mad, which he probably was. He sailed his steamship up a parallel river and forced his labourers – all of them Shuar – to haul it over a hill and down to the Ucayali.

Once the steamer was on the Ucayali, Fitzcarraldo and his companions celebrated with drink. As they did so, Shuar labourers cut the mooring ropes, sending the boat charging towards the rapids. From the start they had planned secretly to sacrifice the vessel, to appease the spirit of the waterfall. The boat plunged over the rapids.

Somehow, Fitzcarraldo survived but never lived to build his opera house. He died soon after, in 1889, drowned in the Urubamba River. He was just thirty-five.

Night falls quickly over the jungle. The patina of dusk diffuses into darkness, a signal for the nocturnal world to wake. In Plaza de Armas the streetlights seethed with insect life; mosquitoes, moths and hornets among them, hurling themselves at the orbs of brilliant white glass. The restaurants and bars, bright with neon lighting, were haunted by them. No one but me was in the least bothered.

The only place in Iquitos free from insects was Ari's Burger. Every few minutes one of the bubbly waitresses would float through, spraying poison gas from an aerosol. I sought refuge there, preferring the gas to the bugs outside.

Even before my backside had met the chrome chair, Florita was standing over me. She had missed me during the afternoon, she said, but would miss me even more later in the night. Three other guys had already asked her to the disco, but she'd rejected them in favour of me. She exclaimed that she would never look at another man. Murmuring more excuses, I ordered another banana split.

I closed my eyes as the poison gas rained down. When I opened them, a robust-looking man was sitting across the table. His skin was tanned, his hair expertly cropped and parted at the side. He had an honest face that seemed out of place in Ari's Burger.

'Iquitos is the best kept secret in the world,' he said in a west-Texan drawl, 'but there's a lot of bad people down here. We're cleaning it up though.'

'I was on the lookout for conmen,' I said.

The Texan tapped his index finger on the raspberry vinyl.

'Don't let down your guard,' he replied. 'The bandits see tourists like you as game… game to be hunted.'

From: *Trail of Feathers*

The Kumbh Mela

THERE'S A BLUR of feet hurrying through ankle-deep mud.

Millions and millions of them. Some in plastic sandals, others in rubber boots, many others in cheap city shoes, or sneakers, or flip-flops, or brogues. Tens of thousands more are barefoot, some limping, others running.

This sea of humanity is surging forward, relentless and unstoppable. Most of them have bundles on their heads. Each one is stuffed with rice and flour, pots and pans, blankets and bedrolls. Many have babies bundled on their backs or toddlers clutched tight to their chests. Eyes squinting into the bright winter sunlight, they are streaming in from all points of the compass towards the vast encampment.

A sense of frantic anticipation and complete exhilaration unites them. As it does so, the unending torrent of pilgrims sets eyes on the glinting waters. It is the point where their journey ends just as it begins.

This is the greatest gathering in human history, a multitude of one hundred million souls. They've come to the Sangam, the confluence point where the subcontinent's two holiest rivers – the Ganges and the Yamuna – converge, at Prayag, outside Allahabad in northern India.

Once every 144 years a Maha Kumbh Mela takes place, Hinduism's vast ritualistic cleansing of souls. Translating as 'The Great Festival of the Urn', the last time it took place, Queen Victoria was on the British throne.

The India that usually makes the headlines is the one abundant with call centres and Rolls-Royce dealerships, and with skyscrapers that reach high above the landscapes of interminable urban sprawl. It's the India of Bollywood bling and of ubiquitous shopping malls, of ritzy brand names, and of the super-rich who can't get enough of all the über-kitsch.

Dedicated to wealth creation, this newfangled India of the twenty-first century defies logic just as it exceeds expectation. It may be a realm that makes the Occidental world drool with envy, but it's only a small fragment of what's really going on.

Travel through the Indian subcontinent and you quickly grasp that this is a land with its feet rooted firmly to the ground. The heads of the jetset oligarchs may be in the clouds, but the majority of rank-and-file Indians have no doubt who they are, and where they've come from. Hailing from villages and small towns, the silent majority may aspire to gaining wealth too, but what's central to their lives is something that runs far deeper.

Faith.

And to most of them there's almost nothing in the ancient spiritual machinery of Mother India quite so auspicious as the Kumbh Mela. An immense cosmic counterbalance, an Indian Woodstock devoted to peace and love, it's the distilled essence of the subcontinent.

Pass a few days at the Mela's world within a world and you can't help but be sucked into it and swept along. As you learn to block out the ubiquitous hum of background noise, you begin to piece together the fragments that form the grand mosaic that is the Kumbh.

I first heard of it as a student backpacking around West Bengal twenty-five years ago. I was taking refuge from the monsoon under a railway bridge. Already sheltering there was a *sadhu*, who was travelling by foot. He was naked, covered in ash, with wizened limbs and an intense stare that has stuck in my mind ever since.

As the rain began to fall harder, he suddenly grabbed my arm.

'I will not get there in time!' he exclaimed anxiously.

'Get where?'

'To the Kumbh Mela!'

I asked him what it was.

'It is the union of the sky, the sun and the moon,' he said.

Unable to forget the holy man's words, I've often wondered if he did make it in time. Had he missed it, there would have been a lengthy wait for the next one, not to mention a long walk home to West Bengal.

Entangled in the astrological sequence of auspicious timings, the Kumbh Mela is held in one of four cities in strict rotation once every three years – at Nasik, Haridwar, Ujjain, and Prayag, where this year's festival was held.

423

The locations of the Melas are said to be points at which droplets of Amrit, the Elixir of Immortality, were spilt in antiquity by the celestial Garuda bird.

Once every twelve years a great Kumbh Mela takes place, when the propitious timing is amplified many thousands of times over. And, in keeping with the lunar cycles, every twelfth great Kumbh Mela is the 'Maha' – held every 144 years.

Remembering the naked *sadhu* taking refuge with me under the railway bridge, and quite certain I wouldn't be here for the next one, I pledged to journey to Allahabad myself, to attend the Maha Kumbh Mela.

As someone well used to the grand scale of India, I assumed deep down that the festival would be nothing more than a whole lot of people whipped up into a spiritual frenzy. But the days and nights I spent there changed the way I view the subcontinent, and even the way I regard my fellow man. A primal human experience, it defied the complexities of contemporary life, while holding up a mirror to our collective souls.

Located a few miles away from Allahabad, most of the festival ground is more normally well underwater, beneath the sacred rivers. Organizers can never be quite sure how far the waters of the Ganges and the Yamuna are going to recede, and exactly which lands will be exposed.

Once the waters have retreated in late November, there's a wait before the ground has drained and hardened. Last year the waters receded much later than usual, which meant that the vast tent city could only be constructed at the last moment.

The festival ground has to be seen to be believed. With a hundred million people traipsing through during the fifty-five-day Mela, it's on a titanic scale. Covering almost five thousand acres, it's divided and sub-divided into numerous sectors on a grid structure.

One of the great difficulties is that the site straddles the intersection of the mighty Ganges and the Yamuna. This leads to a complicated natural arrangement of sandbanks and uneven connection points. To link them all together, dozens of pontoon bridges are erected, each of them buoyed by a series of massive iron drums.

On the surface, the tent city resembles something out of a military campaign. In addition to the pontoons and the neat rows of khaki tents, the main thoroughfares are laid with iron sheets so that vehicles don't get stuck in the mud. There's electric street-lighting too, which bathes the camp in an unnerving yellow glow through the hours of darkness. The lights are run by a series of mobile power stations, set up just for the Kumbh Mela.

But all this is just the tip of the logistical iceberg.

Dozens of police stations pepper the encampment, as do mobile field hospitals, fire stations and government offices. After all, in India, the wheels of bureaucracy die hard. And there are cafés, shrines, and trinket stalls by the thousand, as well as bandstands and rickety-looking fairground rides, and more than 35,000 portable loos.

Spend some time at the Maha Kumbh Mela and you quickly grasp that it's not about mind-numbing statistics. It's about people, and about their utter belief in a system of devotion that forms an unwavering backbone to life from the cradle to the crematorium.

For those of us raised in the cynical nihilism of the West, it may be hard to understand how or why a family living in a village a thousand miles away from Allahabad would blow almost everything they have to bathe at this auspicious moment at the Sangam, the confluence. But, regarded through the eyes of the devout majority, it's an affirmation of unshakeable belief. And central to that belief is the steadfast faith in a system that promises redemption in exchange for devotion.

If the figures are correct, and one in twelve of the entire Indian population passed through the Kumbh this year, then it reflects what this astonishing mass act of piety means to Hindus. They hastened to Allahabad from every corner of India – from each city, town, village and hamlet. They came from the tea plantations of Assam in the extreme north-east and from the desiccated deserts of Rajasthan, from the mountain stronghold of the Himalayas, and from the tranquil waterways of Kerala. They ventured, too, from the smog-filled urban sprawls of Delhi, Bangalore and Mumbai. They came to be united all together but, more importantly, they came to be absolved of their sins.

I reached the Kumbh Mela at dusk on Valentine's Day. Having taken a flight to Varanasi and then driven through the lush countryside for several hours, I knew we were nearing because of a rumbling sound on the wind. We must have still been ten miles out of Allahabad, but I could feel the Kumbh in my bones.

Asking the driver to stop, I got out and listened.

What I heard was like one of those nature films where they stick a microphone into a colony of ants. A cross between frenzied movement and what sounded like every conversation in the world overlaid on top of each other, it filled me with a primeval sense of fear as well as curiosity.

We continued and, as we did so, we began to pass droves of people on foot. Most of them were laden with belongings piled on their heads. Processing forward through wind and light rain they marched with an extraordinary surety of movement. It was as if the Maha Kumbh Mela was somehow in their DNA, that to get there was programmed into them all – whatever the cost may have been.

When in India, foreigners have a way of asking questions for which there are no black-and-white answers. As soon as I arrived, I begged everyone I met to give me facts and figures, and to tell me when the Kumbh Mela began. No one seemed sure. One man told me, 'It started ten million years ago.' Another was less exact. He said: 'It's been going a long, long time, sir.'

The first known foreigner to have written his impressions was the seventh-century Chinese monk Xuanzang (although some scholars have doubted whether he actually saw the Kumbh).

The earliest known account in English was written by the celebrated American traveller and novelist, Mark Twain. He described his visit to the festival of 1894 in *Following The Equator*. Of it, he said: 'It is wonderful, the power of a faith like that, that can make multitudes upon multitudes of the old and weak and the young and frail enter without hesitation or complaint on such incredible journeys and endure the resultant miseries without repining.'

I found myself wondering where Twain would have stayed on his visit more than a century ago. Fortunately for me, I was taken in at the lavish Laxmi Kutir camp, in a prominent position above the main festival site. It was situated between a Hindu temple and a Muslim mosque – both of which strove to outdo the other in terms of noise and commotion through day and night.

The camp boasted tents with ensuite bathrooms, feather quilts, and hot water bottles. There were even chocolates on the pillows at night. Having settled in, I went over to the viewing terrace, and got my first real glimpse of the Kumbh.

Glowing canary-yellow from all the thousands of improvised streetlamps, it was like nothing I had ever imagined. In the struggle to describe the spectacle it seems that only clichés are sufficient. It was like staring through a kaleidoscopic lens into the navel of the world, into a realm that defied both time and space. Humming, murmuring, and with whispers on the breeze, it was electrifying, empowering, and was more radiant in its sheer energy than anything I had ever seen.

After a couple of hours of trying to sleep in my prim tent, I got up. The vibrations from the plateau were calling me to come and join the fun. There was a sense of the Pied Piper about it, something so mesmerizing that I was quite unable to resist.

Clambering down steep steps cut into the rock, I climbed down to where tens of millions of ordinary Indians were camped. It was three a.m. but there were people everywhere. Some were washing or praying, many more were walking alone or with children in arms, all heading in the same direction – down to the Sangam.

Making my way through the unending landscape of tents, my eyes grew accustomed to the creamy yellow light. As for my ears, they were bombarded by the high-pitched chants from a thousand makeshift shrines. And mounted on poles every hundred yards were loudspeakers through which came continuous appeals of family members separated from their clans.

Following the hordes through the mud, I stumbled forward in mist tinged with yellow light over a series of pontoon bridges, down to the confluence. It was bizarre to think that for most of the year the land on which my feet were walking was the sacred riverbed. For the millions of pilgrims this was holy ground, the reason why a great many went barefoot.

The thing that sticks in your mind from the first moment is the sense of goodwill. In the days I spent at the Kumbh Mela, I saw too many spontaneous acts of kindness to recall: a pilgrim pressing a folded bill into a blind beggar's hand; a woman taking off her shoes and giving them to another who had lost hers in the mayhem; a little boy presenting his banana-leaf bowl of rice to a crippled old man on a cart.

Traversing a kind of beach, I finally got down to the actual waterline. Reinforced with sandbags, there was a flimsy wooden stockade screening the area off from a much larger expanse. On the other side of it there were literally millions of people surging into the water. Stripping off their outer garments, they were mesmerized by the auspiciousness of the moment.

The Mela began on 14th January at the Makar Sankranti, when the sun entered Capricorn, the day on which it's said that light returns after its long southward journey. A winter solstice, it signals the start of fifty-five days of providence. And during this festival time there are a series of extra-specially auspicious days. Believing their prayers will be amplified, pilgrims make sure they bathe at the Sangam then.

The day after my arrival was the second-most favourable of all, the reason why so many had got down to the water early – keen to beat the rush. With an ocean of people stretching as far as the eye could see, there was the constant fear of stampede. Kumbh Melas are notorious for masses of innocent people being trampled underfoot. All it takes is for one person to freak out and to run. There is in us all a primal fear of crowds, and it's triggered at such moments.

Like everyone else, I was tanked up with pure adrenalin, ready for fight or flight, and for the stampede. Unlike the pilgrims, however, my purpose was not to enter the freezing waters of the confluence, but to watch.

As I stood there on the less crowded side of the stockade, a policeman on horseback hurtled down the beach. Wielding a *latti*, a long wooden stave, he herded me and others into the narrowest pinprick of land between the water, the stockade, and the countless ordinary folk on the other side.

All of a sudden I made out the muffled cries of what sounded like an army roaring into battle. Turning quickly, squinting through the yellowed light, I saw a sight of true terror, like something from Hollywood's wildest fantasy.

Hundreds of naked men were making a beeline for the spot on which I was standing. Their bodies caked in ash, their hair matted in long twisted dreadlocks, some were waving swords, others tridents or shields. More still were chanting or howling, faces contorted with macabre expressions, feet running in a crazed blur of movement.

Wave upon wave of them charged into the chill water, immersing themselves, before retreating hastily onto the beach. These *naga*s, holy men, are the revered mainstay of a tradition dedicated to prayer, solitude, and to relinquishing the trappings of conventional life. Their brotherhood, the Order of the Juna Akhara, meaning

'Ancient Circle', is a secretive monastic order of *sadhus*, yogis and ascetics.

Such is their reputation for spiritual leadership, they are given VIP pride of place at the Kumbh Mela. When not bathing down at the waterline, they spend their days smoking pipes stuffed with hashish in a special area reserved just for them.

Dedicated to receiving *moksha*, liberation from continual reincarnation, *sadhus* (which simply means 'good men'), crisscross the subcontinent most usually on foot, living lives of stark austerity. They are sworn to celibacy and shun material chattels, and spend a great deal of time crouched beside a smouldering sacred fire known as a *dhuni*. Rubbing the ash onto their naked skin, they pass the hours smoking, meditating, and receiving the veneration of ordinary people.

In the lanes of this VIP area, I came across all manner of *avatar*s and holy men. A few were practising acts of penance, their bodies contorted in strange positions, or their arms having been raised up in the air for decades.

It was there that I found Baba Rampuri.

Bespectacled, with sapphire eyes and with a great bush of teaselled greying beard, he was seated on a low dais. Uncharacteristically clean for a *sadhu*, he had hair that fell in curls to his shoulders; his clothing was spotless too: a loose saffron shirt and pyjama-style trousers.

Baba Rampuri said he had been coming to Kumbh Melas since 1971, the year in which he moved to India from the United States. A throwback to the age of tie-dye and navel-contemplation, he oozed peace, love, and goodwill to all men.

We spent the afternoon together, and in that time Baba Rampuri lifted the veil into the world of the ordained *sadhu*. A mystical fraternity with roots in India's ancient past, it's a society that sits awkwardly with the feverish consumerism that clouds any experience of modern urban India.

Leaning back on his dais, Baba Rampuri looked as though he'd seen it all before – a writer crouching before him eager for a usable soundbite. Then he told me that he had read some of the books I'd written and I punched the air in my mind. His hands churning around him, he said:

'No writer or photographer who's ever come to the Kumbh Mela has ever had a financial or artistic success. None of them. Not a single one.'

I asked why.

Rampuri grinned, albeit a sarcastic grin, one that made me shift my crossed legs uneasily.

'Because,' he said, 'you all tell it like it is, blinkered by the overwhelming seductive imagery. But you never tell the story behind the story. Here at the Kumbh there are a couple of worlds present at the same time. There's the one that's on the surface that intoxicates you, and the other that you hold in your heart.'

Baba Rampuri wagged a finger hard in my direction. 'It's not about me,' he said, 'but about the order of which I'm a small part. This institution has the ability to pass learning down through the time. I've devoted my life to

433

the Ancient Circle of the Juna Akhara. And in that time I've seen that most foreigners miss the point. You all go on about how a pilgrimage like this is about nurturing the self. Well, it's not about the self but the group experience!'

During our conversations, Baba Rampuri would take the *chilam*, a clay pipe, from a fellow American guru, wrap a handkerchief over the end to filter it, and draw hard. His sapphire eyes clouding over, he railed against the foreigners who came to the Kumbh Mela and missed it all because they were too busy peering through camera lenses, and as a result failed to see what was going on.

All of a sudden the American *sadhu* waved a finger in my direction.

'We have to go and feed people now,' he said.

'Who?'

'Ordinary people.'

'How many ordinary people?'

Baba Rampuri pushed his rimless glasses up higher on his nose.

'About five thousand,' he said.

When I asked how he could afford it, the guru seemed a little despondent.

'Every member of the Juna Akhara leaves the Mela penniless,' he told me. 'We always do. It costs us way more than a hundred thousand dollars. Such great social responsibilities go along with it – of which feeding the masses is just one.'

Before I took my leave of Baba Rampuri, he told me to check out his website and to follow him on Facebook. I did a double take.

'You're in cyberspace?'

Reaching for the *chilam*, the American grinned one last time.

'Of course I am,' he said.

Leaving Rampuri to feed a small fraction of the entire pilgrim population, I strolled through the makeshift lanes of the Juna Akhara. Taking in the dozens of holy men, some naked and others not, I felt as though I had reached the innermost layer of onion skin. This seemed to be the spiritual core of an entire religious system, in a land with many hundreds of millions of followers.

I got talking to a Gujarati couple from Ahmedabad who had been prostrating themselves before an elderly *sadhu* – one who had supposedly taken a vow of silence back in 1962. The husband, Rajiv, told me that he worked ten hours a day in a call centre, and that he had brought his entire family to the Kumbh Mela to help balance the malevolent forces in the universe.

I asked what the naked *naga* would be able to do for them.

Rajiv touched a hand to his heart.

'He has given us his love and his blessing,' he said.

'But why do you feel you need it?' I asked cynically.

Rajiv's wife, Mahdvi, broke in.

'Because, it's the counterbalance for the world that we all live in.'

'And how is it – your world?'

Mahdvi shook her head glumly.

'It's a place of deadlines, stress, pollution, and without enough space – a place where you're suspicious of strangers and where you forget to see the beauty.'

'Which beauty?'

Rajiv held out his hands.

'The beauty that's all around us,' he said.

Back up at the deluxe Laxmi Kutir camp, I took a hot shower, scoffed down a four-course dinner, and felt rather ashamed at myself for feeling the need to regroup in the lap of luxury. At the next table I met an Englishman called Ronnie who had come to the Kumbh to look for an old school pal. A big, blustering bear of a man with broken veins speckled over his cheeks, he told me that he had been at Eton with Sir James Mallinson.

'He's down there somewhere,' said Ronnie distantly. 'Although I haven't a clue where to start looking. He's gone native, you see.'

I asked Ronnie what he meant.

'Well, after Oxford, Jim became a *sadhu*, and he was given the name Jadish Das. He's devoted his life to purifying himself.'

I asked Ronnie what his friend was like.

A little overcome with excitement, he exclaimed:

'Jim's a terrific chap – a real chum!'

For all its colour and curious traditions, the brotherhood of the Juna Akhara impressed me for the way it had remained on the rails. It may have been a beacon for eccentric Englishmen and for Californian ex-hippies, but there was something honourable about it. Most of all, I found myself appreciating what it hadn't become – a big-business Disneyland of the Soul.

The same couldn't be said for the dozens of godmen and godwomen who had set up temporary ashrams all over the Kumbh Mela. As the days passed, I couldn't help but become preoccupied by the sleek, well-oiled machinery of their high-flying guru businesses.

One afternoon I was making the long walk across the pontoons to the Sangam, when it began pouring with rain. Seeking shelter, I slipped into a giant canvas marquee in which a *darshan*, a meeting with a holy person, was taking place. Against the rhythmic drone of a tanpura, a woman dressed in a red turban was dispensing blessings to one and all.

Strangely, most of the followers were white Anglo-Saxon foreigners. Dressed identically in costumes of unblemished white, some had shaven heads, except for a Hare Krishna-style pigtail dangling from the back of the scalp. But they were not Hare Krishnas. They were instead zealous devotees of the Mauritius-born godwoman, Her Holiness Sai Maa.

Having jetted in for the Kumbh Mela from the community's Temple of Consciousness Ashram, just south of Denver, most of them were American, with other followers hailing from Germany, France and Spain. Unified by their enthusiasm for neatly packaged mysticism, and by their blinding smiles, the devotees of Sai Maa stuck out a mile, as did the fraternity's organization.

Awash with press packs, plush white vehicles and printed schedules, with merchandising, photo ops and presence on social media sites, the godwoman's setup had to be appreciated for its slickness.

Having whispered that I was a journalist, I was instantly ushered past an office packed with computers and technicians, and welcomed into a pristine audience room decorated with bunches of plastic flowers. It was explained that Sai Maa took a vow of silence for four hours in the middle of each day, but that she was willing to break her vow and speak just to me.

Grunting thanks for the honour, I waited.

From time to time a blue-eyed devotee would shuffle in and out, blinding me with a smile. After I'd waited a little more, there was suddenly a sense of heightened anticipation, as though a VIP – or rather a god – was about to arrive.

A small door opened and the lady in the red turban wafted through.

I have met plenty of self-appointed godmen and godwomen in India before, but Sai Maa was different from all the rest. There was a sense that, despite the abundant trappings of the guru business, she was merely putting on a show. And the show was perfectly configured to be lapped up by the legions of Occidental devotees who were craving a figure such as herself.

All Sai Maa was doing was filling a niche.

Though struggling to speak at first, Her Holiness quickly found her voice. It was soft and mellifluous, gliding out through lips anointed in fuchsia-coloured gloss. During my audience, I learned that Sai Maa had moved from Mauritius to France at twenty-one, that she had sat on the City Council of Bordeaux, and that she still owned a chateau there. I learned, too, that she had two grown-up children. She had been quite late in becoming a self-styled god.

It became clear that there were big plans afoot in the Maa's Temple of Consciousness movement. Construction was at that very moment taking place downriver on the banks of the Ganges at Varanasi, to build an ashram in the shape of two intersecting hearts. Dedicated to Global Enlightenment, Sai Maa's work was already reaching a worldwide following through cyberspace.

In the middle of my audience, a stream of American devotees filed in. With shaved heads bowed low, they prostrated themselves before their deity. Having kissed her feet, some of them snapped pictures with their phones. Almost as soon as they had come, the disciples were ushered out by an officious blue-eyed henchman from LA. I felt like congratulating him because he had understood the crux of the guru business – the art of limiting access.

Once the white-clad devotees were gone, Sai Maa babbled away in florid soundbites for a long while. I wondered how to break free and claw my way back to the glorious human stew of the Kumbh Mela a stone's throw away outside. My break came when the godwoman's

BlackBerry began to buzz. Squinting at the display, Sai Maa took the call, chattering away in French.

Fifty yards from where the godwoman was sitting with scrubbed-clean devotees waiting at the door, a wizened old woman from Bihar was lying on the ground. She was weeping hysterically, her ragged clothing all covered in mud.

'I lost my son in the crowd,' she sobs, 'and I don't know how I will ever find him again.'

As I watched, a stall-keeper selling fried orange jalebis strode up and helped her from the ground. He pointed up to a loudspeaker that was blaring a distraught appeal.

'You're not the only one lost,' he said tenderly. 'I'll take you to the place where you can speak on this thing, and it will find you your son.' He handed her a bowl of hot jalebis and together they set off towards the setting sun.

The next morning I was taken to the scene of a fire. Faulty wiring had short-circuited, setting a Jeep alight, the petrol tank of which had exploded. Miraculously, only two people had been killed. The smouldering remains of dozens of tents and charred belongings had been heaped up in a great pile. Helped by his sons, a slightly built man was picking through it all, his expression forlorn.

'We came all the way from Tamil Nadu,' he said, 'and we have lost everything we brought with us.'

I asked the man about his life. Like most of the people at the Kumbh Mela, he was from India's rock-solid underbelly.

'We are farmers,' he said, 'and we have a little land outside Chennai. We grow rice and have some buffalo as well. We have come here as an act of devotion, a devotion to the river. Of course we hope to be blessed in return, but the reason we are here is to give ourselves to the river.'

All of a sudden the sky darkened as though the end of the world had come. A sense of panic prevailed. Time was running out – before the deluge struck.

A young holy man wrapped in a saffron robe saw me standing in the makeshift street wondering what to do. Tugging at my wrist, he led me fast through the maze of uniform tents, as the wind whipped up once again. It was late morning but the sky was as dark as midnight. As the first raindrops gushed down, the young *sadhu* thrust me into his tent. His name was Hardwar, and his expression was so composed that I couldn't take my eyes off his face.

We sat in silence listening to the rain. Behind him was a cluster of *sadhus* drawing quietly on their pipes. And beside him was a boy of fourteen with almond eyes and an orange turban wrapped tight around his head. Recently ordained into the order of the Juna Akhara, he was lying on his stomach playing a video game on his phone.

'We will be leaving soon,' said Hardwar, straining to make himself heard against the thunderous roar of rain, 'down to Varanasi, where we will camp at the crematorium ghat. Our prayers here are almost done.'

I asked what the Kumbh Mela meant to him. Hardwar's lips were touched with the faintest hint of a smile. 'It's a mirror,' he said, 'in which is reflected the heavens, the universe and the world.'

As the rain flooded down outside, turning the dust into ankle-deep mud, I told Hardwar about Sai Maa and her jetset devotees. He thought for a moment, then tapped me on the knee.

'God descends to Earth and is always present at the Kumbh,' he said softly, 'but to find him you must search for the most unlikely person. In him or her is God.'

The downpour ended and I went back outside to wade through ankle-deep mud. As I struggled through it, I couldn't help thinking of the farmer from Tamil Nadu who had been a random victim of the fire. And my thoughts turned to the millions of farmers, like him, who rely on the Ganges for their lives.

I have heard it said that almost half a billion Indians depend on the waters of Mother Ganga for drinking water and for irrigating their crops. The subcontinent may be urbanizing quickly, but millions spend their lives toiling away on the patchwork of tiny ancestral farms which lie in the Ganges' path.

As a sacred waterway that is herself a goddess, Indians believe the Ganges cannot ever be defiled by the misdeeds of Man. She's above pollution. It's for this reason of course that people are quite happy to gulp down cups of her holy water, even though it's dark grey with silt and grime. Indeed, having bathed at the Sangam, a great many pilgrims filled little containers with the Ganges' hallowed water, to take home to family members and friends who were unable to make the journey to the Kumbh.

With such a colossal tide of humanity clustered on the same stretch of riverbank, local authorities have been increasingly worried about the environmental impact of the fifty-five-day event. Despite a mass of sandbags at the waterline, soil erosion has been considerable. But the real damage to India's goddess-river has been the pollution. Plastic bags may have been outlawed at the Kumbh Mela for the first time, but severe ecological damage was done if only by the mind-numbing amounts of raw sewage flowing into the sacred confluence.

After almost a week at the festival, I headed from my luxurious vantage point down to it one last time.

More people were arriving every moment.

Although I was exhausted from the crowds, the noise, the godmen and the wild hullabaloo, there was a sense of rebirth, as though the Kumbh Mela was reinventing itself for the newcomers.

I watched as an extended family stumbled down to the waterline, clutching a hotchpotch of belongings. So as not to be separated amid the hordes, they had tied a dark blue cord around them all.

Reaching the Sangam in time for dawn, the legions of ordinary souls were stripping off their garments and wading into the water. Almond-eyed Assamese were bathing there along with thickset Punjabis from the north, and with swarthy Tamils from the Bay of Bengal. There were Hindus from the Himalayas and from Kolkata, from the Great Thar Desert and from the vast Indian diaspora that spans the world.

With the pink blush of first light touching the rippling surface, I pondered how little it all could have changed in centuries. And that's what made the Kumbh Mela so special to me – the sense that it was a circle of humanity linking us to our ancestors, to nature, and to our fellow men.

That night I took a taxi to the Allahabad railway station to take my train. The route was flooded and tens of thousands of pilgrims were wading through the overflowing sewers and conduits. With the traffic gridlocked for miles ahead, I abandoned the cab and joined everyone else on foot, my suitcase on my head.

Inside the station there were people everywhere. A great many were sprawled out on the platforms. Some were lying on carpets they had brought from home, others sharing their food with strangers, or in prayer. The atmosphere was convivial, a far cry from how it had been a few days before, when a footbridge had collapsed. In the resulting stampede thirty-six pilgrims had been trampled to death.

The dark blue sleeper train to Delhi rolled in, iron wheels grinding against the tracks. All of a sudden there was a frenzy of commotion as the pilgrims threw themselves at the train.

As I wondered how I would ever get aboard, I saw out of the corner of my eye a familiar face. This time it was smiling – it was the face of the wizened old woman from Bihar, her son's hand clasped tightly in her own.

From: *Cultural Research*

An African Hinterland

NAMIBIA IS ONE of Africa's youngest and most mysterious nations, a land of daunting size and rugged beauty. Within its realm contrasts abound. Rocky plateaux rise hard by expansive deserts; lush watercourses give way to barren vistas and ancient peoples brush with modern technology.

In Namibia's vast desert regions some of the world's most enduring plants, creatures and peoples abide according to an archaic natural scheme. Into these endless tracts, nature cast her richest treasures – diamonds, other precious stones and minerals. Today the country accounts for roughly one-sixth of the world's diamond wealth.

Records from the time of Herodotus indicate that the Phoenicians were the first explorers to circumnavigate the African continent. They were followed, around 600 CE, by a fleet dispatched by the Egyptian Pharaoh, Necho II, whose ships sailed along the continent's eastern seaboard.

But not until two thousand years later, when Portuguese navigators and explorers set out in search of new lands – and a sea route to the Indies – did the continent begin to yield its secrets. In the fifteenth century, King John II of Portugal sent two expeditions under Diego Cão to Africa's western seaboard. History records that the explorer anchored south of what is now Namibia's Skeleton Coast and stepped ashore to set up a stone cross on top of a rocky cape. The cross stood for more than 400 years until the captain of a German vessel removed it late last century and took it to a museum in Berlin. Two years after Diego Cão left his cruciform, Bartolomeu Dias, another Portuguese explorer, positioned a second cross in a bay he named Angra Pequena, Little Bay, now Lüderitz Bay.

Looking at the formidable dunes of the great Namib Desert as they tumble into the icy Atlantic, it is not difficult to understand why so few voyagers chose to venture inland. The oldest desert in the world – some eighty million years – the Namib seems denuded of life, scorched by noonday sun, cooled by chill night mists that billow in from the ocean shutting out the frosty moon. Yet, astonishingly, life exists above and below its surface as plants and creatures draw sustenance from the wind and moisture of its misty phantoms. Such life, from tiny beetles to mighty elephants, have made this improbable wilderness their home. Indeed, many species are found nowhere else in the world. Swept by searing winds, the highest dunes in the world – mountains of sand – roll across the desert like roaming clouds to meet at a place called Sossusvlei.

East of the Namib stand remnants of the time before man walked these lands: dinosaur tracks and petrified forests, the greatest meteorite on earth and ancient castles of clay. From the eroded cliffs of Fish River Canyon, through Namibia's quaint, colonial-style towns, to the wild expanses of Etosha and the Caprivi Strip, Namibia's brittle beauty is vast even by African standards. Yet, although four times the size of Britain, its population numbers fewer than one and a half million people, giving it one of the lowest population densities in the world, with fewer than two people to each square kilometre. This remarkably low number may ensure that the changes ravaging much of Africa never affect its latest republic.

Basking in summer temperatures – ranging from 10-33°C between October and April and from 6–26°C in winter between May and September – Namibia's unspoilt splendour makes it truly a land of the free, for the free. A developing network of well-maintained tar, gravel and dirt roads allows visitors to reach the farthest corners of what has been called Africa's Gem – from the fallen glory of the rocky Finger of God in the south to the majesty of the Okavango River and the rapids of the Popa Falls in the north; from the mystery of the White Lady of the Brandberg to the raw power of the Namib Desert; from the gigantic fossil woods of the Petrified Forest near Khorixas to the Hoba Meteorite near Grootfontein; from the abundant wildlife of that other Eden, Etosha National Park, to the fascination of the Skeleton Coast.

And its people, every bit as unique and colourful, include perhaps Africa's oldest race, the San Bushmen, whose affinity to the trackless desert and savannahs where they live seems almost miraculous. One of their legends underlines this unlikely symbiosis: 'Now you come, now you go. When you come again you will never go.'

The many African tribes and European settlers live in a country of contrasts and vibrant colour. It is bordered in the west by the mighty Atlantic whose shores are lined by the Namib-Naukluft Park, which sprawls across almost 50,000 square kilometres – an area larger than Denmark. The southern border with South Africa is formed by the Orange River. In the north, much of the border between Namibia and Angola is made up of the Kunene and Okavango Rivers. And to the east lies the Kalahari Desert which sweeps into Botswana.

Many contemporary aspects of Namibia bear witness to the Victorian age when the European powers carved up Africa. Even now, Herero women dress in Victorian fashions while the charming buildings of both Swakopmund and Windhoek, the capital, reflect nineteenth-century convention and style. These incongruous vestiges extend beyond costume or architecture to the national boundaries where two particular instances remain curious reminders of colonial days. The first is a narrow corridor of land, 482 kilometres long, extending as far as the Zambezi. The Caprivi Strip, so named after Baron von Caprivi, the German Chancellor of the time, is also known as the Devil's Finger. It was the outcome of the German Kaiser's ambition to join his western and eastern African empires together. The second anachronism, Walvis Bay, midway between the Kunene and Orange Rivers, was annexed in 1878 to become part of Britain's Cape Colony, yet it remained under South African jurisdiction until the end of 1994, when Namibia began to share in its administration.

TAHIR SHAH

Namibia forms three distinct topographical regions – the Namib Desert; the central inland plateau's mountains and plains with, most magnificent of all, Etosha National Park; and finally the Kalahari Desert in the south-east reaches of the country.

The Kalahari's western counterpart, the Namib Desert, stretches more than 2,000 kilometres along the African coast in an arid band between 150 and 200 kilometres wide. In these virtually waterless conditions, its unique animals and plants take their moisture from the cool mists that sweep in from the Atlantic.

The roving dunes along the southern tract of coast are older than any other in the world. To the north lies the legendary Skeleton Coast where the sun-bleached bones of sailors and whales lie side by side with rusting shipwrecks. There, the Namib's dunes are complemented by vast, hard-baked granite flats which stretch from one horizon to the next.

What little takes root in the way of vegetation must rank among the world's most unusual and enduring plants, chief of which is a remarkable dwarf tree that dates back to prehistoric times. Some existing specimens of the tree – *Welwitschia mirabilis* – are more than 2,000 years old. Other marvels have also adapted ingeniously to this cruel land and manage to survive the scorching daytime heat and freezing night temperatures.

Several rivers, most of them seasonal, flow westwards into the Atlantic along Namibia's long seaboard – from the northernmost Kunene River to the Orange River in the extreme south. Three major towns dominate the seaboard. In summertime, elegant Swakopmund, halfway between Angola and South Africa, is woken from its hibernation by masses of tourists who double its wintertime population. A little to the south, Walvis Bay, the deepest harbour on Africa's south-west coast, is another popular haven for tourists. The port serves freight and fishing vessels.

The port of Lüderitz, with its fairy-tale architecture, almost 500 kilometres south of Walvis Bay, has been in use since Bartolomeu Dias moored there in the fifteenth century. East of Walvis Bay, the Namib-Naukluft Park stretches far inland, culminating in dramatic 305-metre mountains of sand at Sossusvlei.

However, the most spectacular feature of the southern region is the deep cleft in the earth's surface, the Fish River Canyon, a colossal gorge more than 160 kilometres long.

On its eastern flank, the Namib Desert meets Namibia's immense inland plateau, the nation's second distinct topographical region, which forms the country's south-north backbone. This varies from brooding mountains with jagged 2,440-metre peaks to wide plains and sandy valleys. Amid the high mountains at Namibia's northernmost extremities, the Kunene and Okavango Rivers flow all year round, the latter feeding the Okavango Delta in neighbouring Botswana.

And it is there in the north, close to the Angolan border, that you find Namibia's most magical landscape – the wilderness wonderlands of Etosha National Park. One of the world's largest game parks, Etosha's 22,270 square kilometres – bigger than Wales – know no seasons. As day melts into night, so the weeks and months merge into one. The Etosha Pan, which gives the park its name, covers some 5,000 square kilometres in the east.

This dry pan used to be the lake into which the Kunene River emptied itself, but following continental shifting, and the subsequent diversion of the Kunene's course to the Atlantic Ocean, the pan became what it is today. This immense shallow bowl, which fills only occasionally after the onset of the rains, is all that remains of that ancient lake. It is the source and sustenance of all life at Etosha, whose plains are home to a variety of creatures – birds, game animals and insects – some of which are found nowhere else in the world. As the scorching heat bakes the bleached and seemingly endless plains, these animals make their way to the rapidly dwindling waterholes in the pan to quench their thirst.

The land between Etosha and Windhoek, the capital city, is dotted with a host of small towns, such as Grootfontein and Otjiwarongo, where you can enjoy the distinctive charms of Namibian society. The most densely populated region of Namibia is Owambo, where the great majority of people live in rural settings.

Windhoek lies almost at the centre of Namibia, linked to the main urban areas and neighbouring countries by an extensive and expanding infrastructure.

The capital's charm – buildings of colonial German design, and modern skyscrapers – is enhanced by its location close to the Auas and Eros Mountains and not far from the Khomas Hochland in the west.

East of Windhoek, the boundless Kalahari Desert, which stretches southwards down the country's eastern flank straddling the border with Botswana, forms Namibia's third distinct landscape, surprisingly different from its western counterpart. For, unlike the Namib, the Kalahari is comparatively rich in plants and grasses, and sustains a great variety of life. Camel-thorn, red ebony and silver terminalia trees mix with a wide range of shrubs and succulents, providing welcome shade and refreshment for the people and creatures that live in the desert.

Keetmanshoop, the largest town at the edge of the Kalahari, grew up in the south around a mission station which later became a German military garrison.

Long before the Europeans first sailed along Africa's south-west coast, Namibia's people enjoyed their ancient ways and age-old beliefs following a destiny diverted only by the first footsteps of Western navigators, explorers, missionaries and carpet-baggers.

Belonging to eleven groups, a rich tapestry of tribes and people has endowed Namibia with its striking and varied cultural legacy. These myriad people have become as one in their new-found freedom. Yet each group retains a distinctive character and language, setting it apart from its neighbours.

Under the old, pre-independence South African administration, these cultures were demarcated geographically by a series of ethnic 'homelands' – such as Koakoland, Owambo, Kavango, Bushmanland, Hereroland and Damaraland. But these were swept away in 1990 by a new local government structure that divided Namibia into

453

thirteen regional authorities, each with its own political constituencies.

Almost one-tenth of Namibia's people, many of them European, make their home in Windhoek. In the few years since independence, the pace of migration from rural areas into the towns and city, spurred by the relentless drought that ravaged southern Africa at the end of the 1980s and in the early 1990s, quickened. Peasants, labourers and village folk flocked to the capital in search of jobs and food.

Namibia's original citizens, long before the other groups migrated to the south-west of the continent, are the San Bushmen. They once occupied the whole of southern Africa; their language is similar to that of their South African kith and kin, the Nama. Fine-boned and lightly coloured, these hunter gatherers, a nomadic people skilled in bushcraft and survival in the harshest conditions, are thought to have roamed Namibia's wildernesses thousands of years ago. Their rock paintings, in caves and on cliffs throughout the country, depict San life, hunting, and the animals around them. For centuries they roamed free, at peace with nature. It was only when they came in contact with outside influences that disaster struck – with the influx of Nama pastoralists, themselves descendants of the Khoikhoi of the Cape Province. This invasion during the early eighteenth century was a tragedy for these peaceful people – and it was compounded when the Wambo and Damara tribes swept in behind the Nama, while the Bantu-speaking Herero filtered into the Kaokoveld in north-west Namibia, before moving through the centre of the country.

Finally large numbers of the Oorlam tribe, themselves Nama who had closer contact with Western influences in the Cape, advanced into Namibia's heartlands. They brought with them weapons as well as a form of the Dutch language from the European communities in southern Africa. This dialect later became Afrikaans, which is still spoken widely in Namibia. It allows communication between indigenous tribes found in the country. Many customs and traditions have been devastated and Namibia's extraordinary cultural heritage is now under threat from modernization and development. But a few remain, as yet untrammelled by Western influence, thus preserving the country's unique legacy.

Namibia has about 70,000 European citizens, most of whom speak Afrikaans, while others are mainly of German or English descent.

The Wambo tribe's 800,000 people, the largest single group, live in the region between Etosha and Angola. To the north-east, Okavango is home to the 180,000 people of the Kavango tribe, the second largest group. Three tribes – the Herero, Himba and Mbanderu – form the 90,000 people of what was Hereroland in Otjozondjupa, which lies to the south of Okavango. During German rule the Herero were almost decimated. Many now roam Windhoek and other towns selling trinkets, or surviving how they can.

The home of the Tjimba and Himba tribes, who are related to the Herero, was Kaokoveld in Kunene. Scorning materialism and the trappings of modern civilization, much like the

Maasai of East Africa, the Himba have become a fascination for Western observers intrigued by their traditional way of life. They were forced into their empty wastelands during the last century by the Nama tribe.

Erongo – where the Damara people endure a harsh existence – is part of the old Damaraland. It is thought the Damara travelled southwards from western Africa through the centre of the continent in a migration lasting many centuries, bringing with them the secrets of extracting iron and making pottery.

The homelands of the Nama lie in the south in Karas, an area dominated by the Orange River. Until the end of the eighteenth century the Nama were at peace. But that was shattered by a massive influx of Herero in search of grazing. The war between the Herero and the Nama lasted for decades and claimed thousands of victims. The most tragic of all Western influences were the firearms brought in by the bellicose Oorlam who propelled South West Africa into an era of unprecedented confrontation. The mixed-race Baster people were driven northwards by the Boers in the 1860s across the Orange River to settle south of what is now Windhoek in the Hardap Region. These protracted migrations over vast areas laid the foundations for today's Namibian cultures. But it was a period characterized by open warfare as tribes found themselves competing for land and scarce resources. Whole generations perished but little was accomplished, except to consolidate the colonialist stranglehold over the land and its people.

Namibia's long history is also stained with the bloodshed from white domination – a tide of terror and belligerence that may never be erased entirely from Namibian soil.

Even before the nineteenth century, Europe's superpowers vied for supremacy of south-western Africa's strategic bays and inlets. To thwart other roving European forces seeking to expand their control of Africa's western flank, the Dutch seized Walvis Bay and Lüderitz Bay in 1793. But when the British took control of the Cape of Good Hope two years later, they also took possession of Walvis Bay and a string of other key locations.

Few Europeans, if any, ventured into the heart of Namibia – it was far too dangerous. The great quests came with the onset of the nineteenth century. The first sorties into Namibia's interior were made by a small corps of hardy explorers, such as Pieter Pienaar who ventured inland by way of rivers like the Swakop. It was not until the arrival of the missionaries, however, that the first major expeditions were accomplished. Among the many Christian pioneers, the names of Abraham and Christian Albrecht, who lived with the Nama and stopped at nothing to spread their faith, ring loudest. Johann Heinrich Schmelen, another Christian missionary, was an extraordinary man who took a Nama bride and set her to work translating the Bible into Nama. The London Missionary Society focused on what is now the Caprivi Strip where the most famous of all missionaries, David Livingstone, was stationed between 1850 and 1851. All across Namibia missionaries spread the word, settling among the Nama, Herero, Wambo and other tribes.

But the Christian message did nothing to prevent the conflicts which marred the final years of the last century. British attempts to end inter-tribal rivalry were feeble, mainly because they had no wish to become enmeshed. And when Adolf Lüderitz, a trader from Bremen, appealed to the Kaiser to do something in 1882, Bismarck decided to act. He annexed the whole of what is now Namibia, except for Walvis Bay and some small islands which the British retained.

At first the small German colonial administration operated a policy of *laissez-faire*. But as the bloodshed between tribes continued, the Germans cut supplies of arms and ammunition, built forts and brought in a military corps, the Schutztruppe. In 1904 these cold-blooded killers instigated a reign of terror in which most of the 80,000-strong Herero men, women and children were slaughtered. By the end of 1907 the tribe counted their numbers in hundreds.

This ethnic slaughter preceded the discovery of a rich diamond field by railway worker Zacharias Lewala, a former miner from South Africa's Kimberley diamond mines. One day, in April 1908, he was shovelling drifting sand from the line near Grasplatz Station, when he noticed the telltale twinkle of a diamond. Lewala scooped up the glistening stone and gave it to his boss, August Stauch, a German railway inspector. Stauch immediately staked a claim to that piece of desert. It came to be called Kolmanskop. The news spread like wildfire and, within weeks, dozens of prospectors had pegged out the entire area south-east of Lüderitz. De Beers, the great South African diamond conglomerate, eager to protect its markets, played down suggestions that the deposits were worth anything, while the colonial administration gave mining concessions only to German syndicates. Prisoners of war from the Herero rebellion were used as slave labour, since there were no other Africans in the diamond zone. Diamond fever continued and new fields were constantly being discovered, particularly in the first two decades of the century. Driven by diamond wealth, the colony's economy grew swiftly. Business expanded and roads, railways and port facilities developed. By 1913, one-fifth of all Africa's mined diamonds came from Namibia.

But at the height of this unparalleled prosperity, German South West Africa became embroiled in World War I. Isolated from the German empire, far from any defensive resources, it was at the mercy of the British forces. But South Africa delayed the push into German South West Africa until the 1914 Boer rebellion was quelled.

Then, in January 1915, South African forces – under the British flag – landed at Swakopmund and Lüderitz. Vastly outnumbered, the Germans surrendered within six months – on 9 July 1915. It was the first German colony to be captured by British forces and a new administration was installed at Windhoek.

But the change did nothing to lift the burden of oppression. Indeed it signalled yet another chapter in the colony's long history of suffering, one that lasted more than seven decades.

In 1919, under the newly formed League of Nations, South West Africa, as Namibia now became known, was entrusted to South Africa as a mandated territory. The

League's intentions could not be doubted. It prohibited South Africa from conscripting Africans into military service, and indeed ordered the trustees to advance the country's social and economic status. But the mandate failed to spell out the need for eventual self-government and this crucial omission allowed South Africa to treat the country as its own colony. In effect this permitted South Africa to plunder its resources and exploit its people. The interests of white South Africans were ever first, and the riches too good to miss. In 1920, Ernest Oppenheimer snapped up the diamond concessions from the nine German companies that operated the syndicate. He paid the bargain price of forty million marks and founded Consolidated Diamond Mines – CDM. In the first twelve years of mining, six and a half million carats of diamonds – a carat is 200 milligrams – were recovered.

Land was wealth, too, and now the Afrikaner settlers threw the peasants off the land to carve out farms on the rich grazing lands of the central plateau. Six years after the war ended, the white population had doubled. By 1926, the indigenous occupiers of their native pastures had been forced out to make way for almost 1,000 white farms, each averaging about 37,000 acres. These reluctant itinerants were destined to wander semi-desert regions seeking pastures for their herds. Under apartheid, black and mixed-race people were forced to live away from white communities. Pretoria established a commission to map out tribal homelands. Known as the Odendaal Plan, after the commission's chairman, it divided the various tribes to prevent them from rebellion and insurgency. Homelands such as Kavango, Owambo and Damaraland were created in the overgrazed and overpopulated regions of Namibia, mainly in the northern wilderness. Residents could only leave if they found work in a white area under a white master.

Freedom for much of the rest of Africa dawned in the 1960s, however, and these new nations changed the balance of power within the United Nations. Their pressure put Namibia's plight on the world agenda. And, in October 1966, the United Nations ended the South African mandate, assuming responsibility for South West Africa under the United Nations Council for Namibia. But South Africa, which accused the UN of acting illegally, refused to relinquish power, sparking off a general strike and rebellions. South Africa responded with a state emergency and imposed virtual martial law.

At the start of the 1970s, the UN recognized the South West African People's Organization (SWAPO) as 'the sole and authentic representative of the Namibian people'. Under Shafiishuna Samuel Nujoma, SWAPO set out to unite all Namibians. Still South Africa refused to loosen its stranglehold.

It was Portugal's eventual departure from Africa as a colonial power in 1975 that acted as the real catalyst for freedom, giving SWAPO a platform in Angola from which to transform its insurrections into a full military offensive. Now Namibia's northern border provided sanctuary for SWAPO's guerrilla arm – the People's Liberation Army of Namibia (PLAN). South Africa labelled SWAPO as a communist organization, as most international support

461

for SWAPO came from communist and Scandinavian countries. As a result, South Africa began a campaign of terror in northern Namibia, and thousands of refugees fled to Angola, Botswana and Zambia. Many of these exiles were recruited by PLAN, strengthening the fight for freedom. SWAPO broadened its political support within Namibia by forging alliances with other political groups, and winning the support of the churches. By the late 1970s, SWAPO was truly national, representing a complete cross-section of Namibian society. But in 1978 South Africa staged unrepresentative elections in Windhoek, which were immediately condemned as a 'sham' by the United Nations.

To combat the thousands of troops that South Africa poured into northern Namibia, SWAPO needed a cohesive military strategy and coordinated initiatives. Roads were mined, ambushes laid and military bases raided.

The liberation war reached its height in the 1980s. Intense fighting in densely populated Owambo spread rapidly to Kavango and the barren Kaoko. PLAN also carried the war to other areas, including the central and southern regions – even Windhoek itself.

PLAN's spy-ring was extraordinarily skilled; the freedom fighters were given food, water, shelter and vital information, allowing raids to have the maximum impact. At the same time, South Africa was able to infiltrate PLAN with spies of its own. SWAPO's discovery of this fact led to many innocent people being accused of spying for the enemy. As a result, South African military operations became increasingly brutal. Namibians were press-ganged into uniform and forced to take up arms against their own kin – while specialized terror units, Koevoets, were sent into battle.

The war drained South Africa of billions of rands – and its enthusiasm for the fight. This war of thirty years, labelled by one side as a liberation struggle, and by the other as the attempted infiltration of communism, reached a stalemate. Neither side could win, and it became clear other means of ending this conflict had to be found.

The 1988 agreement, which the Americans brokered between South Africa and Cuba to end the war in Angola, opened the door for Namibia's independence. Almost 50,000 refugees, the most distinguished of these being Samuel Nujoma himself, flooded back into the country for the November 1989 elections. The turnout was almost 100 per cent. SWAPO won a clear majority with 57.3 per cent of the vote, giving them forty-one of the seventy-two seats in Namibia's fledging parliament. They and the six other parties soon agreed on the constitution. Freedom for all – in religion, association, speech, thought and print – was guaranteed, and all discrimination outlawed.

Finally, on the night of 21 March 1990, after a struggle that had lasted well over a century, thousands of Namibians watched as the proud flag of their new nation was unfurled for the first time. And in the presence of UN Secretary General Javier Perez de Cuellar and world leaders, Sam Nujoma became the first President of Namibia.

From: *Journey Through Namibia*

Finis

THE TAHIR SHAH FICTION READER Timbuctoo Casablanca Blues: The Screenplay Godman Hannibal Fogg and the Supreme Secret of Man Jinn Hunter: The Prism Jinn Hunter: The Perplexity Paris Syndrome Scorpion Soup Tales Told to a Melon The Adventures of Nasrudin The Arabian Nights Adventures The Misadventures of the Mystifying Nasrudin Jinn Hunter: The Jinnslayer The Peregrinations of the Perplexing Nasrudin Timbuctoo: The Screenplay Casablanca Blues Timbuctoo Godman Hannibal Fogg and the Supreme Secret of Man Jinn Hunter: The Prism Jinn Hunter: The Perplexity Paris Syndrome Tales Told to a Melon The Adventures of Nasrudin The Arabian Nights Adventures **THE TAHIR SHAH FICTION READER** The Misadventures of the Mystifying Nasrudin Jinn Hunter: The Jinnslayer The Peregrinations of the Perplexing Nasrudin Timbuctoo: The Screenplay The Voyages and Vicissitudes of Nasrudin Casablanca Blues Timbuctoo Casablanca Blues: The Screenplay Eye Spy Godman Hannibal Fogg and the Supreme Secret of Man Jinn Hunter: The Prism Jinn Hunter: The Perplexity Paris Syndrome Scorpion Soup Tales Told to a Melon The Adventures of Nasrudin The Arabian Nights Adventures The Misadventures of the Mystifying Nasrudin **THE TAHIR SHAH FICTION READER** Jinn Hunter: The Jinnslayer The Peregrinations of the Perplexing Nasrudin Timbuctoo: The Screenplay The Voyages and Vicissitudes of Nasrudin Casablanca Casablanca Blues: The Screenplay Eye Spy Godman Hannibal Fogg and the Supreme Secret of Man Jinn Hunter: The Prism Jinn Hunter: The Perplexity Paris Syndrome Scorpion Soup Tales Told to a Melon The Adventures of Nasrudin The Arabian Nights Adventures The Misadventures of the Mystifying Nasrudin Jinn Hunter: The Jinnslayer The Peregrinations of the Perplexing Nasrudin Timbuctoo: The Screenplay The Voyages and Vicissitudes of Nasrudin Casablanca Blues **THE TAHIR SHAH FICTION READER** Casablanca Blues: The Screenplay Eye Spy Godman Hannibal Fogg and the Supreme Secret of Man Jinn Hunter: The Prism Jinn Hunter: The Perplexity Paris Syndrome Scorpion Soup Tales Told to a Melon The Adventures of Nasrudin The Arabian Nights Adventures The Misadventures of the Mystifying Nasrudin Jinn Hunter: The Jinnslayer The Peregrinations of the Perplexing Nasrudin Timbuctoo: The Screenplay The Voyages and Vicissitudes of Nasrudin Casablanca Blues Timbuctoo Casablanca Blues: The Screenplay Eye Spy **THE TAHIR SHAH FICTION READER** Godman Hannibal Fogg and the Supreme Secret of Man Jinn Hunter: The Prism Jinn Hunter: The Perplexity Paris Syndrome Scorpion Soup Tales Told to a Melon The Adventures of Nasrudin The Arabian Nights Adventures The Misadventures of the Mystifying Nasrudin Jinn Hunter: The Jinnslayer The Peregrinations of the Perplexing Nasrudin Timbuctoo: The Screenplay The Voyages and Vicissitudes of Nasrudin Casablanca Blues Timbuctoo Casablanca Blues: The Screenplay Eye Spy Godman Hannibal Fogg and the Supreme Secret of Man Jinn Hunter: The Prism Jinn Hunter: The Perplexity Paris Syndrome Scorpion Soup **THE TAHIR SHAH FICTION READER** Tales Told to a Melon The Adventures of Nasrudin The Arabian Nights Adventures The Misadventures of the Mystifying Nasrudin Jinn Hunter: The Jinnslayer The Peregrinations of the Perplexing Nasrudin Timbuctoo: The Screenplay The Voyages and Vicissitudes of Nasrudin Casablanca Blues Timbuctoo Casablanca Blues: The Screenplay Eye Spy Godman Hannibal Fogg and the Supreme Secret of Man Jinn Hunter: The Prism Jinn Hunter: The Perplexity Paris Syndrome Scorpion Soup Tales Told to a Melon The Adventures of Nasrudin The Arabian Nights Adventures The Misadventures of the Mystifying Nasrudin Jinn Hunter: The Jinnslayer The Peregrinations of the Perplexing Nasrudin Timbuctoo: The Screenplay The Voyages and Vicissitudes of Nasrudin Casablanca Blues Timbuctoo Casablanca Blues: The Screenplay Godman Hannibal Fogg and the Supreme Secret of Man Jinn Hunter: The Prism Jinn Hunter: The Perplexity Paris Syndrome Scorpion Soup Tales Told to a Melon The Adventures of Nasrudin The Arabian Nights Adventures The Misadventures of the Mystifying Nasrudin Jinn Hunter: The Jinnslayer The Peregrinations of the Perplexing Nasrudin **THE TAHIR SHAH FICTION READER** Casablanca Blues Timbuctoo Casablanca Blues: The Screenplay Eye Spy Godman Hannibal Fogg and the Supreme Secret of Man Jinn Hunter: The Prism Jinn Hunter: The Perplexity Paris Syndrome Scorpion Soup Tales Told to a Melon The Adventures of Nasrudin The Arabian Nights Adventures The Misadventures of the Mystifying Nasrudin Jinn Hunter: Nasrudin Casablanca Blues Casablanca Blues: The Screenplay Eye Spy The Adventures of Nasrudin The Arabian Nights Adventures The Adventures of Nasrudin Casablanca Blues: The Screenplay Eye Spy **THE TAHIR SHAH FICTION READER**

TAHIR SHAH

A REQUEST

If you enjoyed this book, please review it on your favourite online retailer or review website.

Reviews are an author's best friend.

To stay in touch with Tahir Shah, and to hear about his upcoming releases before anyone else, please sign up for his mailing list:

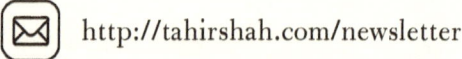 http://tahirshah.com/newsletter

And to follow him on social media, please go to any of the following links:

http://www.twitter.com/humanstew

@tahirshah999

http://www.facebook.com/TahirShahAuthor

http://www.youtube.com/user/tahirshah999

http://www.pinterest.com/tahirshah

https://www.goodreads.com/tahirshahauthor

http://www.tahirshah.com

www.ingramcontent.com/pod-product-compliance
Lightning Source LLC
Chambersburg PA
CBHW030910050726
47498CB00003BA/674